CLARENDON ANCIENT HISTORY SERIES

*General Editors*

Brian Bosworth    Miriam Griffin
David Whitehead

RENEWALS 458-4574

D1738201

The aim of the CLARENDON ANCIENT HISTORY SERIES is to provide authoritative translations, introductions, and commentaries to a wide range of Greek and Latin texts studied by ancient historians. The books will be of interest to scholars, graduate students, and advanced undergraduates.

# SALLUST

## *The Histories*

Translated
with Introduction and Commentary by

Patrick McGushin

VOLUME I

CLARENDON PRESS · OXFORD

# OXFORD

UNIVERSITY PRESS

Great Clarendon Street, Oxford OX2 6DP

Oxford University Press is a department of the University of Oxford
It furthers the University's objective of excellence in research, scholarship,
and education by publishing worldwide in

Oxford New York

Athens Auckland Bangkok Bogotá Buenos Aires Calcutta
Cape Town Chennai Dar es Salaam Delhi Florence Hong Kong Istanbul
Karachi Kuala Lumpur Madrid Melbourne Mexico City Mumbai
Nairobi Paris São Paulo Singapore Taipei Tokyo Toronto Warsaw
and associated companies in Berlin Ibadan

Oxford is a registered trade mark of Oxford University Press
in the UK and in certain other countries

Published in the United States
by Oxford University Press Inc., New York

ISBN 0-19-872141-2
ISBN 0-19-872140-4 Pbk

Printed in Great Britain
on acid-free paper by
Bookcraft (Bath) Short Run Books
Midsomer Norton

# PREFACE

For nearly a century B. Maurenbrecher's *C. Sallusti Crispi Historiarum reliquiae* (Stuttgart 1893) has been the definitive edition of Sallust's major work, the *Histories*. Sallust's political attitude and historical perspective, the close connection between his three historical works, their relevance to our understanding of the last decades of the Roman Republic have, in the period since the appearance of Maurenbrecher's edition, given rise to a considerable body of Sallustian scholarship. Wide-ranging research combined with the discovery of some source material not available to Maurenbrecher justifies a fairly long-held view that the *Histories* in particular need fresh appraisal on matters such as the placement of the fragments, the establishing of coherent contexts, and the provision of a fuller commentary. The introduction of the Clarendon Ancient History Series has provided the opportunity to present the text of the *Histories* to a much wider readership; the commentary will, it is hoped, be of use to scholars of all levels.

My debt to published work on Sallust is apparent from the commentary. I also owe a more immediate debt of thanks to individuals: to my colleague Brian Bosworth for the stimulus of encouragement and advice; markedly to the generosity and scholarship of Dr Miriam Griffin, who read my work in draft. For the blemishes that remain I am totally responsible.

The work has been assisted to a significant degree by the grant of a Senior Honorary Research Fellowship in the University of Western Australia, the benefits of which secured pleasant working conditions and access to research material from many parts of the world. To the secretarial staff of the Department of Classics I record my appreciation for expert assistance in the preparation of my text for publication.

P. McG.

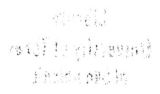

*PARENTUM MANIBUS*

# CONTENTS

*Abbreviations*                           ix

INTRODUCTION                               1
  1. Life of Sallust            1
  2. The writings of Sallust    3
  3. The sources of the *Histories*   5
  4. The transmission of the text   5
  5. Compositional structure   10
  6. Thematic structure        15
  7. The time of writing       18
  8. About this edition        20

TRANSLATION                                23
  Book 1                        23
  Book 2                        45

COMMENTARY                                 64
  Book 1                        64
  Book 2                       185

*Bibliography*                           261

*Index*                                  267

# ABBREVIATIONS

The abbreviations used for ancient authors and their works are, with slight modification in some cases, those found in *The Oxford Classical Dictionary*² (1970), and for periodicals the system used in *L'Année philologique*.

## (a)   Editions of Sallust

| | |
|---|---|
| de Brosses | C. de Brosses, *Histoire de la république romaine dans le cours du septième siècle par Salluste* (1777). |
| Dietsch | R. Dietsch, *Gai Sallusti Crispi quae supersunt*, vol. 2 (1859). |
| Ernout | A. Ernout, *Salluste: Catilina Jugurtha Fragments des Histoires* (Paris 1960). |
| Fighiera | L. S. Fighiera, *Le Orazioni e le Epistole contenute nelle Storie di C. Crispo Sallustio* (Savona 1896). |
| Gerlach | F. D. Gerlach, *C. Crispi Sallusti quae extant*, vol. 3 (1870). |
| Jacobs–Wirz–Kurfess | R. Jacobs, H. Wirz, and A. Kurfess, 'Orationes et epistulae ex Historiis excerptae, in *De Coniuratione Catiline Liber*¹² (Berlin/Zurich 1965). |
| Kritz | F. Kritz, *C. Sallustii Crispi Opera quae supersunt*, vol. 3 (1853). |
| Maurenbrecher | B. Maurenbrecher, *C. Sallusti Crispi Historiarum reliquiae*, vol. 2 (Stuttgart 1893). |
| Paladini | V. Paladini, *Sallustii Crispi orationes et epistulae de historiarum libris excerptae* (Bari 1956). |
| Pasoli | E. Pasoli, *Le historiae e le opere minori di Sallustio*² (Bologna 1967). |

## (b)   Other works

Asconius' commentary on Cicero's speeches is cited in the edition by A. C. Clark (Oxford 1907). The *Scholia Bobiensia* and *Gronoviana*, and the scholia of Pseudo-Asconius, are cited according to the collection of T. Stangl, *Ciceronis orationum scholiastae* (Hildesheim 1964).

| | |
|---|---|
| *AHB* | *The Ancient History Bulletin* (University of Calgary). |
| Badian, *FC* | E. Badian, *Foreign Clientelae* (Oxford 1958). |
| Bauhofer | K. Bauhofer, *Die Komposition des Historien Sallusts*, Diss. Munich 1935. |
| Berne scholiast | *Commenta Bernensia*, ed. H. Usener (Hildesheim 1976). |
| *CAH* | *The Cambridge Ancient History.* |
| *CGL* | *Corpus glossariorum Latinorum.* |
| *CIG* | *Corpus inscriptionum Graecarum.* |
| *CIL* | *Corpus inscriptionum Latinarum.* |
| Ehrenberg | V. Ehrenberg, *Ost und West: Studien zur Geschichtlichen Problematik der Antike* (Prague 1935). |
| Halm | C. Halm, *Rhetores Latini minores* (Leipzig 1863, repr. 1964). |
| *HRR* | H. Peter, *Historicorum Romanorum reliquiae*, vol. $1^2$ (Leipzig 1967). |
| *ILS* | H. Dessau, *Inscriptiones Latinae selectae.* |
| Magie | D. Magie, *Roman Rule in Asia Minor*, 2 vols. (Princeton 1950). |
| *MRR* | T. R. S. Broughton, *The Magistrates of the Roman Republic*, 2 vols. (Amer. Philol. Assoc. 1951–2). |
| *OGIS* | W. Dittenberger, *Orientis Graeci inscriptiones selectae.* |
| *PAS* | *Papers of the American School of Classical Studies at Athens.* |
| Ramsay, *CB* | Sir Wm. Ramsay, *The Cities and Bishoprics of Phrygia* (Oxford 1895–7). |
| *RE* | A. Pauly and G. Wissowa, *Real-Encyclopädie der classischen Altertumswissenschaft* (Stuttgart 1894–1980). |
| *SEG* | *Supplementum epigraphicum Graecum.* |
| Schulten | A. Schulten, *Sertorius* (Leipzig 1926). |
| Spann | P. O. Spann, *Quintus Sertorius: Citizen, Soldier, Exile* (diss. Texas 1976; pub. Fayetteville, 1987). |
| St. | T. Stangl, *Ciceronis orationum scholiastae* (Hildesheim 1964). |
| Syme | R. Syme, *Sallust* (Berkeley, Calif./Cambridge 1964). |
| *SRIL* | *Studi e richerche dell'Istituto de Latino*, Genoa University. |

Thilo–Hagen    *Servii grammatici qui feruntur in Vergili Carmina Commentarii*, ed. G. Thilo and H. Hagen, 3 vols. (Hildesheim 1961).

# INTRODUCTION

## I. LIFE OF SALLUST

In spite of the fact that the writings and life-style of C. Sallustius Crispus aroused a wide variety of comment in the ancient world, surprisingly little reliable information exists for much of his career. It is now generally accepted that Sallust was born at Amiternum in Sabine land, about 50 miles north-east of Rome, in 86 BC and died in 35 BC, four years before the Battle of Actium. These dates depend on scholarly interpretation of the data provided by the *Chronicle* of St Jerome and on the conflicting evidence of the *Chronicon Paschale* (pp. 347, 359 Dindorf) and the *Consularia Constantinopolitana* (Mommsen, *Chron. Min.* I. 214, 217). I have accepted these standard dates even though there is no absolute certainty about them because of Jerome's record of carelessness and inaccuracy in other particulars of literary history. Syme (pp. 13–14) points out that Jerome cannot be accepted on Lucretius and Catullus and that his dates for Livy and Varro are questionable.

Syme (28) notes that no evidence whatever exists concerning Sallust's boyhood, education, political training and beliefs, and public career before he stood for the tribunate in 53. One can therefore merely surmise the influence on Sallust's character and outlook of such external factors as his municipal origin, the effect on the Italian *municipia* of the Social War, the civil war which led to the dictatorship and proscriptions of Sulla, his experience under the oligarchy which Sulla restored, the turbulence and intrigues of the sixties.

Sallust's first attested office was the tribunate of 52. The evidence for this (Asc. 37. 18, 44. 21–45. 1, 49. 24–50. 1, and 51. 8–14) indicates his possible political allegiance at the time and helps to combat a common assumption that Sallust was from first to last a partisan of Caesar. The year 52 opened without consuls, but three candidates were in the field. The Optimates supported Titus Annius Milo; Pompeius' candidates were Quintus Caecilius Metellus Scipio, and Titus Plautius Hypsaeus, who were also strongly supported by Publius Clodius Pulcher, then a candidate for the praetorship. Asconius names the tribunes Quintus Pompeius Rufus and Titus Munatius Plancus as active in hostility to Milo and Cicero and as chief inciters to riot and arson after the murder of Clodius. Asconius also names Sallust as active in support of his fellow tribune, Pompeius Rufus, and as co-operating with Plancus. It could be surmised from this that Sallust was on the side of Clodius and Pompeius Magnus; all three were certainly opposed to Milo, but Sallust's opposition to him is not attested before Clodius' death, and he was allegedly reconciled to him later (Asc. 37. 23C). Roman politics often placed ill-assorted people temporarily on the same side; there is nothing to show what Sallust's motives were in 52.

His transference to the camp of Caesar is to be accounted for by the vicissitudes of political intrigue—Sallust was expelled from the senate in 50 (Dio, 40. 63. 4) and Caesar was prepared to accept allies without question (R. Syme, *The Roman Revolution* (Oxford 1939), 66–7; *Sallust*, 35). Dio gives no hint of the allegations made against Sallust; the censorship was used as a weapon in party strife and Sallust may have paid the penalty for actions and attitudes during his tribunate. He is next heard of commanding one of Caesar's legions in Illyricum late in 49 and failing to stave off the capitulation of the Caesarians under Gaius Antonius on the island of Curicta (Oros. 6. 15. 8). For nearly two years there is no mention of him in history. He re-emerges in 47 when as praetor-elect he is reported to have failed in a mission to quell a mutiny among Caesarian troops in Campania (App. *BC* 2. 92; Dio, 42. 52. 1–2). As praetor in 46 Sallust was active in Caesar's African campaign, where he showed administrative and executive ability in securing much needed supplies from the island of Cercina (*Bell. Afr.* 8. 3, 34. 1, 34. 3). After the victory of Thapsus Caesar took the greater part of Numidia away from King Juba and turned it into a Roman province, Africa Nova. Sallust was appointed its first governor (*Bell. Afr.* 97. 1; App. *BC* 2.

100; Dio, 43. 9. 2). His readmission to the senate was a consequence of this praetorship.

According to Dio (loc. cit.; and *Inv. in Sall.* 19) Sallust so misgoverned his province that he had to face a charge of extortion on his return to Rome. This charge was not pressed and Dio's report (43. 47. 4) that the suppression of bribery charges in 45 was due to bribes paid to Caesar for this favour suggests that this may have been the case with Sallust. Whatever the circumstance, Sallust was spared the humiliation of a second expulsion from the senate and retained riches vast enough to maintain a palatial house. He survived the assassination of Caesar and apparently secured a highly favoured and protected position under the rule of the Triumvirs, Antony, Lepidus, and Octavian (later the Emperor Augustus). He both survived the proscriptions unscathed and wrote with remarkable candour on the pernicious effects of the *potentia paucorum*. In this context it is worth noting that a similar kind of protected status marked the career of Sallustius Crispus the younger, great-nephew and adopted son of the historian. The younger man, who died in AD 20, never attained high office, remaining an *eques* throughout his career, but he succeeded Maecenas as the leading private counsellor to Caesar Augustus and went on to advise his successor Tiberius (see Tac. *Ann.* 3. 30; Syme, 277). While one cannot speak with certainty concerning the effect on Sallust of Caesar's assassination in 44, it is probable that it confirmed his resolve to abandon political ambitions and to devote himself to literary pursuits (*Cat.* 4. 2).

For fuller accounts of Sallust's career see Syme, chs. 4 and 15; G. M. Paul, 'Sallust', ch. 4 of T. A. Dorey (ed.), *Latin Historians* (London, 1966).

## 2. THE WRITINGS OF SALLUST

Three historical works are ascribed without dispute to Sallust. Two of these we possess complete, the monographs *Bellum Catilinae* and *Bellum Iugurthinum*; the third is the fragmentary major work, the *Historiae*, which is here presented in translation. There is no doubt about Sallust's authorship of these three works. There is less agreement concerning other works sometimes ascribed to Sallust. Scholars have long been occupied with the question of the genuineness of the two *Epistulae ad Caesarem senem* which are transmitted in the Codex Vaticanus Latinus 3864 (V) along with the letters and speeches from the historical works. The existing state of the question is that many continental scholars are in support of Sallustian authorship of the *Epistulae*, and some even include the far more dubious *Invectiva in Ciceronem* as part of the Sallustian corpus. Most English-speaking scholars have remained unconvinced. On the topic of authenticity see Syme, 314 ff. and the bibliography cited.

Indications as to the dates of publication of Sallust's three works are few and general in character. His attitude to Caesar and Cato in chapter 54 of the *Bellum Catilinae* and use of the word *fuere* in 53. 6 show that both Caesar and Cato were dead; this provides a *terminus post quem* of 44 BC. The date of death, 35 BC (with the caveat on p. 1 that Jerome is unreliable) gives us a *terminus ante quem*. Otherwise we have only the relative dating which places the *Bellum Catilinae* probably earlier than the *Bellum Iugurthinum* and both these works earlier than the *Historiae*. The lack of precise indication has given scope to scholars to indulge their theories and to make the dates fit in with what they conceived to be the purpose of the work in question. Thus, for example, L. Wohleb (*Phil. Woch.* 48 (1928), 1242 ff.), interpreting the tone of both monographs, claimed that the *Bellum Catilinae* was begun before the death of Caesar and finished during Cicero's lifetime, and that the *Bellum Iugurthinum* was written when the Second Triumvirate was imminent, but not yet established, that is before November 43. None of the theories on dating is compelling; precise dating remains unattainable.

## 3. THE SOURCES OF THE *HISTORIES*

Satisfactory evidence for the sources used by Sallust is hard to come by. In the case of literary sources one can perhaps speak of Varro with some confidence: Varro served under Pompeius in Spain, described his own campaigns, and wrote three books *De Pompeio*. The possibility has been raised that other friends and clients of Pompeius celebrated his deeds in writing: L. Voltacilius Pitholaus, Pompeius' tutor, who was the first freedman to write history (Suet. *Rhet.* 3); Theophanes of Mytilene, the historian of Pompeius who accompanied him in the Third Mithridatic War and, now a Roman citizen, fought in the Civil War. There is evidence that Lucullus, who was fluent in both Latin and Greek (Plut. *Luc.* 1. 4), wrote in Greek a history of the Social War, in which he served under Sulla in 89. There is nothing to suggest that Lucullus later produced his own memoirs, but other writers, Greek and Latin, did commemorate the exploits of his later career (Cic. *Acad. Pr.* 2. 4).

It seems (see my commentary on 2. 44) that scarcely any of the political orations of the seventies survived, but family records will almost surely have preserved the laudatory funeral speeches for ex-consuls, such as Gaius Scribonius Curio and Publius Servilius Vatia Isauricus, who celebrated triumphs. Given the paucity of historical narratives, Sallust will have had recourse to oral tradition, material which would have been available to him from a wide variety of informants such as surviving consuls like Gnaeus Domitius Calvinus and Marcus Valerius Messala Rufus (consuls in 53) and men who had participated in important events like Lucius Cornelius Balbus, who was granted Roman citizenship for services in the Sertorian War, and who survived to become consul suffect in 40.

### 4. THE TRANSMISSION OF THE TEXT

The esteem which kept alive the fame and influence of Sallust's two monographs was clearly shared by his last and greatest work: more than five hundred extant quotations and references from his *Histories* by grammarians, scholiasts, lexicographers, and others form a tribute unequalled among historical works. Unfortunately in this case the fame of the work was not sufficient to secure the preservation of a complete text of the work into the Carolingian period (late eighth century AD) when the devoted scholars of that Renaissance ensured the survival of much of extant Latin literature by restoring and copying manuscripts which had escaped the ravages of the Dark Ages (*c.* AD 600–780). However, something was saved: items from the direct manuscript tradition, some of relatively recent discovery, have survived; all are crucially important for providing a structural framework of the *Histories* and indicating the principles of that structure. The indirect transmission of the text in a series of quotations by grammarians and other types of commentator provides a reasonable, though obviously imperfect, guide to the kind and order of the events within the work.

## (a) *Direct transmission*

*Codex Vaticanus Latinus 3864 (V).*   In the days, probably in the second century AD, when rhetoric was the staple of Roman education, a collection was made of all the speeches and letters contained in Sallust's writings. A manuscript containing this collection is extant (Cod. Vat. Lat. 3864). The six pieces from the *Histories* give speeches first, followed by letters of Pompeius and Mithridates.

*The Fleury manuscript.*  An actual manuscript of the *Histories*, or part of one, also entered the Dark Ages. Written in Italy in the fifth century in Rustic capital, two columns to a page, this codex eventually reached the French monastery of Benoît-sur-Loire (Fleury) where part of it was prepared for different purposes in the seventh or eighth century. At least one double leaf (bifolium) was cut down for binding purposes; now in a miscellaneous manuscript (Cod. Vat. Lat. Reg. 1283B), this bifolium deals with the rebellion of Spartacus at the end of 73 BC (frr. 3. 66 and 68). I refer to it as the Vatican fragment.

Other portions of the Fleury manuscript were cut down to a smaller size and folded in the middle; the original text was removed and replaced with St Jerome's *Commentary on Isaiah*, written in one column. Three double leaves of this Jerome palimpsest have survived. One of these was further cut down and thereby deprived of nearly half its surface; eventually it came apart at its fold. Half of this bifolium ended up with the other two bifolia in the miscellaneous codex in the Municipal Library of Orléans as Codex 192 (169), fo. 20; it is referred to as the Orléans fragment (*fragmentum Aurelianense*, or A). The other half of fo. 20 was presented in 1847 to the Royal Library in Berlin, where it is still kept (Deutsche Staatsbibliothek Lat. Qu. 364). It is referred to as the Berlin fragment (*fragmentum Berolinense*, or B).

The Viennese philologist Edmund Hauler (1859–1941) first identified and deciphered the Sallust palimpsest; he published his findings mainly in *Wiener Studien*, between 1886 and 1931. In my translation of the text I use Hauler's numbering of the columns as part of my identification of the fragments. Schematic reconstructions of the bifolia of the MS are provided in H. Bloch, *Didascaliae* (1961), 62–76.

*Codex P. Vindobonae Latinus 117.* The Vienna fragment, first published in readable form by Bernhardt Bischoff and Herbert Bloch in *WS* 13 (1979), 116–29, contains, two fragments from the *Histories*; these appear as 1. 98 and 1. 100 in the text.

*Papyrus Rylands III 473.* Two pieces of papyrus published by C. H. Roberts in 1938 contain fr. 12 of the 'Fragments of Uncertain Reference' and fr. 2. 9 of the text.

(*b*) *Indirect transmission*

By indirect transmission is meant the quotations from and references to the text of the *Histories* made by grammarians and commentators of various types. The five hundred or so fragments thus provided involve the contributions of some forty-six commentators. Five of these, grammarians all, provide slightly more than three-quarters of the total. The nature of the indirect transmission can be adequately indicated by a brief treatment of the contribution of each of these five. The statistics which emerge from this examination are based on the Latin text of the fragments; I deal only with citations which I have identified as the primary or major sources of the fragments. In the commentary I sometimes refer to additional sources which provide partial versions of the fragments under discussion; I also note fragments whose published form is the result of the combined contributions of more than one source.

*Nonius* (*early fourth century* AD). The primary source of sixty-one quotations from the *Histories*. More than half of these are of two-line length or longer. Book-numbers have been transmitted for all but three of his fragments; the book-numbers allotted to five of his citations have been queried by some editors. It is not surprising that the section 'Fragments of Uncertain Reference' contains no Nonian citations.

Nonius' method of compilation and the sources of his quotations are exhaustively dealt with in W. M. Lindsay, *Nonius Marcellus' Dictionary of Republican Latin* (Oxford 1901) and in a more lucid and compelling fashion by Diana C. White in *Stud. Non.* 8 (1980), 111–211. The reliability of Nonius' book-numbers is dealt with by A. K. Frihagen, *SO* 50 (1975), 149–53, and G. Maggiulli, *Stud. Non.* 6 (1981), 117–22. On errors in Nonius see F. Bertini, *Stud. Non.* 1 (1967), 56–8.

*Servius* (*fourth century* AD). His major work, a commentary on Virgil, supplies 119 quotations, which are the primary source of fragments of the *Histories*. Of this number, thirty-nine quotations are from the augmented Servius (Servius Danielis). Fragments of one-line length predominate in Servius' contribution.

In Book 1 Servius has apparently been credited with the transmission of six book-numbers (frr. 21, 38, 54, 92, 122, 129) but in the case of fr. 92 it should be noted that the book-

number is provided by the scholiast *Anon. Brevis Expositio*
(Thilo–Hagen, 3. 299) on *Georgic* 2. 197. For fr. 129 the
number is supplied by Arusianus, who cites the first clause of
this fragment ('seeing . . . of the enemy'). In Book 2 three
fragments have been transmitted with book-number (frr. 52,
68, 101); the reliability of the number provided for fr. 101
has been questioned by some editors. In Book 3 one of the
two book-numbers connected with Servius (fr. 23M) has
rightly been queried; the other (fr. 83M) owes its book-
number to Nonius, who cites the last part of the fragment
('the other official . . . Perperna'). Likewise, fr. 4. 28M, the
product of a combination of sources, owes its book-number
to Arusianus, who cites the last sentence of the fragment.

While it is not surprising to find that Servian quotations
figure prominently in the section 'Fragments of Uncertain
Reference', it should also be noted that the vast majority
have found a place in the text, a factor due mainly to the
clues provided by their content, at times supplemented by
the evidence of other sources.

*Arusianus Messius* (*late fourth century* AD). Provides 106
primary quotations from the *Histories*, all but three transmitted with book-numbers. Editors have queried the accuracy
of four of his book-numbers. The vast majority of the
citations are of one-line length or less. For a treatment of
Maurenbrecher's handling of cases which involve trans-
missions shared by Arusianus with other sources see L. Di
Salvo, *SRIL* 5 (1981), 29–52.

*Aelius Donatus.* The most notable grammarian of the
fourth century AD, whose extant commentary on the plays of
Terence owed much to Aemilius Asper whose late second-
century AD commentaries on Terence and on Sallust
(*Catiline* and *Histories*) are now lost. The vast majority of his
thirty-two quotations are of one-line length or less; six have
been transmitted with book-number.

*Priscianus* (*early sixth-century* AD *grammarian*). Gives fifty-
five quotations from the *Histories*, the majority being one-
line length or less. Three quotations have been transmitted

without book-numbers, while the accuracy of just one of the transmitted book-numbers has been unanimously queried by editors. On the reliability of Priscian's book-numbers see G. Perl, *Philologus* III (1967), 285–8 and the commentary on 2. 83.

## 5. COMPOSITIONAL STRUCTURE

Editors before Maurenbrecher took different approaches to the structure of the *Histories*. The first attempt at a systematic arrangement of the fragments was that of C. de Brosses (1777). He arranged all the fragments known to him in a chronological sequence without paying heed to the division into books as transmitted in the tradition. Since in the case of many fragments there was no hint of a specific situation, he often assigned the same fragment to two different places, and occasionally used a fragment even more often. The lack of method and of rigour in his procedure naturally aroused criticism, but the perceptiveness of his location of numerous fragments remained a redeeming feature. In his 1831 edition Gerlach, working on the annalistic framework of the twelve years mentioned by Ausonius (*Ep.* 22. 62 ff.), allocated the fragments according to specific events and books without paying much attention to the transmitted book-numbers. This procedure was censured by Kritz, who in his 1853 edition maintained that the book-numbers transmitted were a vital clue to the content and time-frame of individual books. Within the books as Kritz arranged them the fragments were placed according to the arena of activity; on the analogy of the monographs, a whole complex of connected events covering more than one year was at times reported in one place. Dietsch (1859) followed a more rigorous and more cautious procedure of allocating the fragments, with the result that many fragments were relegated to the section 'Fragments of Uncertain Reference'. Somewhat harshly dismissed by Maurenbrecher, Dietsch's scholarly commentary is often the source of valuable information.

Hauler's decipherment of the Fleury manuscript revealed

a fresh basis for deciding on the structure of the work. Two transitions from one year to the following have been preserved in this palimpsest (see 2. 40 and 2. 82 D). These show that Sallust followed the annalistic tradition with a statement on consuls and an annual organization of events in their chronological order. Wars extending over several years were not dealt with in a continuous narrative; their narration was sometimes interrupted by the changeover to a new year. In addition, the Fleury manuscript, cols. XI–XII (frr. 2. 75–6), shows that Sallust's report of the Sertorian War for 75 has been divided into summer and winter campaigning seasons, interrupted by events from other theatres in the same year. Maurenbrecher had the advantage of these discoveries for his 1893 edition of the text, a work, for its time, of considerable merit. However, he appears to have overlooked some of the implications of the manuscript evidence.

Presentation of the structure of the *Histories* in tabular form may be of use when dealing with what I believe are questionable assumptions on Maurenbrecher's part regarding structure.

**Book I (78–77 BC)**
Personal preface.
Introduction:
> (1) General considerations on the moral, social, and political history of Rome.
> (2) Treatment of the historical period which preceded his own subject-matter—the Social War; conflict between Marius and Cinna; Sulla's conquest of Italy and Rome; the proscriptions which ushered in the Sullan restoration.

Revolt of Lepidus—speeches of Lepidus and Philippus.
Sertorius' career from 105 to 80 BC—a brief report on urban affairs 78.
Early stages of Sertorian War.
Preliminary treatment of operations in Cilicia and Macedonia.
Expedition of P. Servilius Vatia against the Cilician pirates.

**Book 2 (late 77–early 74 BC)**
Excursus on Sardinia—Corsica.
Final phase of Lepidus' revolt.
Transfer of command in Spain from Metellus to Pompeius;
  character-sketch of Pompeius.
Urban affairs of 76.
Events of Sertorian War in 76.
Foreign wars elsewhere—Macedonia, Dalmatia, Illyria,
  province of Asia.
Urban affairs of 75—civil unrest.
Course of Sertorian War in 75—summer campaign.
Curio's campaign in Macedonia; P. Servilius Vatia against
  the Isauri.
Winter campaign in Spain in 75.
Pompeius' letter to the senate.
Urban affairs of early 74.

**Book 3 (74–72 BC)**
M. Antonius against the pirates.
Urban affairs of 74.
Opening campaign of Third Mithridatic War (74–73);
  siege of Cyzicus.
Sertorian War in 74.
Urban affairs in 73—speech of Licinius Macer.
Mithridatic War in 73–72; siege of Amisus.
Excursus on topography of Pontus.
Outbreak of slave rebellion under Spartacus (73).
Antonius' campaign against Crete (73–72).
Final phase of Sertorian War (72).
The slave rebellion in 72.
Events in Macedonia (72).

**Book 4 (72–68 BC)**
Urban affairs of 72.
Events of Mithridatic War 72; fall of Cabeira.
Activity of M. Terentius Varro Lucullus in Thrace (72).
Last phase of the Spartacus war, incorporating an excursus
  on topography of southernmost Italy and the Strait of
  Sicily (72–71).
Urban affairs of 71.
Mithridatic War (71).

Activity of M. Aurelius Cotta (71).
Urban affairs of 70.
Lucullus' campaign in Armenia (69); the Letter of
Mithridates.
Urban affairs of 69.
Lucullus invades northern Armenia (68).
Urban affairs of 68.

**Book 5 (68–67 BC)**
Final phase of the campaign of Lucullus.
The pirate threat—the Gabinian Law of 67 BC.

From this outline of the content and architecture of the
*Histories* some additional points can be deduced concerning
the compositional principles on which it was structured. The
fact that Sallust was strongly influenced in the monographs by
the work of the Greek historian Thucydides in matters of style
and concept suggests that the structure of his *Histories* may
have come under the same influence. Deductions concerning
this feature of Sallust's work are naturally hazardous because
of the fragmentary nature of the tradition: the fragments,
excerpted for the most part for linguistic and not historical
interest, only rarely provide a composite text of some detail.
The chronology of events within the period dealt with is by no
means established throughout; specific dates are rare, as are
indications of summer or winter half-years.

   Maurenbrecher considered events such as the operations of
C. Cosconius in Dalmatia as *res minores* ('minor matters') and
held that it was Sallust's practice to deal in a single combined
passage with minor matters which covered more than one year
(2. 57). Consequently he believed that 2. 37–8 were part of a
combined treatment of about two years' campaigning by
Cosconius, governor of Illyricum, and that 2. 63–8 were part
of a narrative dealing with the campaigns conducted by P.
Servilius Vatia over the triennium 77–75. He dismissed the
apparent contradiction posed by the fact that campaigns in
Macedonia are dealt with in two different segments of Book 2
(2. 35–6 and 60–2) with the statement that these are two
different Macedonian wars, the former conducted by Appius
Claudius, the latter by Scribonius Curio (see notes ad loc.). On

the contrary, the partition of the treatment of the Macedonian campaign in this case is evidence of a basic structural principle used by Sallust, after the manner of Thucydides, of providing an exact chronological development of events inside a year's report; in this case the first treatment deals with 76, the second with 75 BC. It is not known how Sallust dealt with campaigns which overlapped normal campaigning seasons, such as those involving the sieges of Cyzicus and Amisus in Book 3 and the fall of Cabeira in Book 4. I have assumed an extended campaigning season in each case.

Apart from the use of half-yearly campaigning seasons as a chronological indicator Sallust seems also to have followed the Thucydidean practice of providing a change of book inside a year's report, corresponding to a change of subject-matter, of war-theatre, or of campaigning season. Such a change is certainly the case with Sallust's Books 1/2 and the year 77, and Books 2/3 and the year 74; it is probably also the case with Books 3/4 and the year 72 and with Books 4/5 and the year 68.

Thucydides' influence can more confidently be assumed with regard to the speeches and letters in the *Histories*. Like Thucydides, Sallust uses speeches to provide a variation in narrative method; in each of his works speeches and letters are used to highlight the background and the atmosphere of important events and decisions. The two speeches of Book 1 of the *Histories* conform to some extent to the Thucydidean device of using a pair of speeches to reflect the crucial alternatives governing a decision. By using the words of men who play an important role in the events he is dealing with, Sallust is able to present a deeper and more varied analysis of the political and social problems which form the essence of his theme. In the monographs, which have been preserved intact, and in the *Histories* Sallust apparently allows his characters to present their own points of view, to explain or justify conduct or policy, and to present assessments of event or motive as the only true version. In the monographs one can detect an ironical contrast between what is stated in speech or letter and the facts of the situation as Sallust narrates them. Even from the fragmentary text of the *Histories* one can surmise a similar contrast, especially in

the case of Cotta's speech (2. 47) and Pompeius' letter to the
senate (2. 72).

In the commentary, a preface to each speech and letter
discusses to what extent each is a genuine document and
how far its content and thrust is the work of the historian
himself.

## 6. THEMATIC STRUCTURE

The few autobiographical details which appear in Sallust's
work are concerned with the circumstances on account of
which he abandoned his political career. His personal crisis
had its cause in the crisis of state and society which had
reduced Roman political life to a stage of corruption
threatening the fabric of contemporary Rome and for which
he saw no remedy. All of Sallust's writings are directed at
illuminating salient points of this social and political turmoil
and revealing as far as possible how deeply rooted its
symptoms were.

From early in his political life Sallust realized that the
abandonment of the moral and social values which had led
to the ancient greatness of Rome must inevitably produce
disastrous results. This he expressed pungently in all three
works (*Cat.* 5. 9, 10. 6; *Iug.* 41. 3–5, 9–10; *Hist.* 1. 10, 12–
13). He labelled the Catilian conspiracy as 'worthy of special
notice because of the extraordinary nature of the crime and
the danger arising from it' (*Cat.* 4. 4). By this he meant that
the conspiracy was simply an external manifestation of
unrest behind which there lurked the committed seekers of
personal power (*Cat.* 17. 5, 7: cf. 36. 4, 39. 4). This emphasis
on the hidden dangers presented by civil unrest, factional
conflict, and the obdurate stupidity of the ruling clique is
present in his treatment of similar developments in the
*Bellum Iugurthinum* and the *Historiae*. Common to all are
the developments which followed the significant changes in
army service introduced by Marius, the emergence of the
mercenary army, the failure of the government to handle
emergencies by constitutional procedures, and the opportunities thereby presented to men of ability and ambition to

pursue goals of personal power. The developments which ensued showed that the civil conflicts of the final half-century of the crisis were fought by protagonists working for their own interests.

The reasons given by Sallust for the selection of the Jugurthine War as the topic of his second monograph are bluntly expressed: 'first because it was long, bloody, and of varying fortune; and secondly, because then for the first time resistance was offered to the arrogance of the nobles'. This latter factor, he says, was the beginning of a struggle which led to civil wars and the devastation of Italy. This Numidian War exacerbated the rivalry of parties and factions (*Iug.* 41. 6) and was the precursor to the Social War, the civil war of Marius and Sulla, the dictatorship of Sulla—events which are outlined in the second part of the Introduction to the *Histories*. Sallust's treatment of it was designed to illustrate the aspects of the Roman crisis in its external development and in its military character.

The pressure exerted by external wars on the ability and willingness of an inept ruling oligarchy firmly to govern a growing imperial system was to increase in the succeeding decades; the ineptitude and indecision which marked official Roman administration in these years gave rise to dissension and unrest, and presented opportunities for ambitious individuals to aim at personal dominance.

Such opportunities were enhanced by another factor. Appointed consul for 107 BC and confirmed in the command against Jugurtha, Marius introduced a series of innovations in the recruitment of Roman legions which became the crucial factor in bringing about the series of civil wars which ended only with the establishment of the Principate. Enlistment was opened to members of the lowest class (*capite censi*); in time the Roman army was composed of men who made soldiering a profession, who depended on general-patrons for their needs both during and after their service years. These close ties with commanders and the building up of an *esprit de corps* over years of active service led to a type of military dictatorship. The five successive consulships of Marius anticipated the series of consulships of Caesar and Octavian Augustus. The last sentence of the monograph, 'At that time the hopes and welfare of our country were in his hands', would eventually apply in a more permanent form to Octavian Augustus. The *Histories* embrace the period from the death of Sulla in 78 to the extraordinary command conferred on Pompeius by the Gabinian law of 67 BC. The basic views and discussions of the two monographs on how the contemporary situation had developed are once more summarized in the introduction to Sallust's major work.

The narrative of the *Histories* (see tabular analysis) deals with the incompetent handling of problems at home and abroad by a ruling oligarchy which continued to demonstrate its lack of ability to administer a Roman imperial system. This unsatisfactory state of affairs leads to the revolt of Lepidus, the Sertorian war, civil unrest in 75, the pirate threat, the third Mithridatic War, and the slave rebellion, all of which play a part in contributing to the rise of Pompeius. This general, competent, ruthless, ambitious, is the dominant character of the *Histories*; his career was the prelude to the demise of the Republican constitution and of political freedom.

The importance which Sallust attached to the role of Pompeius is indicated by the inclusion of the general's early career as part of the introduction to the narrative proper (comm. 1. 44–6) and by the character-sketch which preceded the narrative of Pompeius' role in the Sertorian War (2. 17–20). The fragmentary nature of the extant narrative makes accurate assessment of the scope and tenor of Sallust's treatment of Pompeius' personality and activities hazardous. The immediate impression from what remains of the character-portrait and Pompeius' conduct of the Sertorian War (2. 26–31, 46–57, 70–8; 3. 43–6, 81–9M) is that the historian has concentrated on character traits and activity unfavourable to Pompeius' reputation. Sallust's chief interest was the political factor. Pompeius' letter to the senate (2. 82) illustrates graphically the political motivation which compels him to action. The demagogic practices he resorted to, the use of venal tribunes to achieve his goal of personal domination emerge clearly in a few fragments of Book 4 (42–9M), while all the traits noted in earlier fragments—

demagogy, hypocrisy, conceit—mark his attitude during the
heated debate on the *Lex Gabinia* (5. 19–22, 24M).

The outcome is an unbalanced treatment of a very
complex personality. It is possible that by accident of
transmission discreditable aspects of Pompeius' career out-
number the less reprehensible. It is certain that Pompeius'
role in accelerating the crisis of the Roman Republic would
rule out the glossing-over of aspects less favourable to his
reputation. That the historian's strong feelings led him to
concentrate only on the negative side of Pompeius' activity
cannot be dogmatically asserted, but it remains a strong
possibility.

Works on the formative years of Pompeius' career include
the following: E. Badian, *FC* (1958), 267–84; R. E. Smith,
*Phoenix* 14 (1960), 1–13; A. La Penna, *Athenaeum* 41
(1963), 232–8; Syme, 201–2, 206, 212, 224; B. R. Katz, *Riv.
stor. di antichità* (1982), 111–39.

The crisis of the Roman Republic has been dealt with by
several modern scholars. Major treatments include: Syme,
*Roman Revolution*; A. La Penna, *Sallustio e la rivoluzione
Romana*[3] (Milan 1973); Ch. Meier, *Res Publica Amissa*[2]
(Wiesbaden 1980); P. A. Brunt, *The Fall of the Roman
Republic* (Oxford 1988). Briefer treatments in Syme, *passim*,
and G. Perl, *Philologus* 113 (1969), 201–16.

### 7. THE TIME OF WRITING

The monographs and the *Histories* were written during the
period of the Second Triumvirate. Sallust, who must have
had high hopes that Caesar's victory in the civil war would
be followed by the restoration of the Republican constitution,
realized after Caesar's one-year dictatorship and the political
disturbance which followed the assassination that his fore-
bodings concerning the dangers connected with political and
moral decay (*Cat.* 5. 9) were well founded—the *libera res
publica* was no longer a viable constitutional organ.

This final stage of realization affected the tone and
manner of the proems and narratives of his works. Events
dealt with in the monographs and the *Histories* are viewed,

not in isolation and with reference to their individual content, but from Sallust's experience and knowledge of these later developments. In the note on 1. 67. 22, **on his own authority** I draw attention to widely recognized parallels between the *tumultus Lepidi* and the civil war which broke out late in 44, exemplified particularly by the manifold echoes, in the speech of Philippus, of Cicero's *Philippics* against Antony. In the note on 2. 42, **They then demolished the defensive wall** attention is drawn to the similarities between the attack by a Roman mob on the consuls of 75 and the attack in 40 on the triumvirs Octavian and Antony which is described in App. *BC* 5. 67–8. Thus in the *Histories* events in the past which had a paradigmatic usefulness for developments in Sallust's present were especially stressed. Less immediately obvious events and statements may also have been introduced for their exemplary significance: thus the remarks on the futility of *vis* ('violence') as an instrument for reform, and the failure of more enlightened measures because of moral and political corruption (*Iug.* 3. 2–3) may be a comment on Caesar's failure to set things right; similarly, it has been deduced from the description of 'these degenerate ways' (*Iug.* 4. 7) that Sallust reacted with bitterness against the policy of Caesar and Antony which by debasing the membership of the senate had lowered the dignity and effectiveness of that body. In some cases his writing carries an emphasis which does not flow naturally from the material as such and is perhaps to be accounted for by his passionate attitude to events at his time of writing. Phrases in Catiline's speech, for example, such as: 'For ever since the state fell under the jurisdiction and way of a few powerful men, it is always to them that kings and potentates are tributary, and peoples and nations pay taxes. All the rest of us, good and bad, nobles and commons alike, have made up the mob, without influence, without weight, and subservient to those to whom in a free state we should be an object of fear' (*Cat.* 20. 7; cf. 33. 4, 36. 4), have some application to Pompeius in the east, but are more vividly relevant to the rule of the Triumvirate.

Sallust was able without fear to express his feelings on Sulla's later career: 'As to what he did later, I know not if one should speak of it rather with shame or with sorrow' (*Iug.* 95. 4). Direct criticism of the power-lords of his writing years was out of the question; it would have been an almost suicidal act. He had, therefore, to give expression to his strong antipathy to political despotism by means of indirect remarks and veiled allusions. It is a manner of communication which demands alertness from the reader. It is also an indicator of his political stance during those years.

No direct evidence exists concerning Sallust's political alignment after Caesar's death. The view put forward by W. Allen (*Stud. in Philol.* 51 (1954), 1–14) that Sallust was a follower of Antonius has rightly been dismissed: see A. La Penna, *SIFC* 31 (1959), 168; 33 (1961), 253; *Athenaeum* 41 (1963), 244; Syme, 223; G. Perl, *DLZ* (1964), 880; *Klio* 48 (1967), 105; *WZ Rostock* 18 (1969), 379–90. A suggestion made, with no proof provided, of a connection with Octavian (A. Rosenberg, *Einleitung und Quellenkunde zur römischen Geschichte* (Berlin 1921), 174) has also been rejected; Syme (122, 224, 237–8) has noted that probable Sallustian allusions to Octavian are uniformly negative. Moreover, the sundry statements and allusions in his writings which reveal his rejection of despotism as a form of government would clearly apply to the members of the Second Triumvirate. For Sallust this form of rule was not, as its official description has it, *rei publicae constituendae* ('for the purpose of setting up the republic'), but rather a definitive casting aside of the *libera res publica*.

Sallust's achievement as a historical thinker is that he recognized the decline of the Roman Republic as a historically unavoidable development, even though he deplored that development. His power as a writer lies in the passion with which he expressed his sorrow at the destruction of a political system and of its moral basis, which had earlier opened up for Rome the way to greatness.

## 8. ABOUT THIS EDITION

I have retained Maurenbrecher's convention of using an asterisk (e.g. 1. 5*) to designate fragments which have been transmitted without book-number.

Reference is made in the commentary to philological and grammatical points only where they have a bearing on the historical content of the fragments.

In translating the text I have used italics where the source material is in the form of an indirect reference to Sallust's text (e.g. 1. 30). Where a word or phrase inside such an indirect reference is assumed to be a direct quotation from the *Histories* it is printed in roman type (e.g. 1. 3).

At the end of the text of each book is a small group of fragments transmitted with book number which cannot be placed within the text of the book. These are described in the commentary as 'Fragments *incertae sedis*' (of uncertain placement). The group 'Fragments of Uncertain Reference' in Vol. 2 is used for fragments transmitted without book number which cannot be placed with confidence in a specific context.

Reference in this introduction and in the commentary on Books 1 and 2 to fragments in Books 4-5 have been made according to Maurenbrecher's organization of the fragments (e.g. 4. 2M). The reason is that I have not yet dealt with the last two books of the work and I anticipate that my translation of their texts will involve changes to Maurenbrecher's ordering of the fragments. A concordance provided in Volume 2 will make clear the connection between the order of fragments in this edition with the order established by Maurenbrecher.

# SALLUST
# *THE HISTORIES*

**1.** Rufinus, 575. 18

I have compiled the military and civil history of the Roman
people for the consular year of Marcus Lepidus and Quintus
Catulus, and for the years thereafter.

**2.** Priscianus, 3. 188. 15

For from the beginning of the city to the Macedonian War
against Perseus . . .

**3.** Victorinus, 203. 24

*For history in its expression ought to be concise and lucid and
credible, all of which qualities Sallust attributed to himself in
the* Catilina: *'I shall write briefly and as truthfully as I can' (4.
3). In the first book of his* Histories *he attributed individual
desirable qualities to other writers of history. To Cato he
granted brevity:* 'The most eloquent Roman of all made his
descriptions brief'; *to Fannius he granted the quality of truth.*

**4.** Charisius, 280. 11

recently wrote / written . . .

**5.** * Servius Dan. *Aen.* 2. 89

I, in so great an abundance of very learned men . . .

**6.** *Adnot. super Luc.* 3. 164

*The fact that this* Cato, on the proposal of Clodius, was sent
to Cyprus to make formal acceptance of the inheritance
which king Ptolemy on his death had bequeathed to the
Roman people. *Sallust records this at the beginning of the
first book of the* Histories.

**7.** Arusianus Messius, 494. 4

Nor has the fact that I fought on a different side in a civil war
diverted me from the truth.

**8.** Priscianus, 2. 58. 1

The first quarrels arose among us through a defect of human nature which, restless and unbridled, is always immersed in struggles for liberty or for glory or for power.

**9.** Victorinus, 158. 7

The Roman state reached the height of its power in the consulship of Servius Sulpicius and Marcus Marcellus, after all Gaul this side of the Rhine and in the region between the Mediterranean and the Ocean had, except for places rendered inaccessible because of swamps, been totally subjugated. On the other hand, the state conducted its affairs according to the highest moral standards and with the greatest harmony in the period between the second and last Punic wars.

**10.** Augustinus, *CD* 2. 18

But discord and avarice and ambition and other vices which tend to emerge in times of prosperity increased to a very great extent after the destruction of Carthage. Indeed the injustices inflicted by the more powerful, the resultant secessions of the plebs from the patrician class and other types of disagreement occurred in Rome from the very beginning. After the expulsion of the kings a regime of equal justice and restraint lasted only until fear of Tarquinius and the serious war with Etruria came to an end. From that time on the patricians treated the people as slaves, made decisions, as the kings had done, concerning their execution and flogging, drove them from their lands and acted like tyrants over the rest of the population who were now landless. Crushed by these cruel practices and above all by a load of debt occasioned by the necessity to contribute both money and military service for continual wars, the common people, armed, took up position on the Mons Sacer and on the Aventine and acquired for themselves tribunes of the people and some legal rights. The contention and strife between the two groups came to an end with the advent of the second Punic War.

**11.** Arusianus Messius, 504. 21

a city free from wars . . .

**12.** Gellius, 9. 12. 15 and Augustinus, *CD* 3. 17

Once the fear of the Carthaginians was removed the way was clear for the exercise of political feuds. Frequent riots, party strife, and finally civil wars broke out, during which a few powerful men, to whose influential position most people had lent their support, were attempting to win absolute rule masquerading as champions of the senate or of the people. The terms 'good' and 'bad' were applied to citizens, not on the yardstick of services rendered or injuries inflicted on the state, since all were equally corrupt; any individual of outstanding wealth and irresistible in his lawlessness was considered 'good' because he was the preserver of existing conditions.

**13.\*** Augustinus, *CD* 2. 18

From that time the moral standards of our ancestors, which before this had been declining gradually, were swept away with the velocity of a torrent; the young were so corrupted by self-indulgence and by avarice that it could truly be said that men had been born who could not preserve their own patrimonies nor allow others to preserve theirs.

**14.** Arusianus Messius, 484. 19

The honour of all parties had degenerated into a commodity for barter.

**15.\*** Augustinus, *CD* 2. 21

*Indeed at the time when this discussion is supposed to have taken place the death had already occurred of one of the Gracchi,* an action, *says Sallust,* which gave rise to serious political discord.

**16.\*** Servius, *G.* 2. 209

So great was the sense of responsibility exercised by our forefathers towards the Italian race.

**17.\*** Cledonius, 76. 24

The Licinian law was detrimental to everyone this side of the Po.

**18.*** *Adnot. super Luc.* 3. 632
and all Italy defected in spirit.

**19.*** Donatus, Ter. *Adelph.* 458
after the revolt of the allies and the Latins.

**20.*** Servius Dan. *Aen.* 8. 8
In effect Italy was ravaged by plundering, by the flight of inhabitants, and by massacres.

**21.** Servius Dan. *Aen.* 10. 45
Finally he begged the settlers themselves in the name of the distresses and the uncertainties of the human condition.

**22.** Nonius, 543. 29
During the night by chance he came upon a fisherman's small craft.

**23.*** Servius Dan. *Ecl.* 5. 19
that the war should come to an end under whatever conditions were available.

**24.** Arusianus Messius, 498. 8
that nothing had been settled concerning the constitution or the liberty of the Roman people.

**25.** Priscianus, 2. 536. 10
He tied . . . together after the manner of a chain.

**26.** Arusianus Messius, 486. 16
unaccustomed to freedom . . .

**27.** Arusianus Messius, 487. 1
Sulla, having suspicions concerning these matters and especially concerning the ferocious temperament of King Mithridates, who would renew the war at the opportune time . . .

**28.** Arusianus Messius, 459. 13
they hastened to muster the army at Dyrrhachium.

**29.** \* Donatus, Ter. *Eun.* 978

Then arose a dialogue, with questions being put from both sides concerning their respective states of well-being, the relationships with their respective generals, the extent of their personal possessions.

**30.** \* *Adnot. super Luc.* 2. 134

[*Near Sacriportus*] *Sulla, after his return from Asia, fought and defeated the young Marius, who fled to Praeneste. This is the Marius who attained the consulship against his mother's will, as Sallust records.*

**31.** \* Servius, *Ecl.* 2. 67

and the defeat of Marius had enlarged the war.

**32.** Priscianus, 3. 67. 1

stationed near Praeneste . . .

**33.** \* Servius, *Aen.* 2. 400

Seized by a base fear, Carbo abandoned Italy and his army.

**34.** Arusianus Messius, 484. 13

so that the Sullani were planning their escape for the night-time.

**35.** \* *Adnot. super Luc.* 2. 139

so that the domination which he had taken vengeance on was being longed for.

**36.** *Adnot. super Luc.* 2. 174

as in the case of Marcus Marius whose eyes were gouged out after his arms and legs had first been broken, evidently in order that he might expire member by member.

**37.** Donatus, Ter. *Hecyr.* 258

and he was the uncle of his children.

**38.** Servius Dan. *Aen.* 2. 502

since the altars and other things set aside for the service of the gods were being defiled by the blood of suppliants.

**39.**\*  Lydus, *De magistr.* 3. 8

*The nomenclators, as Aemilius [Asper] says in his commentary
on the* Histories *of Sallust, are those who indicate and name
the citizens.*

**40.**  Priscianus, 2. 392. 22

Since, therefore, the goods of the proscribed had been sold
or simply given away . . .

**41.**  Arusianus Messius, 450. 16

that they would refuse him nothing because of so generous a
reward.

**42.**  Arusianus Messius, 506. 31

by which it was revealed that a return to the republican
constitution had been sought for the acquisition of booty,
not for the restoration of freedom.

**43.**  *Adnot. super Luc.* 1. 175

there was a reversion to the custom of the barbarous past in
which all right was based on might.

**44.**\*  Servius, *Aen.* 2. 20

pretending that his bowels were being purged.

**45.**  Gellius, 9. 12. 14

That war was aroused by fear of the victorious Pompeius
who was restoring Hiempsal to his throne.

**46.**  Festus, 210. 9

When the great siege works had been completed, he
appointed his lieutenant Lucius Catilina to conduct the
siege.

**47.**  Arusianus Messius, 499. 1

both were competing against each other with great bitterness
about the prefecture of the city as if it were about the control
of the state.

**48.**  Codex Vaticanus Lat. 3864 (V): Speech of Lepidus to
the Roman people

(**1**)  Your clemency and your honesty, fellow citizens,

qualities which have made you supreme and renowned throughout all other nations, fill me with the greatest fear in dealing with the tyranny of Lucius Sulla. On the one hand I am afraid that you may be tricked through not believing others capable of acts which you yourselves consider abominable—especially since all Sulla's expectations are dependent upon crime and treachery, and he thinks that he cannot be safe unless he has shown himself even worse and more detestable than you fear, so that when you have been completely duped by him your wretchedness may wipe out your concern for freedom. Then again, if you do take precautions, I fear that you may be more occupied in averting dangers than in exacting retribution for wrongs committed. (2) As for his satellites, I cannot adequately express my amazement that men who bear names made great by the most distinguished deeds of their ancestors are willing to pay for dominion over you with their own slavery, and, without regard for equity, prefer this state of affairs to living as free men according to the highest principles of justice. (3) Distinguished offspring of the Bruti, Aemilii, and Lutatii, born to overthrow what their ancestors acquired by their prowess! (4) For what did these forefathers defend against Pyrrhus, Hannibal, Philip, and Antiochus other than our liberty and each his own dwelling-place and our right of submitting to nothing but the laws? (5) But all of these benefits this caricature of a Romulus of ours holds in his hands as if they had been wrested from foreigners; not fully sated with the destruction of so many armies, consuls, and other leading men whom the fortune of war had destroyed, he shows more cruelty at a time when success turns most men from anger to pity. (6) But more than that, he alone of all within the memory of man has devised punishment for those yet unborn, who are thus assured of outrage before they are assured of life. Worst of all, up to this time he has been protected by the enormity of his crimes while you are being deterred from taking steps to recover your liberty by the fear of an even more cruel servitude.

(7) Now is the time for action, citizens; now is the time to face up to the tyrant in order that your spoils may not be bestowed on him. This is not the time for putting things off,

nor for looking for help by prayers to the gods—unless, perchance, you hope he is now weary or ashamed of his tyranny and that what he has seized through crime he will, with even greater danger to himself, let go. (8) On the contrary, he has sunk to the point where he regards no position as illustrious unless it is safe, and considers every device for retaining his supremacy as honourable. (9) And so that state of tranquillity and peace combined with freedom, which many good men used to choose rather than an active career with honours as a reward, is a thing of the past; (10) in these times, citizens, one must either be slave or master, one must feel fear or inspire it. (11) For what else is left to us? What human laws are left? What divine laws have not been violated? The Roman people, a short while ago the ruler of nations, now stripped of power, repute, and rights, without the power to administer its own affairs, an object of contempt, does not even retain the rations of slaves. (12) A considerable part of our allies and of the people of Latium are being debarred by this one man from the citizenship granted them by you in return for their many and distinguished services, while a few of his underlings, as a reward for their crimes, have taken possession of the ancestral homes of the guiltless common people. (13) The laws, the courts, the treasury, the provinces, client-kings, nay even the power of life and death over our citizens are in the hands of one man. (14) At the same time you have witnessed human sacrifices and seen tombs stained with the blood of citizens. (15) Is there anything left to those who are truly men except to rid themselves of oppression or to die valiantly? For in truth nature has appointed one and the same end for all, even for those flanked by armed might, and no man waits for the final inevitability doing nothing, unless he has the heart of a woman.

(16) But Sulla says that I am a cause of political turmoil because I protest against the rewards paid to inciters of civil disorder; he calls me a lover of war because I seek to restore the rights which apply in times of peace. (17) Of course I do, since you will not be safe and fully protected under Sulla's domination unless Vettius of Picenum and the clerk

Cornelius may squander the goods which others have
honestly acquired; unless you all approve the proscription of
innocent men because of their wealth, the torture of
distinguished citizens, a city depopulated by exile and
murder, the goods of wretched citizens sold or given away as
if they were the spoils of the Cimbri. (18) Sulla charges
me with having possessions which are derived from the
goods of the proscribed, but in fact the very greatest of his
crimes is that neither I nor anyone else would have been
sufficiently safe if we were doing what was right. Moreover
the property which at that time I bought through fear, I am
disposed nevertheless to restore to those who, having paid
the price, are their rightful owners; it is not my intention to
allow any depredations at the expense of citizens. (19) Let
it be enough to have endured what our madness has brought
upon us—Roman armies pitted against each other, our arms
turned away from the enemy and against ourselves. Let
there be an end to crime and outrage—of which, however,
Sulla is so far from repenting that he counts them among his
claims to glory, and, if he were allowed, would even more
eagerly do them again.

(20) But now, while I no longer have qualms about what
you think of him, I do have fears about how far you are
prepared to go. My anxiety is that, while you are waiting for
someone else to give a lead, you may be caught, not by his
forces which are unreliable and venal, but through your
inaction which allows one to continue on a course of robbery
with violence and to appear fortunate in proportion to one's
audacity. (21) For, apart from his crime-stained underlings, who has the same aspirations or who does not desire a
complete change, retaining only the achievement of victory?
Is it, think you, the soldiers at the cost of whose blood riches
have been won for slaves such as Tarrula and Scirtus? (22)
Or is it those who in seeking office were thought less worthy
than Fufidius, a vile wench, the degradation of all honours?
And so I place my greatest confidence in that victorious
army which has gained nothing by so many wounds and
hardships except a tyrant. (23) Unless perchance their
mission was the overthrow by force of arms of the power of
the tribunes which their forefathers had established by force

of arms, and to rob themselves with their own hands of their rights and jurisdiction. Extraordinary indeed the reward they received when, banished to swamps and woods, they find that insult and hatred are their portion, that just a few carry off the prizes. (24) Why then, you might ask, does the tyrant parade about with so great a following and with such assurance? Because success is a wonderful screen for vices; but if success falters he will be despised as much as he is now feared. Or perhaps he acts in this way under the pretext of maintaining peace and harmony, which are the names he has bestowed on his guilt and treason. Furthermore, he declares that the republic cannot otherwise stand firm and the war be ended unless the common people are permanently driven from their lands, the citizens cruelly plundered, and all rights and jurisdiction which once belonged to the Roman people placed in his own hands. (25) If this seems to you to be peace and order, then show your approval of the utter demoralization and overthrow of the republic; assent to the laws that have been imposed on you; accept a peace combined with servitude and hand on to future generations a model of how to ruin their country at the price of their own citizens' blood. (26) As far as I am concerned, although by reaching this highest of offices I had done enough to live up to the fame of my ancestors, as well as to secure my own dignity and even my safety, it was not my intention to pursue my private interests; I regarded freedom united with danger preferable to peace with slavery. (27) If you share this view, citizens of Rome, rouse yourselves, and with the good help of the gods follow Marcus Aemilius, your consul, who will be your leader and champion in recovering your freedom.

**49.** Arusianus Messius, 504. 11

in fact he did not dare to complain about the domination of Sulla . . . at which he took offence.

**50.*** *Schol. Gronov. Rosc.* 90 (312. 4 St.)

Quickly it becomes a matter of shame to catalogue outrageous conduct in so prominent a personage.

**51.** Arusianus Messius, 488. 10
flaunting his conduct before the eyes of all peoples.

**52.** Charisius, 253. 3
that he was, by his own admission, insatiable in other respects and in his lusting after other men's wives.

**53.**\* Plutarch, *Comp. Lysandri et Sullae*, 3. 2
*But Sulla allowed neither the poverty of his youth nor the years of his old age to put limits on his desires; he continued to introduce marriage and sumptuary laws for the citizens, while he himself was living in lewdness and adultery, as Sallust says.*

**54.** Servius Dan. *Aen.* 4. 283
Octavius and Q. Caepio did the same thing without any serious expectation on the part of anyone and clearly without being publicly requested to do so.

**55.** Nonius, 257. 47
In fact pimps and wine-merchants and butchers and other artisans of the type used by the common people in their daily pursuits were organized for a price.

**56.**\* Servius Dan. *Aen.* 4. 214
addressing him at the top of his voice as 'tyrant' and 'Cinna'.

**57.**\* Servius Dan. *Aen.* 1. 270
A large crowd of men had assembled, driven from their fields or expelled from their city.

**58.** Charisius, 266. 29
that Lepidus and Catulus with armies allotted to them by decree should set out as early as possible.

**59.** Nonius, 31. 30
Then the Etruscans and the other people who supported the same cause, thinking that they had at last found a leader, provoked war with the greatest delight.

**60.** Arusianus Messius, 503. 7
having a good understanding of all that the senate had recommended.

**61.*** Donatus, Ter. *Andr.* 365

Was he therefore bound to submit to the decree of the senate?

**62.** Priscianus, 2. 243. 10

the tribunician power, a prerogative of the people.

**63.** Charisius, 331. 13

[that] Lepidus, repenting of his decision . . .

**64.** Arusianus Messius, 484. 20

It was suspected that all of Etruria had joined the revolt behind Lepidus.

**65.*** Donatus, *Aen.* 1. 37

For enterprises of that kind, if they did not turn to the detriment of their authors, would bring ruin to the Republic.

**66.*** Servius, *Aen.* 9. 244

[Philippus] who in age and wisdom surpassed the rest.

**67.** Codex Vaticanus Lat. 3864 (V): Speech of Philippus in the senate

(**1**)  My greatest wish, Fathers of the Senate, would be that our country might be at peace or that in the midst of dangers it might be defended by all of its ablest citizens; or at least that evil designs should cause harm to their contrivers. But on the contrary, everything is in turmoil, the result of civil dissensions fomented by those whose duty it was rather to suppress them; and finally, the wise and the good are forced to do what the worst and most foolish of men have decided.  (**2**)  For even though you may detest war and arms, you must nevertheless take them up because it is what Lepidus wants, unless perchance anyone has a policy of preserving peace and at the same time allowing aggression. (**3**)  O ye good gods, who still watch over this city about which we have ceased to worry: Marcus Aemilius, lowest of all criminals—it is difficult to say whether he is more vicious or more cowardly—has an army for the purpose of overthrowing our liberty, and from being an object of contempt has transformed himself into something to be feared. You, meanwhile, mumbling and dithering, look for peace with words and the incantations of soothsayers instead of fighting for it; you do not realize that by your irresolute decisions you are losing your prestige and Lepidus his fear. (4) This is a natural outcome, since he reached a consulship because of his robberies, and obtained a command and an army because of acts of sedition. What might he not have gained by good conduct when you have rewarded his crimes so generously?

(5) But of course it is those who up to the very last have voted for embassies, for peace, for harmony and the like that have won his favour! Quite the opposite. Despised, considered unworthy of a share in government, they are regarded as fair game since fear it was that made them sue for the peace which fear had made them lose. (6) For my own part, from the very outset, when I saw Etruria conspiring, the proscribed being recalled, and the state rent asunder by bribery, I thought there was no time to be wasted, and with a few others I supported the policy of Catulus. But those who extolled the great deeds of the Aemilian clan and who maintained that they had added to the greatness of the Roman people by taking a lenient view said that even at that stage Lepidus had taken no irrevocable step, in spite of the fact that he had taken up arms on his own responsibility to overthrow freedom. And so, while seeking power or protection for themselves, each of them has suborned the deliberations of the senate. (7) At that time, however, Lepidus was a brigand at the head of some camp-followers and a few cutthroats, not one of whom could have got a day's pay for his life. Now he is a proconsul with military power which he did not buy but which you gave him, with staff officers who are still bound by law to obey him. The most vicious characters of every social class flock to his standard inflamed by poverty and greed, driven by the consciousness of their crimes, men who find repose in times of discord, disquiet in times of peace. These are the men who sow the seeds of rebellion after rebellion, of war after war, followers once of Saturninus, then of Sulpicius, next of Marius and Damasippus, and now of Lepidus. (8) Moreover, Etruria and all the other smouldering embers of

war are aroused; the Spanish provinces are stirred to revolt,
Mithridates, in close proximity to those of the tributary
peoples from whom we still receive support, is looking for an
opportunity for war; in short, for the overthrow of our
empire nothing is lacking save a competent leader.

(9)    Wherefore, senators, I beg and implore you to watch
out; do not allow the unbounded licence of crime, like a
madness, to infect those who are still sound; for when the
wicked are rewarded, it is not easy for anyone to remain
virtuous just for virtue's sake.    (10)    Or are you waiting for
Lepidus to come again with an army and enter our city with
fire and sword? In truth that eventuality is much nearer the
position in which he now finds himself than is civil war to
peace and concord.    (11)    He has taken up arms against
the state in defiance of all human and divine law, not in
order to avenge the wrongs inflicted on himself or the
wrongs of those whom he pretends to represent, but to
overthrow our laws and our liberty. For he is driven and
tormented in mind by ambition and fear resulting from his
crimes; uneasy and cut off from advice, he is resorting now
to this plan, now to that. He fears peace, hates war; he sees
that he must abstain from luxury and licence, and meantime
he takes advantage of your indolence.    (12)    As for your
conduct, I lack sufficient wisdom to know whether I should
call it fear or laziness or madness, when each one of you
seems to be praying that such great evils which threaten you
like a thunderbolt may not touch him, and yet makes no
effort to prevent them.

(13)    I ask you to reflect how the order of things is
reversed: formerly, public mischief was planned secretly,
public defence openly, and hence the good easily forestalled
the wicked; nowadays peace and harmony are disturbed
openly, defended secretly; those who desire disorder are in
arms, you are in fear. What are you waiting for, unless
perchance you are ashamed or weary of doing the right
thing?    (14)    Or is it that the demands of Lepidus have
influenced your thinking? He says that it is his wish to render
to each his own and keeps the property belonging to others;
to annul laws set up in time of war, while he uses armed
compulsion; to validate the citizenship of those from whom

he denies it has been taken, and in the interests of harmony to restore the power of the tribunes, from which all our discords have been kindled. (15) O worst and most shameless of all men, are the poverty and grief of our citizens of any concern to you? To you who have nothing in your possession which was not seized by arms or by injustice? You ask for a second consulship—as if you had ever given up your first! You seek harmony through war, by which the harmony which we had attained is being broken, a traitor to us, unfaithful to your party, the enemy of all good men. That you stand ashamed neither before men nor before the gods, whom you have outraged by your perfidy and your perjury! (16) Since such is your character I urge you to hold to your purpose and to retain your arms, lest by postponing your plans for rebellion, you may be unsettled yourself and keep us in a state of watchful concern. Neither the provinces nor the laws nor your country's gods tolerate you as a citizen. Continue as you have begun, so that you may meet with your deserts as soon as possible.

(17) And you, my fellow senators, how long, by your hesitation, will you allow your country to be undefended, and how long will you continue to meet arms with words? Forces have been levied against you, money extorted from individuals and from the treasury, garrisons removed from some places and stationed in others; laws are being issued in arbitrary fashion, and in the meantime you are thinking about sending envoys and making decrees! But by Hercules, the more eagerly you seek peace, the more bitter will the war be, since he finds that he is being encouraged in his objectives more by your fear than by the justice and righteousness of his cause. (18) For whoever says that he hates turmoil and the death of citizens, and as a consequence keeps you unarmed while Lepidus is in arms, is really advising you to suffer what the conquered must endure, although you yourselves have the power to inflict such a fate upon others. Such counsellors are advising you to keep peace with him and encouraging him to make war upon you. (19) If this is what you want, if such great torpor has stolen upon your spirits that, forgetting the crimes of Cinna upon whose return to our city the flower of this senatorial

order perished, you will nevertheless entrust yourselves, your wives, and your children to Lepidus, what need is there of decrees? What need of Catulus' help? (**20**)   Surely it is in vain that he and other good citizens are taking thought for the republic. But have it your way. Acquire the protection of Cethegus and other traitors who are eager to renew the regime of pillage and fire, and once more to arm their bands against our country's gods. If on the other hand you stand for liberty and for what is good and true, pass decrees worthy of your name and so increase the courage of our brave defenders. (**21**)   A new army is ready, to which are added the colonies of veteran soldiers, all the nobles and the best leaders. Fortune favours the stronger; soon the forces which our negligence has allowed to develop will melt away. (**22**)   Therefore, this is what I recommend: whereas [Marcus] Lepidus, in defiance of the authority of this body, in concert with the worst enemies of their country, is leading against this city an army raised on his own authority, therefore let it be resolved that Appius Claudius the *interrex*, with Quintus Catulus the proconsul and others who have *imperium*, shall defend the city and see to it that the Republic comes to no harm.

**68.**   Arusianus Messius, 492. 24
he was hastening his flight.

**69.**   Arusianus Messius, 503. 4
superior in numbers, but being himself devoid of military experience . . .

**70.**   Priscianus, 3. 67. 2
near Mutina . . .

**71.***   Servius, *Aen.* 10. 168
*To Cosae, a city of Etruria, which, according to Sallust, is expressed in the singular number.*

**72.**   Arusianus Messius, 474. 31
speeding up their departure.

**73.*** Victorinus, 205. 30

After the expulsion of M. Lepidus and the whole of his army from Italy, an anxiety less urgent but by no means less serious and complex was worrying the senators.

**74.*** *Adnot. super Luc.* 2. 534

the whole of hither Spain was in turmoil.

**75.** Priscianus, 2. 535. 16

He requested Curio as a younger man and one who had not been repulsed by the votes of the people to concede priority to Mamercus on the ground of age.

**76.*** Servius Dan. *G.* 1. 8

He exchanged the toga for a military cloak.

**77.*** Gellius 2. 72. 2

Under the command of Titus Didius in Spain he covered himself in glory as a military tribune. In the Marsic War he made himself very useful in the preparation of troops and weaponry; and yet many achievements carried out under his command were left unrecorded, principally because he was not a noble, thus arousing the spite of historians. However, during his lifetime his face bore the record of such deeds in numerous battle scars and an empty eye-socket. Far from being worried about them, he took the greatest delight in these disfigurements in so far as he was keeping, to his greater glory, the rest of his body intact.

**78.*** Donatus, Ter. *Andr.* 939

and they were greeting him with enthusiastic shouts of congratulation.

**79.*** Seneca, *Ep.* 114. 19

In the midst of civil war he seeks a reputation for justice and virtue.

**80.*** Donatus, Ter. *Eun.* 92

unless counteraction were taken against him in concert.

**81.*** Donatus, Ter. *Eun*. 467
when a conference was granted to the troops against his will,
a few were corrupted and the army was handed over to
Sulla.

**82.*** Servius, *Aen*. 1. 380
that Spain was his ancient motherland.

**83.*** *Adnot. super Luc*. 7. 267
He was greatly loved for the moderation and punctiliousness
with which he exercised command.

**84.*** *Comm. Bern. ad Luc*. 1. 478
Salinator is killed while on the march.

**85.*** Jerome, *Ep*. 70. 6
Calpurnius surnamed Lanarius.

**86.** Arusianus Messius, 480. 16
a few men who were occupying the pass.

**87.** Gellius, 10. 26. 10
Some of these [ships], after going just a little way, began to
sink, the load being excessive—and unstable when panic
had thrown the passengers into disorder.

**88.*** Servius Dan. *Aen*. 2. 564
since Sertorius with so small a force was unable to make a
sortie with his ships.

**89.*** Gellius, 9. 12. 22
with the natural desire of mankind to visit unknown places.

**90.** Nonius, 495. 40
It was known that the two islands, near to each other and ten
thousand furlongs distant from Cadize, spontaneously produce food for their inhabitants.

**91.*** Servius, *Aen*. 5. 735
*According to the philosophers Elysium is the Fortunate Isles*
which, *says Sallust,* have been celebrated in the songs of
Homer.

**92.** Servius Dan. *Aen.* 2. 640
It is said that he had planned a flight to distant stretches of Ocean.

**93.** Gellius, 10. 26. 2
And so Sertorius, having left a small garrison in Mauretania, took advantage of a dark night and a favourable tide and tried by stealth and by speed to avoid a battle while making the crossing.

**94.** Gellius, 10. 26. 2
When they had crossed, a mountain, seized in advance by the Lusitanians, gave them all shelter.

**95.** Nonius, 231. 22
And soon Fufidius, arriving with his legions, after he sees such steep banks and just one ford, which was by no means an easy crossing for combatants (everything in fact more favourable to the enemy than to his own troops) . . .

**96.** Priscianus, 2. 534. 21
He summoned Domitius the proconsul from hither Spain with all the forces which he had assembled.

**97.** Arusianus Messius, 469. 28
a people who had rarely gone beyond the borders of their own region.

**98.** *Schol. Veron. Aen.* 4. 178/Cod. P. Vindob. Lat. 117
(A)
and throughout the whole province there spread exaggerated and fearsome rumours, as each witness, obeying the impulses of his own terror, was alleging that there were fifty thousand or more enemy troops, men of strange and monstrous aspect, eaters of human flesh fetched from the confines of Ocean . . .
. . . by Domitius . . .

**99.** Priscianus, 2. 436. 5
The horses, terrified or wounded and without their riders, are throwing ⟨the combatants⟩ into confusion.

**100.** Cod. P. Vindob. Lat. 117 (B)

they were in favour of submitting, not so much because of
the horses and the weapons as through their own fear. But
Domitius, as he was standing forth and beseeching those
whom he recognized not to deliver him, their general, into
the hands of the enemy . . . killed . . . the legatus Septimius
. . . struck[?].

He, however, as if paralysed by fear, was not sufficiently
in control of his mind or of his hearing or speaking, and was
in every way preoccupied ⟨*as to how he might withdraw
himself from danger*⟩ . . . had lost much blood . . . was
calling himself . . . four days. . .

**101.** Arusianus Messius, 476. 18

and Metellus was informed of their numbers by letter.

**102.** Nonius, 310. 11

Setting out for that region he burned villages and fortresses,
and laid waste by fire fields deserted by the farmers; but his
depredations were neither wide-ranging nor carried out with
any great speed, because of his fear of a people expert in the
laying of ambushes.

**103.*** Servius Dan. *Aen.* 10. 103

Now all at once the Tagus was seen to subside.

**104.*** Servius Dan. *Aen.* 3. 516

He took up a position in a valley covered with brushwood
and low trees.

**105.** Priscianus, 2. 539. 20

and they did not have time to withdraw or to array
themselves for battle.

**106.** Nonius, 526. 12

He took by storm Dipo, a strongly fortified town which had
held out for many days.

**107.*** Servius Dan. *Aen.* 12. 458

a heavily fortified town of Lusitania.

**108.*** Pompeius, 273. 11
He came to Conisturgis, the leading town of the region.

**109.** Diomedes, 374. 1
At the command of Metellus the trumpeters interposed a call.

**110.** Charisius, 235. 1
irreproachable in other respects and of outstanding ability.

**111.** Priscianus, 3. 79. 25
although driven off on more than one occasion, he does not lose his confidence . . .

**112.** Nonius, 282. 22
While the gates were causing the people to crowd together, and, as usual in such terrified confusion, no distinction was being made regarding birth or rank, Sertorius was raised about half-way up the wall on the shoulders of his servants and then hoisted over the wall by the hands of soldiers positioned on the top of the wall.

**113.** Arusianus Messius, 460. 6
A very high hill near Ilerda was occupied and around it they built many defensive works.

**114.** Pompeius, 163. 6
Sertorius had transformed that pirate emporium into a naval base.

**115.*** Priscianus, 3. 64. 19
And so Servilius, leaving his sick colleague at Tarentum, crossed the sea ahead of him.

**116.*** Servius, *Aen.* 1. 420
overlooking the lands of Lycia and Pisidia.

**117.** Priscianus, 3. 66. 19
towards Olympus and Phaselis . . .

**118.** Priscianus, 3. 66. 20
towards Corycus . . .

**119.** Priscianus, 3. 66. 20
near Corycus . . .

**120.** Priscianus, 3. 66. 21
near the town of Lete . . .

**121.** Priscianus, 3. 66. 21
driven back from the town of Lete . . .

**122.** Servius Dan. *Aen.* 12. 694
a few who possessed expertise and genuine talent rejected
these ⟨practices⟩.

**123.** Arusianus Messius, 514. 10
that the city referred to was devoid of men of military age.

**124.** Priscianus, 2. 366. 10
part of the army was in two minds.

**125.** Arusianus Messius, 462. 6
to face up to and to die with the enemy.

**126.** Arusianus Messius, 465. 2
he chose a location higher than was becoming for victors.

**127.** Arusianus Messius, 509. 9
and he was moving the sentries back under the penthouses.

**128.** Priscianus, 2. 367. 7
but from there, without pausing for defensive works or for
rest, he advanced against the town.

**129.** Servius Dan. *Ecl.* 5. 5
seeing that he had come close to the wall of the enemy, he
had paid the penalty.

**130.** Priscianus, 2. 512. 10
unless it had faded away along with the frenzy for war.

**131.** Arusianus Messius, 493. 13
practised in war . . .

**132.** Arusianus Messius, 464. 20
trained in warfare . . .

**133.** Arusianus Messius, 470. 18
outstanding in war . . .

**134.** Arusianus Messius, 493. 17
in the middle of the day . . .

**135.** Donatus, Ter. *Phorm.* 979
by deserted tracks . . .

**136.** Arusianus Messius, 484. 17
immoderate in his feelings . . .

**137.** Charisius, 154. 23
wild . . .

**138.** Charisius, 308. 1
mainly among those who . . .

**139.** Eutyches, 483. 8
*the defective forms quaeso, quaesis, the infinitive of which,
quaesere, Sallust placed in the first book of the* Histories.

BOOK 2

**1.*** Donatus, Ter. *Phorm.* 97
when I have dealt with the geography of the island.

**2.** Gellius, 13. 30. 5
Sardinia, in the African Sea, has the shape of a human foot
and projects to a larger extent to the east than to the west.

**3.*** Solinus, 4. 1
*Concerning Sardinia, which is called Sandaliotis in* Timaeus
*and* Ichnusa *in Crispus, it is quite well known in what sea it is
situated and who the ancestors of its inhabitants are.*

**4.*** Servius, *Aen.* 1. 299
*At that time one cause of invasions was sea-voyaging, which made it easy for people to change their abodes, as Sallust records.*

**5.** Charisius, 278. 5
from regions far away and distant from each other.

**6.*** Servius, *Aen.* 7. 662
of Geryon . . .

**7.** Priscianus, 2. 154. 2
[or] as others have related, Tartessus, a Spanish city which the Carthaginians now inhabit under the name of Gaddir.

**8.*** Probus, *Catholica* 7. 27
the son of Apollo and Cyrene . . .

**9.** Pap. Rylands III 473
or to Iolaus . . . it being uncertain whether [the name] is . . . or evidence of their foreign origin. The Balari were runaways from the Carthaginian army—according to the Corsicans they were Pallantians, while some think them Numidians and others Spaniards—a race whom either their fickle temperament or fear of their allies rendered disloyal, recognized by their dark-coloured clothing, their manners, and their beards. In the Celtiberian war . . . Daedalus after he had set out from Sicily, whither he had fled to escape the anger ⟨and power⟩ of Minos.

**10.*** Servius, *Aen.* 1. 601
*many settled in different places after the fall of Troy . . . others, according to Sallust, settled in Sardinia.*

**11.** Arusianus Messius, 490. 4
country rich in crops and fodder . . .

**12.*** Servius, *Ecl.* 7. 41
for in Sardinia there grows a plant similar to balm, *as Sallust says.* If it is eaten, it contracts men's faces with the pain of the rictus and kills them, causing a grimace like a smile.

**13.** Priscianus, 2. 264. 8

But they themselves speak of a bull belonging to a herd which a Ligurian woman called Corsa used to tend near the shore.

**14.*** Probus, *Catholica* 22. 26

to Tarrhi . . .

**15.** Arusianus Messius, 472. 6

people banished from the [Roman] world . . .

**16.** Nonius, 385. 2

In addition, in their gossip, by depreciating his failures as perversity, his successes as chance, his luck in warfare as recklessness, they were destroying . . .

**17.*** Suetonius, *Gram.* 15

*so that Lenaeus . . . savaged Sallust the historian in a bitter satire because he had written of him* [Pompeius] *as noble of countenance, shameless in character.*

**18.** Donatus, Ter. *Phorm.* 170

moderate in all things except in his thirst for power.

**19.*** Donatus, Ter. *Eun.* 285

nevertheless from young manhood he had behaved insultingly towards many honourable men.

**20.*** Vegetius, *Mil.* 1. 9

He used to compete in jumping with the agile, in running with the fleet of foot, in using a crowbar with the muscular.

**21.** Gellius, 10. 20. 10

for the tribune of the plebs Gaius Herennius had, by previous arrangement with him, vetoed a law proposed by the consul Sulla concerning his return.

**22.*** Cledonius, 22. 12

at Narbonne through an assembly of the Gauls . . .

**23.** Priscianus, 2. 243. 3

Because he was excitable and restless in both movements

and words he used to call him Burbuleius, the name of a half-mad actor.

**24.**   Arusianus Messius, 489. 5

. . . and his colleague Octavius, good-natured and suffering from gout.

**25.**   Arusianus Messius, 467. 3

that he might cease from pursuing that course of action.

**26.***   Jerome, *Abac.* 2. 9

the Saguntines, renowned among mankind for their loyalty and their misfortunes, their devotion outstripping their resources, since in their city even then walls half-demolished, houses unroofed, and the inner walls of temples blackened by smoke were showing clear evidence of the Punic invasion.

**27.***   Charisius, 128. 10

of the Saguntines . . .

**28.***   Servius, *G.* 2. 98

Against them Sertorius had set up three separate ambushes in narrow tracks through the forest which were ideal for the purpose: the first, it was hoped, would pick off the advancing enemy.

**29.***   Rufinianus, 57. 10

and they rush on them from the rear.

**30.***   *Schol. Bob.* Cic. *Flac.* 14 (98 St.)

*I think this must refer to the time of the Sertorian War because there Laelius, the father of this Laelius, was killed by the soldiers of Hirtuleius. As Sallust says:* a great number of military standards were seized along with the body of Laelius.

**31.***   Servius, *Aen.* 11. 544

and since Metellus was operating a long distance away the hope of receiving reinforcements was a remote one.

**32.***   Probus, *Catholica* 20. 2

Ucurbis . . .

**33.** Arusianus Messius, 480. 24

unimpaired, as far as supplies were concerned.

**34.*** Porphyrion, Hor. *Ep.* 2. 2. 81

but during the winter Sertorius had the opportunity to augment his forces.

**35.*** Probus, *Catholica* 20. 10

to Stobi . . .

**36.** Arusianus Messius, 488. 5

an impressive man, inferior to none in any type of activity.

**37.** Arusianus Messius, 486. 19

a race fierce in war and unaccustomed to subjection.

**38.*** Servius, *G.* 3. 475

he advanced only into the nearest part of Iapydia.

**39.** Priscianus, 2. 246. 3

the senate, informed through messengers of Orestes, gave its approval to the act of surrender.

**40.** Fleury MS col. 1 (AB)

. . . who had commanded the army, sent one legion in spite of the contempt he felt for his lack of judgement, a gesture which had earned for him a reputation for wisdom. Then L. Octavius and C. Cotta entered upon their consulship. Of these, Octavius conducted himself in a careless and apathetic manner; Cotta was more quick to act, but was through ambition and by nature a briber, desirous of the favour of individuals.

**41.** Fleury MS col. 2 (B)

and on the motion of the same speaker Publius Lentulus Marcellinus was sent as quaestor to the new province of Cyrene although that province, bequeathed to us by the dead king Apion, needed to be secured by an administration more prudent than that of a young man, and to be exercised in a less greedy manner. Moreover, ⟨in this year there flared up rivalries⟩ of the different orders . . .

**42.** Fleury MS col. 3 B

. . . an intolerable shortage [of corn]. This development distressed the people to the point that, when they chanced upon the two consuls as they were escorting along the Sacred Way one of the candidates for the praetorship (that Q. Metellus who was afterwards given the *cognomen* Creticus), they attacked them in an outbreak of violence and, when the consuls fled, followed them to the house of Octavius which was close by. Then they demolished the defensive wall.

**43.**\* Donatus, Ter. *Eun.* 650

with the senators acting promptly in a period of great scarcity.

**44.** Fleury MS col. 4 (BA) / Codex Vaticanus Lat. 3864 (V)

A few days later, Cotta, in mourning garb, very much distressed because the commons were displaying an un-friendly attitude towards him instead of the goodwill he longed for, addressed the people in assembly in the following manner:

(**1**) 'Citizens of Rome, I have encountered many dangers at home and abroad, and many adversities, some of which I have endured, some fended off by the help of the gods and my own courage; in all of these I have never lacked the resolution to make a decision or the energy to act. Adversity and success kept changing my resources, but not my character. (**2**) But in these present troubles my situation is different; my good fortune has deserted me and taken everything else with it. Moreover, old age, an affliction in itself, is doubling my anxiety, in that it is my wretched misfortune as I near the end of my life not to be able even to hope for an honourable death. (**3**) For if I am a traitor to you, and, though twice born into this state, I hold cheap my household gods, my country, and its highest office, what torture in life, what retribution after death is adequate punishment for me? My crime in fact would be too great for any of those well-known punishments of the damned.

(**4**) 'From early youth I have lived my life before your eyes, both as a private citizen and as a magistrate; those who had need of my tongue, my counsel, my money, have had the use of them; nor have I exercised my gift of oratory nor used my talents for evil purposes. Most eager for private goodwill, I have incurred the most bitter personal enmities for my country's sake. When the state and I were overcome and I was expecting even worse misfortune since I could not count on help from others, you, citizens of Rome, restored to me my country and my household gods, and added to them your highest mark of distinction. (5) For such favours I should scarcely seem grateful enough even if I were to give up my life for each one of you. That I cannot do, for life and death are subject to natural laws; but to live without disgrace amongst one's fellow citizens, with reputation and fortune intact, that is something that may be given and received.

(6) 'You have elected us consuls, citizens of Rome, at a time when the state faces the severest difficulties at home and abroad. Our commanders in Spain are calling for pay, soldiers, weapons, and food; circumstances compel them to do so, since the defection of our allies, the flight of Sertorius through the mountains prevent them from either engaging in battle or providing for their necessities. (7) Armies are being maintained in the provinces of Asia and Cilicia because of the excessive strength of Mithridates. Macedonia is full of foes, and so are the coastal regions of Italy and of the provinces. In the mean time our revenues, made scanty and uncertain by war, barely suffice for a part of our expenditures; hence the fleet which we keep at sea is much smaller than the one which formerly used to protect our food supplies. (8) If this state of affairs has been brought about by treason or negligence on our part, then follow the urgings of your anger, exact punishment from us; but if fortune which affects us all is frowning on us why do you resort to acts unworthy of you, of us, and of Rome?

(9) 'As for me who because of my years am close to it, I do not pray to be spared death if that will lessen any of your ills; nor could my life come to an end, as by the law of nature it soon must, in a manner more honourable than in securing your well-being. (10) Behold, here I stand, Gaius Cotta your consul! I do what our ancestors often did in hard-fought wars—I consecrate and offer my life to my

country.    (11) Look around you then for one to whom you
may entrust the state; for no good man will want such an
honour when one must take responsibility for the chances of
fortune, for the uncertainties of the sea, and for war brought
on by others, or else must die a shameful death.    (12) Only
bear this in mind, that it was not for crime or avarice that I
went to my death, but that I willingly gave my life in return
for great benefits.    (13)  In your own name, fellow citizens,
and by the glory of your ancestors, I beseech you, endure
adversity and take thought for your country.    (14)  Imperial
power involves great anxiety, many heavy burdens; it is in
vain for you to seek to avoid them and to look for peace and
prosperity when all the provinces and kingdoms, all lands
and seas are racked by hatred or exhausted by wars.'

**45.\***    Asconius, Cic. *Corn.* 67. 2–3

*for also in Sallust . . . there is no mention of any law proposed
by him, other than that which he carried in his consulship
against the wishes of the nobility and which was greeted with
great enthusiasm by the people,* that it should be permitted to
those who had been tribunes of the people to take on other
magistracies.

**46.**    Priscianus, 2. 201. 18

having on the left the walls of the town, on the right the
River Turia which, a small distance away, flows past
Valentia.

**47.\***    Servius Dan. *Aen.* 12. 694

since he had taken so few precautions the real ⟨blame⟩
must be attached to Perperna.

**48.**    Nonius, 503. 53

It could be taken for an island, given that it is washed all
around by waves thrown up from the east and the south-
west.

**49.\***    Servius, *Aen.* 1. 576

and on the flanks he had stationed men who were absolutely
dependable.

**50.** Nonius, 538. 22

[soldiers on each side] rushed to confront the opposing general and so intensified the battle that missiles fell on Metellus' cloak and struck Hirtuleius on the arm.

**51.** Charisius, 288. 17

in the evening . . .

**52.** Servius Dan. *Aen.* 4. 23

and that no one would acknowledge as men people who came away unarmed from a battlefield.

**53.*** Priscianus, 3. 39. 7

He was of above average height and build.

**54.*** Servius, *Aen.* 10. 539

[they seized] his horse and its splendid trappings.

**55.** Arusianus Messius, 481. 10

before Sertorius, who had returned, was able to draw up his troops for battle.

**56.** Priscianus, 2. 489. 9

nor had the support troops he had arranged for according to his usual practice been assembled.

**57.** Nonius, 389. 6

the generals being so eager for battle and so keen in action that Metellus was wounded by a blow from a javelin.

**58.** Arusianus Messius, 488. 12

after Varro had heard these things, exaggerated in the manner of rumours.

**59.** Macrobius, *Sat.* 3. 13. 7–9

(1) But Metellus, having returned after a year to farther Spain, was greeted with great honours by the inhabitants who, both men and women, rushed from all sides in the streets and in houses to crowd around him. (2) Then when the quaestor C. Urbinus and others, knowing his desires, invited him to dinner he was entertained in a manner far more sumptuous than was the normal Roman

practice or indeed that of any other people. The house was decked with tapestries and decorations, stages were erected for the shows of the actors, the floor was strewn with saffron, and other features recalled the magnificence of a temple. (3) In addition to that, when he was seated, a statue of Victory, let down by a rope and accompanied by the artificially produced sound of thunder, used to place a crown on his head; then when he ventured abroad he was worshipped with incense as if he were a god. (4) The *toga picta* was generally his dress when he was reclining at the table. The courses he was served were most elaborate; they included not only the products of the entire province but also many types of birds and animals from Mauretania across the sea, not met with up till now. With this kind of behaviour Metellus was diminished in his glory to a considerable extent, especially in the estimation of men of the old Roman type, men of irreproachable character who judged such an attitude as arrogant, unsupportable, and unworthy of the authority of Rome.

**60.**   Nonius, 280. 25

In the same year in Macedonia at the beginning of spring C. Curio set out for Dardania with his whole army, and collected by whatever means he could the payments agreed upon with Appius.

**61.**   Servius Dan. *G*. 4. 144

that warfare in a restricted area would go on too long.

**62.**   Nonius, 127. 30

Their anger flared to a tremendous degree.

**63.**   Nonius, 202. 7

He changed direction towards the city of Corycus, renowned for its harbour and for a wood in which saffron blooms.

**64.***   Servius, *Aen*. 8. 232

Exhausted, he had returned to Pamphylia.

**65.**   Arusianus Messius, 503. 9

they overtop by two thousand feet all the [mountains] around.

**66.** Priscianus, 2. 202. 9

except for areas watered by the Clurda, which flows down from the Taurus mountain.

**67.** Arusianus Messius, 510. 8

a race of nomads more used to pillaging than to planting.

**68.** Servius Dan. *Aen.* 8. 278

For use in banquets they buy drinking vessels and other gold utensils which were chattels consecrated to the service of the gods.

**69.** Fleury MS cols. 7 and 8 (A):

(A) Then the signal was suddenly given when the second watch was already well advanced and they began fighting simultaneously from both sides. At first they made a great din and threw their missiles from a distance and at random in the darkness. Then, when the Romans deliberately did not respond either with shouts or with missiles, they thought they were terrified or that the fortifications had been abandoned, and eagerly rushed across the ditches; from there the swiftest of them tried to surmount the rampart. But the Romans standing on top began finally to pelt them with stones, spears, and stakes and repelled in confusion many who had almost reached the top by blows inflicted at close quarters or with their shields. In the sudden panic which ensued some were run through on the earthwork itself, others fell upon their own weapons. (B) The ditches were half filled with the bodies of the many killed; for the remainder safety was found through flight since they were protected by the Romans' uncertainty in the darkness and their fear of ambush. Then, after a few days, shortage of water compelled them to surrender; their town was burnt and the rural population sold into slavery. The terror thus produced soon caused envoys to come from Isaura Nova to ask for peace; they promised to give hostages and to obey orders. So Servilius, mindful of the ferocity of the enemy, and aware of the fact that in their case it was not war-weariness but a sudden fear which had prompted their peace overtures, moved his entire force in front of the walls as soon as possible. He did so for fear that by sending back their envoys they might cause them to change their minds.  **(C)**  In the mean time he dealt in a conciliatory manner with the envoys and said that a surrender would be more easily arranged when all the people were present. In addition he restrained his troops from ravaging the fields and from every other kind of damage; the townspeople out of goodwill towards the troops were supplying them with corn and other goods. In order that he might not be an object of suspicion he placed his camp on the open plain. Then, after the handing over of one hundred hostages in compliance with Roman orders, he asked them to surrender refugees, weapons, and all engines of war. The younger men, at first under a prior agreement and later as it occurred to individuals, created a commotion throughout the city by hostile demonstrations and proclaimed that as long as they were alive they would never surrender their arms or their allies.  **(D)**  But those of less warlike age whose years had given them much experience of Roman strength wanted peace; but, knowing that they had participated in violent behaviour, they feared that once they had given up their weapons they would suffer the ultimate fate of the conquered. While they were all thus hesitating and discussing matters confusedly together, Servilius concluded that any surrender was pointless unless it was imposed through fear. Without warning he took up a position on a mountain sacred to the Great Mother which was only a javelin's throw from the town's escape route. It was believed that the goddess to whom the mountain was dedicated banqueted there on certain days and that sounds could be heard . . .


**70.**\*   Servius, *G*. 4. 218

*He derived this from a custom of the Celtiberians who, as we read in Sallust,* dedicate their lives to their kings and after their demise refuse to go on living.


**71.**   Arusianus Messius, 510. 7

a type of soldier accustomed to brigandage from boyhood.

**72.** Charisius, 268. 24

by night and by day to test the vigilance of watches and pickets.

**73.** Arusianus Messius, 503. 3

nor were maidens handed over in marriage by their parents; instead, they themselves used to select the most active in war.

**74.** Nonius, 535. 2

in addition a few pirate vessels and light passenger craft.

**75.** Fleury MS col. 11 (A)

The mothers used to remind the menfolk setting out to war or brigandage of the warlike exploits of their fathers when they celebrated in song the brave deeds of these heroes. When it was discovered that Pompeius was approaching with hostile intent the older men were trying to persuade them to make peace and obey his orders. The women's objections fell on deaf ears, so they separated from the men, armed themselves, and took up as secure position as they could near Meo⟨riga?⟩. They called upon the men to witness that they were deprived of country, of those who could give birth, and of freedom; as a result, the tasks of giving suck, of giving birth and other duties of women remained with the men. This roused the young men, and scorning the decisions of the elders . . .

**76.** Fleury MS col. 12 (A)

[The townspeople, resorting to the sanction of an oath] affirmed that if they were relieved from the siege they would conclude an alliance in good faith; they had not been able to make up their minds between him and Pompeius during the period of uncertain peace. Then the Roman army was withdrawn to the territory of the Vascones for provisioning purposes; Sertorius also struck camp because it was of great concern to him not to lose the hopes he had of Asia. Because of the convenience offered by a ford Pompeius held his troops in a stationary camp for some days, the enemy being separated from him only by a shallow valley. Since the neighbouring cities of the Mutudurei and the [N]eores helped neither him nor Sertorius with supplies, both armies suffered from hunger. Finally, Pompeius marched on with his troops in battle-square formation . . .

**77.**   Arusianus Messius, 498. 24

he ordered his legate Titurius to spend the winter in Celtiberia with fifteen cohorts and to watch over their allies.

**78.**   Nonius, 172. 11

Having occupied all the passes, they invaded the fields of the Termestini and made a great haul of corn after having experienced great scarcity.

**79.**   Nonius, 449. 26

and many convoys had been destroyed through ambushes by robbers.

**80.\***   Donatus, Ter. *Phorm.* 38

money which had been provided to give Metellus the means to conduct the war in Spain.

**81.**   Priscianus, 2. 534. 23

he raised money on loan.

**82.**   Codex Vaticanus Lat. 3864 (V) / Fleury MS cols. 13–16 (A): *Letter of Pompeius to the senate*
(1)   'If it had been against you and my country's gods that I had undertaken all the toils and dangers which have accompanied the many occasions since my early manhood when under my leadership the most dangerous enemies have been routed and your safety secured, you could not, Fathers of the senate, have taken more severe measures against me in my absence than you are now doing. For, in spite of my youth, having exposed me to a most cruel war, you have as far as you were able destroyed by starvation, the most wretched of all deaths, me and an army which deserves your highest gratitude.   (2)   Was it with such expectations that the Roman people sent its sons to war? Are these the rewards for wounds, for blood shed so often for our country? Tired of writing letters and sending envoys, I have exhausted all my personal resources and even my future prospects, while in the mean time for a three-year period

you have barely given me the means of meeting even one year's expenses. (3) By the immortal gods, do you think I [A] can play the part of a treasury or maintain an army without food and pay?

(4) 'For my part I admit that I set out for this war with more eagerness than discretion, for, having received from you only a titular command, within forty days I raised and equipped an army and drove an enemy who was already at the very throat of Italy from the Alps into Spain; and through those mountains I opened up a route different from that which Hannibal had taken and more convenient for us. (5) I recovered Gaul, the Pyrenees, Lacetania, and the Indicetes; I withstood the first onslaught of the victorious Sertorius in spite of the rawness of my troops and the enemy's superiority in numbers. I spent the winter in camp surrounded by the most savage of foes, not in the towns nor [B] in boosting my own popularity. (6) Why need I enumerate battles or winter expeditions or the towns we have destroyed or captured? Actions speak louder than words: the taking of the enemy's camp at the Sucro, the battle at the River Turia, the destruction of the enemy general Gaius Herennius together with his army and the city of Valentia—all these are sufficiently known to you. In exchange for them, grateful senators, you present me with famine and shortages.

(7) 'Thus the situation of my army and that of the enemy is the same: for neither is being paid and either, if victorious, can march into Italy. (8) I draw your attention to this state of affairs and ask you to take notice of it and not to force me to solve my difficulties by abandoning the interests [C] of the state for my own. (9) That part of hither Spain which is not in enemy hands has been laid waste, either by us or by Sertorius, to the point of extermination, except for the coast towns, to the stage where it is actually an expense and a burden to us. Last year Gaul provided Metellus' army with pay and provisions; now, because of a failure of the crops, it can hardly support itself. I myself have exhausted not only my means, but even my credit. (10) You are our last resort; unless you come to our aid my army, against my wish but as I have already warned you, will cross to Italy and bring with it the whole Spanish war.'

[D] This letter was read in the senate at the beginning of the following year. The consuls agreed among themselves on the provinces which had been allotted to them by the senate: Cotta took Cisalpine Gaul, Octavius Cilicia. Then their successors, Lucius Lucullus and Marcus Cotta, greatly disturbed by Pompeius' letter and messages, both because of the interests of the state and because they were afraid that, if he led an army into Italy, they themselves would have neither glory nor status, used every means to provide him with pay and reinforcements. In this they were aided especially by the nobles, the greater number of whom were already giving voice to their fighting spirit and were backing their words with deeds.

**83.**   Priscianus, 2. 505. 5

Opposing them were many who wished to come from Bithynia to prove that the son was an impostor.

**84.***   Seneca, *Ben.* 4. 1. 1

a man about whom one cannot speak except with concern.

**85.***   Ampelius, 30. 5

*So Darius reached the throne and from him descended* Artabazes who, *according to Sallust,* was the founder of the kingdom of Mithridates.

**86.**   Arusianus Messius, 455. 24

he himself was of a cruel disposition.

**87.***   Servius, *Aen.* 5. 295

But Mithridates at the end of his boyhood entered into his rule after removing his mother by poison.

**88.***   *Schol. Gronov.* 318 (27 St.)

*The example which compares a woman with a ruler appears incongruous, but is shown to be fitting in all respects: firstly, by reason of place, because Mithridates was from Pontus, the native land of Medea; secondly, because of the fact that she murdered close relatives, as did this ruler* who, *according to Sallust,* killed both a brother and a sister.

**89.*** Quintilianus, *Inst.* 8. 3. 82
Mithridates being of huge stature bore weapons of a comparable size.

**90.** Nonius, 215. 33
As a result of the Fimbrian revolt there were present at the court men who, because of their compliance in discussions, and particularly their hatred of Sulla, were respected and favoured by the king.

**91.*** Arusianus Messius, 463. 6
They arrived in Pontus in the third month, much more quickly than Mithridates expected.

**92.** Arusianus Messius, 509. 25
truly expert in the art of war . . .

**93.** Priscianus, 2. 143. 12
whom King Leptasta had sent in custody from Mauretania under a charge of treachery.

**94.** Arusianus Messius, 490. 25
since he was addressing many meetings while the games in honour of Apollo were being held in the Circus Maximus.

**95.** Nonius, 315. 5
and the serious [situation] is being kept under control.

**96.** Arusianus Messius, 495. 16
Afterwards when with too much confidence in himself . . .

**97.** Arusianus Messius, 513. 22
when some of the legions were led across the river he extended the camp.

**98.** Arusianus Messius, 513. 27
having encouraged his cavalry, he led them across via a ford.

**99.** Donatus, Ter. *Adelph.* 319
they were being killed by the impact of those who were rushing headlong into the river.

**100.**  Nonius, 497. 29

In the headlong rush a large number were run through by
their own weapons or by the weapons of those nearest to
them and the remainder were butchered like sheep.

**101.**  Servius Dan. *Aen.* I. 423

He extended the wall from the corner of the right side to a
swamp not far distant.

**102.**  Arusianus Messius, 483. 28

that [they] had placed all the wounded bodies on rafts.

**103.**  Eutyches, 482. 22

He hastened to augment his leading ranks with reinforcements and to crowd together his front line.

**104.**  Arusianus Messius, 488. 1

Terror seized the enemy while confidence emboldened his
own men.

**105.**  Arusianus Messius, 456. 6

in the case of those who were surrounded, iron blades,
stones, and missiles of a similar type were striking their
heads, which were exposed on the right-hand side.

**106.**  Nonius, 177. 17

They were letting down bread from the walls in baskets.

**107.**  Nonius, 101. 13

He casts them headlong from the walls.

**108.**  Donatus, Ter. *Andr.* 706

still less are they comparable to a bull.

**109.**  Nonius, 310. 19

So they are dismissed, cleared of blame more because of
their brazen self-assurance than because of the evidence
produced.

**110.**  Charisius, 209. 1

They were at hand.

**III.** Priscianus, 3. 76. 27

boldly . . .

**112.** Donatus, Ter. *Phorm.* 171

and the Carthaginians bring ⟨an accusation?⟩ against . . .

# COMMENTARY

As I have already pointed out (Introd. section 2), Sallust's decision to change from the monographic treatment of historical topics to the traditional annalistic form of historiography involved significant compositional and structural changes in the ordering of the narrative. The change also affected the nature of the material which formed the introduction to the narrative proper of his last and major work.

While the loss of much of the introductory material is to be regretted, sufficient fragments do remain to allow a reasonably satisfactory understanding of the basic content and thrust of this section. Two factors play a part in the work of analysis and reconstruction: the annalistic form involved the use of traditional elements of procedure and content; Klingner's careful analysis of Maurenbrecher's edition in his 1928 paper (*Hermes* 63) and the subsequent refinement of his conclusions by a succession of scholars, notably La Penna and Pasoli, have made it possible to apply more rigour in the choosing and the collocation of the fragments deemed to have their place in this part of the work.

Investigation reveals that the material prior to the narrative of Sallust's specific topic falls into three segments: a personal preface (frr. 1–7); a two-part introduction comprising (i) general considerations concerning the moral, social, and political history of Rome (frr. 8–15), a segment which corresponds in some measure to the opening segment (the 'Archaeology') of Thucydides (1. 2–22), and the content of chapters 6–13 of Sallust's *Bellum Catilinae*; (ii) a more detailed narrative (frr. 16–46) of the historical period which preceded the true and proper beginning of his own historical topic.

**1. 1–7.** The exordium or personal statement of the writer of history involved a more or less fixed group of elements and formed an indispensable part of both Greek and Roman historical works. The vast gaps in the ancient historiography transmitted to us prevent our tracing the development of such traditional elements in detail, but we can glimpse the general picture from chs. 52–4 of Lucian's *How to Write History* (2nd cent. AD). Speaking of the historian's duties Lucian observes: 'After all his preparations are made he will sometimes begin without a preface, when the subject-matter requires no preliminary exposition. But even then he will use a virtual preface to clarify what he is going to say . . . For they [his audience] will give him their attention if he shows that what he is going to say will be important, personal, or useful' (52–3). Amplification is given to Lucian's points by the anonymous rhetorician in Halm (588. 18 ff.); he named the chief headings of the material contained in an exordium as *de historia*: a general statement on the usefulness of history; *de persona*: personal details, reasons for writing etc.; *de materia*: reasons why the topic chosen is deserving of a historical treatment.

Besides such precepts of traditional practice, some guidance as to the content of Sallust's preface is afforded by Tacitus, who apparently took as his model, when he wrote his own *Histories*, the structure of Sallust's exordium. Livy's preface, in addition to confirming our impression of a common store of traditional material used by Roman historians, also provides, because of its polemic attitude to Sallust's viewpoint, some insight into Sallust's philosophy of history.

Sallust's exordium as we now possess it begins with a statement of theme (1) and follows this with mention of his predecessors in the writing of Roman history (2–4). He then refers to his specific purpose and, presumably, to the personal circumstances under which he was writing (5–6) and ends with a promise of impartiality in dealing with his material (7).

**1. 1.** Priscianus repeats all of this fragment, except for the verb, at 3. 73. 11 and part of it at 3. 64. 18. Donatus, *Aen.* 1. 1, confirms that Sallust began his work with these words.

**for the consular year.** Means that the year 78 BC was the *terminus a quo* of Sallust's narrative. A traditional motive could have induced him to begin with the year 78. This was the year of Sulla's death and it is possible that the *Histories* of Sisenna, Sallust's immediate predecessor, had concluded with this event (*HRR*, cccxl).

**Marcus Lepidus.**    Sallust's narrative begins with the revolt led by this man.

**Quintus Catulus.**    A patrician with political views diametrically opposed to those of Lepidus.

**thereafter.**    A vague expression of the *terminus ad quem* which is given somewhat firmer substance in Ausonius, *Epist.* 22. 61 ff.: 'Now, Catiline, thy monstrous plot, now Lepidus' sedition, now from the year of Lepidus and Catulus the fortunes and vicissitude of Rome do I commence and trace their sequence through twice six years.' This statement brings the conclusion of the work down to the end of 67 BC. Some scholars, however, share with Gerlach the view that the *Histories* contained a narrative of events down to the consulship of Cicero and Antonius in 63 BC. A variation of this is the hypothesis expressed by Maurenbrecher (*Proleg.* 73) that death prevented the historian from bringing his narrative down to the Catilinarian conspiracy. This was also the year which witnessed the death of Mithridates, and falls in with the theory of Bauhofer, that the historian thought of adding a Book 6 to conclude his *Histories* with the death of Mithridates. Bauhofer's theory that the structure of the *Histories* revolved around leading figures in the narrative has received no support. It is true that the *Histories* to some extent filled the lacuna between the monographs and it is to this that Ausonius may be referring when he remarks on the connection of the *Histories* with the Catilinarian conspiracy. But it does not seem likely that he would have repeated material he had already dealt with, when, for example, he prefaced the story of Catiline in 64–63 with a synopsis of the so-called First Conspiracy. The work as we have it ends with some fragments dealing with internal affairs such as the *Lex Gabinia* of 67 and such foreign affairs as the conquest of the pirates by Pompeius. It has been stated (Jacobs–Wirz–Kurfess, *Einleitung*, 5–6) that the year 67, signalling the rise of Pompeius, constituted a satisfactory conclusion, analogous to that of the *Bellum Iugurthinum* with the rise to power of Marius. It could be assumed that Sallust's use of the vague 'thereafter' indicates cautiousness, leaving open the bottom time-limit. Whether he had the possibility of premature death in mind or had not yet fixed upon an ending acceptable to his purpose cannot, given the state of the text as we have it, be determined with certainty.

**1. 2–4.** The content of these fragments allows us to assume with some confidence that Sallust enumerated his most important predecessors in Roman historiography from the elder Cato down to Sisenna; that, in addition, he provided an evaluation of the quality of their literary presentation and the reliability of their research. The reference to 'very learned men' in 5 would indicate that his verdict on the predecessors was in many respects favourable, even if it is tempered at times by specific reservations.

**1. 2.** This fragment is repeated in full in Servius, *Aen.* 1. 30. The second half is cited in Priscianus, 3. 30. 20, and in several other grammarians.

Maurenbrecher accepted Kritz's view that the fragment was part of an overview of the growth of Roman power; consequently he placed it as fr. 8 and followed it with two other fragments (9* and 10M) in order to demonstrate that Sallust had indeed dealt with the topic of Roman expansion. It must be stressed that no fragment that we possess can be referred with any certainty to a historical review of the type envisaged by Kritz and Maurenbrecher. It should also be noted that Sallust cannot have viewed the end of the Macedonian War either as a climax of the Roman rise to power or as a crucial turning-point in the development of Roman political life. In fr.9 below he clearly states that the conquest of Gaul marked the acme of Roman external expansion, and in fr. 10 that the destruction of Carthage marked the turning-point of Roman internal history.

In framing his interpretation Kritz had rejected the earlier view expressed by C. Linker (diss. Marburg, 1850) that this fragment was part of the enumeration of Sallust's Roman predecessors. Modern scholarship, led by F. Klingner

(*Hermes* 63 (1928) ), A. La Penna (*SIFC* 35 (1963), and E. Pasoli (*Stud. Urb.* 49 (1975) ) has accepted Linker's interpretation, but has not reached unanimous agreement on the placing or on the precise context of the fragment.

My decision to place it in the exordium, despite the caution counselled by La Penna (p. 21), is based largely on the fact that Tacitus modelled himself on Sallust in the preface to his own *Histories*. I assume, therefore, that both historians, after naming the consular year from which their narratives would begin, embarked on a discussion of preceding historiography with sentences beginning with 'For' (*nam*).

**the Macedonian War against Perseus.**   The war brought to a successful conclusion by Paulus Aemilius after the battle of Pydna, 168 BC. See Livy's summary, 45. 9–10. Such a reference makes it less easy to be definite about the exact context of this fragment. The wording has given rise to a variety of conjectures regarding the role of historiography within such a time-span. The conjecture by D. Flach, *Philologus* 117 (1973), 76–86, that the context was one in which Sallust was justifying his choice of theme by emphasizing that Roman history down to the Macedonian war had already been dealt with by the elder Cato, while the long lapse of time down to 78 had received exhaustive treatment on the part of Roman historians, is quite an interesting one. It has, however, been rejected on somewhat tenuous grounds by G. Petrone (*Pan* 4 (1976), 39–67), who offers a hypothesis that cannot readily be accepted. She puts forward the theory of a complete and critical examination, brief of necessity, of all Roman historiography from the earliest annalists to the historians closer to Sallust's time; Sallust therefore must have used material which covered the long historical period between the foundation of Rome and the Macedonian war and used it to put into prominence the role exercised by Cato in his historiography.

In *Cat.* 8. 5, after discussing the advantage that the Athenians enjoyed in having such noteworthy historians as Herodotus, Thucydides, and Xenophon, Sallust continues: 'But the Roman people never had that advantage since their ablest men were always totally engrossed in affairs; their minds were never employed apart from their bodies; the best citizen preferred action to words, and considered that his own good deeds should be praised by others rather than that theirs should be narrated by him.' It is likely that Sallust began his survey with a reference to the long period in which historiography of a developed kind was lacking in Rome and that with his reference to the Macedonian War he was alluding to the appearance of the first truly Roman historical work, the *Origines* of the elder Cato.

**1. 3.** The phrase 'the most eloquent Roman of all' appears in Servius, *Aen.* 1. 96, in Ampelius, 19. 8, and in Pompeius, 158. 23. I have quoted the Victorinus passage in full because I believe it enables us properly to interpret the two fragments which contain the statements made by Sallust.

**The most eloquent Roman . . . truth.** Maurenbrecher was of the opinion that Sallust here implicitly denied veracity to the elder Cato, an assumption which led him to nominate Cato as the distorter of history in his 1. 5*M, a fragment which I have relegated to Fragments of Uncertain Reference (see Introd. section 8). Klingner (*Hermes* 63 (1928), 168) talks of an antithesis between Cato and Fannius and holds that it originated not from Sallust but from Victorinus. I do not believe that any antithesis is involved. Sallust is represented as having embarked upon a discussion of the qualities which characterized specific historians. His attribution of brevity to Cato is not a denial of veracity to that historian, but simply the naming of the quality which most notably marked his work and was in keeping with that severity of character for which the elder Cato was famous. His implacable opposition to the flattery of senatorial historiography led him, as Nepos, *Cato* 3. 4, and Pliny, *NH* 8. 11, indicate, to exclude from his narrative even the names of protagonists of battles and of winners of victories. Sallust would have been acquainted with the debates in Cicero's *Leg.* 1. 6–7 and *De Or.* 53 on the manner of writing history. The general tenor of these debates is indicated by a statement such as: 'For after the annals of the chief pontiffs, than which nothing can be drier, when we come to Fabius or to Cato (whose name is always on your lips) or to Piso, Fannius, or Vennonius, although one of these may display more vigour than another, yet what could be more lifeless than the whole group?' Cicero is dealing solely with the aspect of style. As a historian, Sallust may have felt that he could discern more expertly qualities which Cicero had overlooked or underestimated.

**Cato.**    Marcus Porcius Cato, the elder (234–149 BC). A man of considerable ability in legal, political, and military arenas, he achieved an enduring reputation for unbending observation of a stern traditional morality. In this respect, the influence of his writings on Sallust was profound. Cato's *Origines*, in seven books, was in summary form (*capitulatim*). The first work of its kind in Latin, it set the standards for historical research and initiated a Latin prose style. The influence of this style on Sallust is shown by his liking for archaisms in vocabulary, forms of expression and structure, and in an energetic and combative narrative style. See Syme, 262–3, 267–8.

**Fannius.**    Gaius Fannius had gained the consulship of 122 as a friend of C. Gracchus and had then turned against him (Plut. *C. Gracch.* 8. 2–3). As a historian he was the first representative of the Optimate tradition concerning the Gracchan phenomenon and may have laid the foundation of the hostile attitude to the Gracchi; Cicero (*Brut.* 101) knew and approved of his work. Sallust's attribution of veracity as the leading characteristic of Fannius' work is probably in the spirit of his own avowal of impartiality in fr. 7: personal political leanings did not lead him to distort the truth. See *HRR* cxciii–cxcix and 139–41; F. Münzer, *Hermes* 55 (1920), 427–42; E. Badian in T. A. Dorey (ed.), *Latin Historians* (London 1966), 14–15.

**1. 4.**    The Latin version of this fragment—*recens scrip*—is corrupt in that the second word is truncated and could be completed in several ways, e.g. *scrip ⟨si⟩* I wrote; *scrip ⟨sit⟩* he wrote; *scrip ⟨tum⟩* written; the other Latin word, *recens*, can be taken either as an adverb ('recently') or as a noun ('recent work').

The fragment is generally interpreted as referring to the work of Sallust's predecessor, L. Cornelius Sisenna, whose

*Histories* covered the period from the Social War (91–87 BC) down to the beginning of 78 BC, or perhaps down to the death of Sulla. The tradition of a historical exordium involved paying one's immediate predecessor the compliment of not repeating material dealt with by him. That is not to say that shortcomings in the work of the predecessor were necessarily overlooked or excused. Thus Thucydides pays Herodotus the compliment of starting his history of the Peloponnesian War from the point where his predecessor had concluded the history of the Persian invasions. Nevertheless, Thucydides obviously had Herodotus in mind when he alluded to the absence of romance in his own work (1. 22).

In similar fashion Sallust had earlier referred in *Iug.* 95. 2–4 to his intention not to speak elsewhere of Sulla's period, on the grounds that it has already been dealt with by Sisenna. He adds, however, the opinion that 'Lucius Sisenna, whose account of him is altogether the best and most careful, has not . . . spoken with sufficient frankness.' This probably indicates Sallust's feeling that Sisenna's narrative was deficient in its treatment of events either because of fear or because of sympathy with the Sullan solution to the Roman crisis. In any case, he did not adhere to his decision not to deal with Sulla elsewhere (see notes on 1. 48 *passim*: 49–53). A very useful treatment of Sisenna's work is that of E. Rawson, *CQ* 29 (1979), 327–46. See also E. Badian, *JRS* 52 (1962), 50–1 (= *Studies in Greek and Roman History* (Oxford 1968) 212–14).

**1. 5.\*** This fragment is repeated in full at Servius, *Aen.* 4. 213. Sallust now turns to discuss matters relating to himself. Although the fragment is cited without book-number, its placing in the exordium seems to be justified, as several scholars have noted, by the almost exact imitation of its wording by Livy in his *Praef.* 3: 'and if in so vast a company of writers my own reputation should be obscure, my consolation would be the fame and greatness of those who will overshadow me.'

It is possible that with this statement, as Flach (*Philologus* 117 (1973), 78) argues, Sallust acknowledged that he did not presume that he could emulate his predecessors successfully, but had decided to deal with a period which was still awaiting a satisfactory treatment. I doubt very much, however, if the Sallustian passage carried on in the same diffident tone as that of the corresponding Livian extract. Sallust's monographs had set in train a new fashion of dealing with history; his essay into the more traditional form of Roman historiography would not be marked by a slavish adherence to traditional conventions. It is more likely that the contrast 'I . . . abundance of very learned men' indicates that his treatment of his material will show differences of attitude and tone from the works of his predecessors. The two remaining fragments of this segment show him firmly speaking as his own man.

**1. 6.   at the beginning of the first book . . .**   The fact that this fragment refers to the mission entrusted to the younger Cato in 58 BC and that the scholiast firmly places it in the first book of the *Histories* raises problems concerning the context in which Sallust discussed this episode. Maurenbrecher suggested that the annexation of Cyprus was mentioned in connection with a Sallustian treatment of the expansion of Roman imperial rule, and placed it, as 1. 10M, in a conjectural segment dealing with this topic. This conjecture is, however, untenable (see notes to 1. 2).

One further fact will serve to strengthen the rejection of Maurenbrecher's view and may also point the way to a more satisfactory solution. It is to be noted that the scholiast also reports, in all probability from the text of Sallust himself, that the assignment was entrusted to Cato on the basis of a law proposed by Clodius and was designed as a pretext to remove from Rome a senator who was incorruptible and an implacable enemy of change. The other sources we possess are unanimous and explicit on this—Cic. *Dom.* 20–1; Vell. Pat. 2. 45. 4; Plut. *Cato min.* 34. 2–3; *Pomp.* 48. 6; *Caes.* 21. 4. Cato's mission is discussed by S. I. Oost, *CPh.* 50 (1955), 98–112 and by E. Badian, *JRS* 55 (1965), 110–21. Thus the mission could not truly be presented as an example of the expansion of Rome rule. Here, it may have been used as a sad sign of the times in which a man with the integrity of a

Cato could be removed from the political scene by the machination of an agitator like Clodius.

The more likely solution concerning the context is that suggested by Klingner, *Hermes* 63 (1928), 170, developed by La Penna, *SIFC* 35 (1963), 9–10, and accepted by E. Pasoli, *Atti Accad. d. Lincei* (1966), 27. The fragment forms part of a discussion of Sallust's own thinking on the deteriorating quality of Roman rule and is designed partly to substantiate his credentials as a historian, as a man who has participated in public life and has subsequently viewed political developments with an expert eye. It would also serve to convey his opinion of the political climate in which he is actually writing, a climate which might well have affected his presentation of events. The latter is an aspect which he mentions in the final fragment of his exordium.

The fact that Sallust as tribune in 52 supported his fellow tribunes M. Plancus and Pompeius Rufus in their opposition to Milo (Asc. 37, 44–5, 49) has led to the view that he was on the side of Pompeius and Clodius in this period (Syme, 31–2; D. C. Earl, *Historia* 15 (1966), 310). Even if that were the case, it would not have affected Sallust's confirmed view that the decline of republican Rome was the result of abuse of power by individuals and groups.

**1. 7.** This statement clearly marks the end of the exordium. In the same way Tacitus, towards the end of the corresponding segment of his *Histories*, forswore hatred and partiality: 'those who profess inviolable fidelity to truth must write of no man with affection or with hatred'. Cf. *Ann.* 1. 1. 6: 'without anger and without partiality, from the reasons for which I am sufficiently removed'.

**different side in a civil war.** Sallust, who receives no mention in Caesar's *Bellum Civile*, did play some part in the civil war of 49–46. He commanded one of Caesar's legions in Illyricum late in 49 (Oros. 6. 15. 8). He re-emerged in 47 when as praetor-elect he failed in an attempt to quell a mutiny among the Caesarian troops in Campania (App. *BC* 2. 29; Dio, 45. 52. 2). As praetor in 46 Sallust was active in Caesar's African campaign, where he showed administrative and executive ability in securing much-needed supplies from the island of Cercina (*Bell. Afr.* 8. 3, 34. 3).

Unlike Livy, who would wish to avoid the animosities inevitably aroused by writers who dealt with topics such as civil wars, Sallust comes out with a firm statement of his own position regarding the politics of the troubled period about which he is writing. His declaration of impartiality is all the stronger for this blunt frankness; it is matched by Tacitus' confession of his own advancement under Domitian in *Histories* 1. 1.

**1. 8–15.** A distinctive feature of the Sallustian narrative method was his selection of a brief, crucial period of Roman history and the analysis of it in terms of the general forces and motivations which were determining the course of that history. In this segment of the *Histories* the events of his chosen period are set within a general interpretation of Roman history. Much of what he says is familiar from the monographs, but there are some important differences of detail and of emphasis. Two features are important for our understanding of Sallust's philosophy of history, namely the concept of *metus hostilis* ('fear of an outside enemy') coupled with the fall of Carthage, and the tone of pessimism which can be detected in his treatment of Rome's moral and political degeneration.

Maurenbrecher places seven fragments in this final section of the first part of the introductory material, i.e. 1. 12–18M. He rejected Kritz's contention that there had to be a close relationship between the two fragments which he, Maurenbrecher, had collocated as 12 and 16 (our 12 and 13). He did so because of an assumption that there intervened a detailed description of Italian peace and prosperity in the period between the second and last Punic wars. He could find only two fragments to support this view; of these, his 1. 14 I have relegated to fragments of Uncertain Reference (Introd. section 8) for reasons which I give ad loc.; his 1. 15 I have collocated as 1. 11 above. The third fragment, 1. 18M, I have placed as fr. 43 of this Book.

**1. 8.** The final phrase of the fragment, 'in struggles . . . power', is found in Servius Dan. *Aen.* 4. 245.

**A defect of human nature.** Many commentators have seized on this expression to support their conviction that Sallust had a deep scepticism concerning the nature of man, a feeling which in the development of his thinking through the monographs to the *Histories* perceptibly developed into pessimism. Given the possibilities that Sallust attached to moral excellence in his earlier works, it is not necessary to conclude that by 'defect' (*vitium*) Sallust is here referring to an organic incapacity for *virtus*. He could simply be pointing to an innate perversity in man which renders him always dissatisfied with the fruits of the struggles for liberty and national glory.

**struggles for liberty . . . power.** The propensity in man to debase the laudable energy expended in the acquisition of liberty and glory into a ruthless pursuit of personal power is surely what Sallust had in mind here. Thucydides, 3. 82. 2, talks of 'an inherent characteristic' and Tacitus is clearly reflecting the Sallustian thought when he writes of 'the old greed for power, long ingrained in mankind' (*Hist.* 2. 38).

The sequence liberty, glory, power is exactly the process by which Sallust traced the developing causation of civil wars in Rome. Civil dissension arose from struggles of the people against kings and patricians (*Cat.* 6. 7, 7. 1–4; *Hist.* 1. 10). After the fall of Carthage the pursuit of glory degenerated under the influence of ambition (*Cat.* 10–11; *Iug.* 41) to the point where each man who attacked the government did so 'under the pretence of the public good but in reality he was striving for his own personal power' (*Cat.* 38. 3). Finally, because of the degeneration in moral and political life a few powerful men (*pauci potentes*) aimed at personal domination —men such as Marius, Cinna, Carbo, Sulla.

Under the influence of his continuing researches into the crisis of the Roman Republic Sallust came to realize that struggles with worthy motives could easily degenerate and create a favourable climate for the aspirations of demagogues and tyrants. Ironically, the dynamism which could bring about the benefits of political harmony is more often the obstacle to the attainment of a stable balance. There is no doubt that there was a change in Sallust's outlook; that it amounted in the *Histories* to a complete reversal is highly debatable.

The tone and content of this fragment are clearly of the character of an 'archaeology'. Klingner, however, has shown that the archaeology of the *Histories* probably began with the opening words of I. 9: 'The Roman state reached the height of its power etc.' on the grounds that neither the archaeology of the *Bellum Catilinae* (6–13) nor the excursus on parties and factions in the *Bellum Jugurthinum* (41) has a reference in the first person to correspond with 'among us' of our fragment. Pasoli, *Stud. Urb.* 49 (1975), 372, adds in support of Klingner's view that this fragment forms part of a suitable formula of transition between the personal recall (7) of civil disorders lived through by Sallust and the consideration of the origin and prime causes (9) and (10) of civil discord in Rome.

**I. 9.**    Parts of this fragment are either cited or paraphrased in other sources: thus Nonius, 92. 6, speaks of [Gaul] 'this side of the Rhine . . . totally subjugated'. Augustinus gives a summary paraphrase of the second sentence in *CD* 3. 21.

It was Augustinus' habit either to cite again material already cited earlier or to paraphrase all or part of a quotation already cited. This habit has led Maurenbrecher to join the content of I. 9 and 10 to form one fragment (I. 11M). He provides as the connection what he considers to have been the direct Sallustian form of part of a sentence which preceded the direct citation of his I. 11: 'and the cause of this happy state [i.e. second sentence of this fragment] was not any love of justice but fear of a treacherous peace, as long as Carthage remained standing'. Klingner objected that the Latin version of Maurenbrecher's connecting sentence contained forms of expression not used by Sallust. I have found it more convenient to follow Kritz in dealing with two separate fragments drawn from separate sources.

**The Roman state reached . . . power.**    It was this opening sentence which caused Maurenbrecher to assume that a discussion of the external power of Rome was included in the *Histories* (see note on I. 2). While Klingner argued on textual and conceptual grounds against such an assumption, it seems to me that the second sentence of this fragment sufficiently clinches the matter.

**the consulship of Servius . . . Marcellus.** That is, the year 51 BC.

**all of Gaul . . . totally subjugated.** Given Sallust's official career (Introd. section 1), it is not surprising that he should light upon the achievement of Caesar as the highlight of Roman expansion. He was, of course, writing in the decade which followed the assassination of Caesar and the extinguishing of whatever expectation he had entertained of finding in Caesar a solution to the crisis of the Republic. I have referred elsewhere (Introd. section 6) to possible echoes of Sallust's own final decade and its effect on his viewpoint and his treatment of events.

**On the other hand.** Introduces a typically Sallustian antithesis: external dominion reached its zenith in 51 BC while the height of moral health and political harmony was attained in a different age—between the second and the last Punic wars. The ironic contrast between the acme of Roman imperial expansion and a concurrent almost total degeneration of moral and political ideals is picked up again in fr. 10, where the crucial factor of decay and degeneration is related to the transfers of political power at Rome.

**the period between . . . Punic wars.** This period of internal concord and perfect morality (201–150 BC) was due to *metus hostilis*, the fear of an external enemy. Since Sallust subsequently extends the scope of this general concept (see note on I. 10, **after the destruction of Carthage**), we would be more correct in using the term *metus Punicus* in this context—the fear caused by Rome's great rival for control of the Mediterranean basin, the city of Carthage. Many scholars have indicated Posidonius as responsible for the theory of *metus hostilis* and as source for Sallust's use of the concept. It was a very Roman concept, however, and constituted the chief argument supposedly used by Scipio Nasica in his opposition to the elder Cato's cry that 'Carthage should be destroyed' by means of a third Punic war: cf. Diodorus 34/5. 33. 4–6; Plutarch, *Cato maior* 27; Florus, I. 31. 5; Appian, *Punica* 69.

**I. 10.** Augustinus, 3. 17, repeats the citation from 'From that time on' down to the end of the fragment; at 3. 16 he gives a summary paraphrase of the sentence: 'A regime of equal justice . . . came to an end.'

**But discord and avarice and ambition . . . increased to a very great extent.** The restless energy which gave rise to struggles for liberty and glory also forms the basis of civil discord. The word 'increased' forms a contrast not with the immediately preceding period when *metus hostilis* (1.9) had ensured sustained concord and moral conduct of the highest order, but with the period before the Punic wars when absence of *metus hostilis* of any kind involved a breakdown of concord and strife between the orders.

**after the destruction of Carthage.** The theme of degeneration is also dealt with in the monographs (*Cat.* 6–13; *Iug.* 41) and this enables us to trace a development in Sallust's views on this topic. In *Cat.* a generation which is good by nature is assumed for the beginning of the Roman story; only the unexpected could bring a reversal of the justice and the uprightness which was 'due not so much to laws but to nature' (9. 1). The unexpected came with the fall of Carthage, but the cause of the subsequent decay was not the removal of *metus hostilis* but an irrational and vague fortune which 'began to grow cruel and to bring confusion into our affairs' (10. 1). In *Iug.* 41 the fall of Carthage is again the turning-point, but now the emphasis is on the consequent removal of the *metus Punicus* which had kept the Romans from internal strife. Now, in the *Histories*, there occurs a significant expansion of the *metus hostilis* motif. The fear which could specifically be labelled *Punicus* because it concerned confrontation with Carthage had, as the general concept *metus hostilis*, been in existence from the very beginning of the Republic when harmony inside the city was held together by fear of the deposed Tarquinius and war against the Etruscans. After the removal of these early threats concord between the classes disintegrated and long-drawn-out strife between patricians and plebs continued as long as a *metus hostilis* did not emerge to impose concord again. Such an extension of the fear motif indicates a deepening of pessimism or a sharpening of rationalism which is remote from the idealization of the past in his earlier work. This darker picture which could even raise doubts about the destiny of Rome apparently worried Livy, who indirectly opposes this Sallustian view in *Praef.* 11: 'either love of the task I have set myself deceives me or no state was ever greater or more righteous or richer in good examples'. In choosing 146 BC as the critical turning-point in Rome's path to degeneration, Sallust rejects a well-established tradition that by the middle of the 2nd cent. the processes which eventually destroyed the Republic were already at work. The annalistic tradition, represented by Livy, 39. 6–7, ascribes the crisis to the return of Manlius Vulso's army from Asia in 187 BC. Polybius, conscious of a change in moral standards from 200 BC onwards, places the crisis in the years in which Rome had achieved world dominion after 168 BC (31. 25. 3 ff.; cf. Diod. 31. 26). The annalist L. Piso dated the onset of degeneration at 154 BC (Pliny, *NH* 17. 244 = Piso fr. 38 *HRR*). None of these accounts, as D. C. Earl, *The Political Thought of Sallust* (Cambridge 1961), 44, remarks, precludes the possibility of the truth of the others. Elsewhere (P. McGushin, *C. Sallustius Crispus: Bellum Catilinae. A Commentary* (Leiden 1977), 87–8.) I have suggested that the reason for Sallust's rejection of the annalistic tradition seems to lie in his concentration on an aspect of the early period different from that which appears in Cato, Polybius, Piso, and Livy. His emphasis is on *concordia*, and his over-simplified view of the Roman past is modified in 1.9 where the 'greatest concord' is claimed only for the half-century preceding 146. His idealized view in the monographs made him overlook other factors of a very complex situation—factions among the nobility, increase in public and private wealth and the like are ignored. It should be noted, however, that subsequent writers adopted Sallust's choice of 146 as an epochal year in Roman history. Cf. Pliny, *NH* 33. 150; Vell. Pat. 2. 1. 1; Florus, 1. 33. 1; Augustinus, *CD* 1. 30; Orosius, 5. 8. 2.

**secessions of the plebs.** Three secessions are recorded in Roman history: the first in 494 on account of the severity exercised by creditors (Liv. 2. 32); the second, caused by the conduct of the *decemvir*, Appius Claudius, in 449 (Liv. 3.

51); the third, to the Ianiculum in 287 because of a dispute over public land (Liv. *Per.* 11; Pliny, *NH* 16. 37). Some confusion exists concerning the sites of these secessions. R. M. Ogilvie, *A Commentary on Livy 1–5* (Oxford 1965), 311 ff. and 489–90, fiercely rejects the opinion of some modern ancient historians that the secessions are fictitious, and puts forward an attractive hypothesis as to the origin of this confusion. In the oldest account, based on Piso, the plebs seceded to the Aventine hill on the first and second occasions (Liv. 2. 32. 3; cf. Diod. 12. 24 and Sall. *Iug.* 31. 17). The first secession is connected with the establishment of the tribunate, an institution safeguarded by *leges sacratae* (sacred laws) whose origin was naturally connected with the *Mons Sacer* (sacred mount)—App. *BC* 1. 1. Hence there was a development of the tradition which sited both secessions on the two hills (Cic. *Rep.* 2. 58 and 63). This clumsy solution was later improved by allotting the first secession to the Mons Sacer and the second to the Aventine, and this became the standard version (Cic. *Brut.* 54 Asc. *Corn.* 76. 17 and 77. 20; Liv. 3. 51. 10). It is to be noted that whereas in the course of a digression Livy (3. 54. 9–10) adopts this standard version, in the main narrative (3. 52. 1) he prefers the older and clumsier version that the plebs moved from the Aventine to the Mons Sacer.

**Tarquinius . . . Etruria.** There is little doubt about the substantial historicity of Tarquinius Superbus, last king of Rome, in so far as he represents a renewed domination of Rome by the Etruscans, a domination which ended with their violent expulsion (Ogilvie 1965, 194 ff.). Expulsion was followed by an attempt by Veii, most southern of the Etruscan cities, and the Tarquinii to restore Tarquinius to his throne (ibid. 247–8).

**debt.** The sources give a mixture of motives for the secession but all emphasize debt as the major cause. Livy places great emphasis on the economic factor (2. 23, 27, 28. 7, 31. 7), as does Dion. Hal. in Book 6 of *Ant. Rom.* (23. 3, 26, 28. 2, 34. 2). The mention of additional factors such as political rights (Cic. *Rep.* 2. 57; Dion. Hal. *Ant. Rom.* 6. 53. 1, 79. 2) is probably an anachronism or a rationalization of the fact that the plebs did secure their own officials, the tribunes of the people.

**Mons Sacer . . . Aventine.** Sallust appears to have his own version, a variation of Livy's 3. 52. 1 report of a movement from the Aventine to the Mons Sacer (cf. Cic. *Rep.* 2. 58).

**tribunes of the people.** All sources connect the establishment of the tribunate with the first secession of 494. The problem of debt, exacerbated for the plebs by the responsibilities of the military service demanded of them, found an appropriate solution in the appointment of their own officials. In fact the tribunate with its powers of *auxilium* (protection) guaranteed by the sacrosanctity of the tribune provided a solution which was mutually satisfactory. The patricians were content that the tribunate agreed upon was not a magistracy with powers to propose measures to the people; it was a watch committee. The oldest tradition gave the original number of tribunes as two, presumably to match the two consuls. The number was raised to four when the assembly of the tribes (*comitia tributa*), established in 471, officially elected the tribunes.

**1. 11.** This fragment is cited as belonging to Book 1. I follow the tentative suggestion of Pasoli, *Stud. Urb.* 49 (1975), 369, that it could be part of the material subsequent to the final sentence of 1. 10, illustrating the effect of *metus hostilis*, and also the appropriately antithetical prelude to 1. 12 which describes the disastrous effects of the removal of *metus Punicus*. Maurenbrecher's collocation is discussed below.

**1. 12.** The first sentence of the fragment has been preserved in Gellius; the rest in Augustinus. Arusianus Messius, 463. 2 cites the phrase 'to whose influential . . . lent support'.

The fragment begins with a comprehensive picture of the process of disintegration, one which inevitably led to civil wars. The specific emphasis here is on ambition and the importance of the role of economic power in the political struggles which marked these decades.

**a few powerful men.** Both M. Paananen, *Sallust's Politico-Social Terminology* (Helsinki 1972), 53, and Bartole, *Boll.*

*Stud. Lat.* III (1973), 395, have considered as inaccurate R. Hanell's view (*Eranos* 43 (1945), 271–2) that in Sallust's works *pauci* (*potentes*) can be taken to mean *nobiles/ nobilitas*. The powerful few were indeed members of the nobility but the term *pauci* (*potentes*) is applied only to the most prominent and most active politicians of that class; in *Cat.* 20. 7 Sallust makes this fact absolutely clear.

**masquerading . . . senate or people.**   Sallust in *Cat.* 38. 3 expands this accusation: 'all who . . . assailed the government used specious pretexts, some maintaining that they were defending the rights of the commons, others that they were upholding the prestige of the senate; but . . . each in reality was working for his own advancement.'

**all were equally corrupt.**   Even if this censure is restricted to aspirants to personal power, it is a singularly harsh judgement; it may well reflect the more pessimistic mood at the time of writing.

**was considered 'good'.**   Perversion of political vocabulary was an inevitable feature of political strife; it receives powerful emphasis and illustration in Thucydides, 3. 82. 4. The Latin word *boni* was used commonly to include men of substance who were loyal upholders of the constitution: Cicero tries to expound and expand this meaning of *boni* in *Att.* 7. 7. 5 ff., and in *Sest.* 97 ff. to extend the term to all men, irrespective of class or wealth, who supported preservation of the republican constitution. But it was a word prone to perversion. Here it is applied to the so-called defenders of the status quo, and is simply a false label to screen their acts of oppression.

**the preserver of existing conditions.**   Precisely the attitude of the conservative optimates who lacked the initiative to take firm action against the obvious threat to the republican constitution.

**1. 13\*.**   This summary of internal developments in Rome after the removal of *metus hostilis* is a later rephrasing of the material already dealt with by Sallust in *Cat.* 10. 3–11, to which 1. 12 corresponds, and in *Cat.* 12. 2, to which this fragment corresponds (Klingner 1928, 177). It thus appears that Kritz was correct in positing a close connection between these fragments. In both cases Sallust deals first with the effects of ambition aided by economic resources and then proceeds to the vice of avarice and its attendant excesses.

**From that time.** The dating implied by this remark is indicated by statements made by Augustinus before his citation of this fragment, and by Vell. Pat. 2. 1. 1. Augustinus, quoting Sallust's *Cat.* 5. 9 'by gradual changes it [the Roman state] ceased to be the fairest and best and became the worst and most vicious', reports that this refers to the period after the destruction of Carthage. Velleius is even more explicit: 'when Rome was freed of the fear of Carthage . . . the path of virtue was abandoned for that of corruption, not gradually, but in headlong course.' Augustinus' reference to civil wars just before he quotes this fragment can be taken simply to mean that the description of precipitate moral decay after 146 BC amounts to a historical explanation of the civil wars. The fact that Augustinus follows his citation with a reference to the Sullan regime and that Sallust, before his treatment of the specific evil of avarice in *Cat.* 12. 1–2, had dealt expressly with the evils attendant upon Sulla's regime has led to a presumption that the period referred to was the Sullan era. It seems preferable to follow the observation of Klingner and Pasoli that the content of 1. 13 confirms the concept, already expressed in 1. 11, that the crisis which had begun from the very beginning of the city became a headlong collapse from the end of the Punic wars.

**the young were so corrupted . . . that it could truly be said.** A repetition of the censure of the younger set which appears several times in the *Bellum Catilinae*—12. 2, 13. 4–5, 14. 5–7, 16. 1–2.

**1. 14.** This trenchant phrase has several echoes in Sallust and these serve to clarify its meaning. Thus *Cat.* 10. 3: 'Hence at first the lust for power, then for money grew upon them; these were, as it were, the root of all evil'; *Iug.* 31. 12: 'Men stained with crime, with bloodied hands, men of monstrous greed, guilty yet full of arrogance, men who have made honour, reputation, loyalty, in short everything honourable and dishonourable a source of gain.' Honour is the victim of their bartering, either for political power or for the pleasures of the body.

**1. 15.**\*    The discussion to which Augustinus refers is the debate on the corruption of the Roman government in Cicero's *Rep*. 3. 45–8. Cicero introduces Scipio Aemilianus, the destroyer of Carthage, who discusses the republic at a time—129 BC—when there were already presentiments that it would perish because of the corruption that Sallust has described here in 1. 12–14. The reference is to the murder of the reforming tribune of 133 BC, Tiberius Gracchus, who was cut down when he attempted to win re-election to the tribunate against fierce opposition.

**an action . . . serious political discord.**    A general statement that fits in with the common sentiment that the failure of the Gracchi to introduce reforms marked the beginning of the crisis of the Roman Republic. A comment in Cicero's *Rep*. 1. 31: 'For as you observe, the death of Tiberius Gracchus and, even before his death, the character of his tribunate, divided one people into two factions' embraces two aspects, the impact of the nature of the Gracchan tribunate, and the effect of Tiberius' murder, brought about by senate-inspired violence.

Sallust may well have commented on both aspects, but our fragment deals only with the consequences of the manner of Tiberius' death. This receives explanatory amplification in Vell. Pat. 2. 3. 3: 'this was the beginning in Rome of civil bloodshed, and of the licence of the sword. From this time on right was crushed by might, the most powerful now took precedence in the state' etc.

**1. 16–46.**    The second part of the Introduction is a treatment of the period preceding the beginning of Sallust's specific subject-matter. Just as the first part could be said to fulfil the function served by Thucydides' 'archaeology' (1. 2–19), this second part resembles Thucydides' *Pentecontaetia* (1. 89–119) in establishing the climate of political thought and civil and military activity which preceded and influenced the events of the narrative proper. Tacitus' *Histories* follows a fairly similar pattern: an exordium (ch. 1), an introduction of general reflections on ethical–political matters (2–3), a second introduction consisting of a general picture of armies and provinces (4–11).

The fragments which we can allocate with some confidence to this segment indicate a treatment of the Social War and its preliminaries (16–20) followed by a narrative of Roman domestic conflicts in the period 88–79 BC. That is to say, Sallust selected from material already systematically dealt with by Sisenna the events and aspects which he could use to reinforce the thrust of his own narrative, and to highlight the basic causes of the Roman crisis.

**1. 16–20.** The Social War of 91–87 BC suffers from a lack of adequate documentation.[1] Since the relevant books of Livy have been lost, Appian remains our principal source. While the first book of Appian's *Civil Wars* gives a clear and coherent account of the origin of the Italian problem (1. 21, 34), the historian simply explains how the Social War occurred and does not deal with the complex of underlying causes which led to the conflict. Not surprisingly, then, scholarly controversy persists over points of detail; there is, however, general agreement on the history of the relations between Rome, the Latins (*Latini*), and the Italian allies (*socii*) during the second century BC and on the factors which brought about the confrontation which is known as the Social War. On the source material for the actual conflict see *CAH* vol. 9.

Even though all the fragments here allocated to this segment have been transmitted without book-number, the content of each fragment, sometimes supported by evidence from other sources, makes its position fairly secure. Their content also indicates that Sallust's treatment of the conflict was on broad general lines, apparently concentrating on aspects which illustrated the breakdown of the strong moral principles which had marked Roman contacts with the Italian allies over many decades and on the ruthlessness which marked the crushing of resistance to the corporate and private ambitions of many members of the ruling class.

---

[1] This conflict was variously designated: *bellum sociale* (social war); *bellum Italicum* (Italic War); *bellum Marsicum* (Marsic War—from the Marsi, a leading Italian tribe).

**1. 16\*. So great was the sense of responsibility.** This fragment also appears in Fronto (M. P. J. van den Hout, *Frontonis Epistulae* (Leiden 1954), 154. 23). As Maurenbrecher observes, the form of this statement indicates that it was preceded by a description of measures favourable to the conditions and rights of the Italian peoples. Maurenbrecher mentions tribunes or knights (*equites*) as the agents of such services, referring probably to the measures proposed by activists such as C. Gracchus and M. Fulvius Flaccus. While it is not unlikely that Sallust would have been in sympathy with such measures, his use of the word 'ancestors' (*maiores*) makes it more likely that he is referring to Roman attitudes to the peoples of Italy during the period of Rome's expansion (Kritz, ad loc.). Acquisition of Roman citizenship at the time when Rome was extending her sphere of influence and her tribal system in Italy was relatively easy; new tribes would include non-Romans, the original inhabitants being enrolled together with Roman and Latin settlers. A typical example is that of Veii, (L. R. Taylor, *The Voting Districts of the Roman Republic* (Rome 1960), 66–7). In similar fashion Sallust had turned to ancient Rome in *Cat.* 6–9 when dealing with Rome's moral strength before the onset of degeneration.

It should be stressed that the granting of citizenship at these early stages was confined to individuals. When, in the second and first centuries BC, it became a question of granting citizenship to whole communities, sections of the ruling class resisted the move; reactions to this set the stage for open confrontation between Rome and the peoples of Italy.

**1. 17.\*** The Latin text of this fragment is corrupt: *citra Padum omnibus lex* †*Lucania fratra*† *fuit*. I follow a certain Casselius who in 1593 emended *Lucania* to *Licinia* and conjectured *fraudi* ('detrimental') for the meaningless *fratra*. Maurenbrecher conjectured ⟨*in*⟩*grata* ('unwelcome') and put it into his text, but 'unwelcome' seems too weak a description of a law which had such profound effects on the relations between Rome and the allies (W. Clausen, *AJP* 68 (1947), 293–4). The same applies to Landgraf's 1895 conjecture *parata* ('devised against') in spite of Renehan's attempt, *RhM* 105 (1962), 257–60, to revive it with copious documentation of Sallust's use of the various forms of the verb *parare* ('devise').

**The Licinian law . . .** The *Lex Licinia Mucia*, sponsored by the consuls of 95, L. Licinius Crassus and Q. Mucius Scaevola, struck from the lists allies who had illegally assumed Roman citizenship: it set up a *quaestio* ('court' or 'judicial inquiry') to investigate doubtful cases. Cicero, *Off.* 2. 47, confirms that this was the thrust of the law: 'It may not be right, of course, for one who is not a citizen to exercise the rights and privileges of citizenship; and the law on this point was secured by two of our wisest consuls, Crassus and Scaevola.' The law is still commonly referred to in textbooks as an expulsion act, driving non-citizens from Rome, an interpretation based on the unreliable scholiast in *Schol. Bob.* 129 St. (on Cic. *Sest.* 30) who gives as the thrust of the new law: 'so that the allies and the Latins were ordered to return to their own communities'.

**On this side of the Po.** At this time Italy proper extended northward little beyond Ancona and Florence. The land stretching further northward to the Alps was known as *Gallia Cisalpina* (further subdivided into Transpadane and Cispadane with reference to the River Po which intersects it). Till about 82 BC when it became an ordinary Roman province this region in administration and colonization passed as part of Italy. The region south of the Po was hardly distinguishable from Italy proper.

**1. 18.\*** The fragment is repeated at *Adnot. super Luc.* 6. 348 with the order of the final two words reversed.

Since Asconius (Cic. *Corn.* 67) remarks concerning the Licinian law that 'by this law the attitude of the leaders of the Italians changed to one of hostility so that this law became the chief cause of the Italic War which broke out three years later', Sallust must in this fragment be talking about the immediate effect of the promulgation of the law.

The war actually broke out four years after the passage of the law, i.e. late in 91 (Florus, 2. 18. 8; Obsequens, 54; Orosius 5. 18. 1; cf. Diodorus, 37. 2. 2). P. A. Brunt, *The*

*Fall of the Roman Republic* (Oxford 1988), 100–1, accepts that the Licinian law was the chief cause and accounts for the delay of over three years before the outbreak of hostilities on two grounds: so widespread and concerted a rebellion as that which occurred in the winter of 91–90 would have required a long period of preparation—the fate of Fregellae had demonstrated the perils of precipitate action; even up to the beginning of armed revolt the Italians had hoped that persuasion and negotiation might obviate recourse to arms.

Asconius' view of the Licinian law as the prime cause of the Italian War is acceptable in the sense that it marked the culmination of a series of events, enactments, and anxieties connected with the process of enfranchisement from the time of the Gracchi. For the leaders of the Italian communities the threat to their interests posed by the effects of the agrarian law of Tiberius Gracchus, their subsequent concern about threats to their overseas business dealings, the possibility of future legislation prejudicial to their well-being gradually brought the realization that their deteriorating situation could be redressed only by their attainment of full Roman citizenship. The attitude of the Roman senate and of the Roman people, astutely counselled, was reflected in the failure of the measures put forward by M. Fulvius Flaccus in 125 BC and C. Gracchus in 122. By 95 the Licinian law further illustrated the intransigence of the Roman attitude. The Italians seem to have held on to the hope that the situation would be ameliorated by peaceful negotiation. The events of M. Livius Drusus' tribunate of 91 BC made it clear that the Roman government would not willingly agree to the conferment of citizenship on the Italian communities.

The leading modern discussions on the causes and aims of the Social War are those of E. Gabba, *Athenaeum*, 32 (1954), 41–114, 293–345; P. A. Brunt, *JRS* 55 (1965), 90 ff.; F. T. Salmon, *Phoenix*, 16 (1962), 107 ff.; idem, *Samnium* etc., chs. 9, 10; Badian, *FC*, chs. 8, 9; idem, 'Roman Politics and the Italians', *Dialoghi di archeologia* (1972), 385 ff.

**1. 19.\*   allies and the Latins.** The Italian peoples, *socii Italici*, were allied to Rome by formal treaties which might mean a *foedus aequum* which set both parties on an equal footing and provided for military assistance in defensive wars. The other type of treaty, *foedus iniquum*, indicated the superiority of Rome and bound such allies to assist Rome in offensive wars as well.

The Latins (*Latini*) by their origin as the original inhabitants of *Latium* and their special social position formed an intermediate category between Romans and the *socii Italici*. Latin colonies were autonomous states subject to Rome in foreign policy only. They provided numerous troops to Roman armies and garrisoned Italy at strategic points with conspicuous loyalty.

**allies.** A coin bearing the name Q. Silo and showing eight warriors swearing allegiance may be a record of the membership of the binary league of two cantons, the Marsic and Samnite, which formed the nucleus of the allies who seceded from Rome. These were the Picentines, Marsi, Peligni,Vestini, Marrucini, Frentani, Samnites, and Hirpini. Appian, *BC* 1. 39, adds four names to this list in his catalogue of the rebellious peoples: Pompeiians, Venusini, Apulians, Lucanians.

**Latins.** Sallust is one of the few sources which indicate that Latins participated in the Social War. That their involvement was minimal is indicated by the fact that Appian's list includes only one Latin tribe, the Venusini. Florus (2. 6. 6–7) speaks of all Latium as a participant and names an Afranius as commanding the Latin participants. Florus, however, is notoriously untrustworthy in some matters. There is ample evidence of the loyalty of the Latin colonies, exemplified by Alba Fucens (*ad Her.* 2. 45; Florus, 2. 6. 11) and Aesernia (App. *BC* 1. 41; Sisenna, fr. 16P; Diod. 37. 19. 1–2). This conspicuous loyalty to Rome of the majority of the Latins had its origins in the attempts by Rome's ruling oligarchy to assuage the allied reaction to the failure of Flaccus' enfranchisement bill of 125 BC. In that year, one which was also marked by the revolt and subsequent destruction of the Latin colony of Fregellae, it appears that Rome conferred on the leaders of the Latin communities the right to acquire citizenship *per magistratum*—all Latin magistrates were given the right to become citizens by virtue of their local office (Asc. *in Pis.* 3; cf. Liv. 23. 22. 5; Pliny, *NH* 7. 136). The policy of conciliation was reflected in the exemption of the Latins from the expulsion edict of Fannius in 122 BC and in the terms of C. Gracchus' enfranchisement bill of the same year which provided for full citizenship for the Latins and Latin status for the other allies. Despite the failure of this bill, it appears from Latin loyalty in the Social War that the citizenship *per magistratum* satisfied the leading men of the Latin communities; it was these who determined Latin policy. Nowhere do we find any indication that the lower classes were dissatisfied with this outcome.

**I. 20.**\*   Most sources allude to the ferocity of the fighting on both sides and the savagery with which the defeated were treated. The atrocities committed by the allied armies in the first two years are highlighted in particular (Sisenna, fr. 16P; Diod. 37. 19–21;). Sallust's very general summary of this aspect of the war may be part of a general statement on the lack of judgement and the stubbornness based on greed and exclusiveness which caused devastation of property and loss of life (cf. Vell. Pat. 2. 15. 3) on such a scale.

The early realization by the Roman government of the serious implications of the conflict is indicated by the promulgation late in 90 of the *Lex Iulia*, which offered full citizenship to all Latins and to all communities in Italy which had not revolted (App. *BC* 1. 49; Cic. *Balb.* 21; Gell. 4. 4. 3; cf. Sisenna fr. 119P; Vell. Pat. 2. 16. 4).

**I. 21–46.**   The inadequacy of the sources for the history of the eighties had been underlined by E. Badian, *JRS* 52 (1962), 48–51 (= *Studies* 209–14). He notes the deficiencies represented by Appian's concentration on reports of terror and massacre, by Plutarch's moralizing and fanciful presentation of the last days of Marius, and the contrast between the detail of his narrative of Sulla's war in the East and his victorious return and the cursory treatment of what was happening in Rome during the years of his absence. Apart from some references in Cicero, Livy is our principal source. But the relevant part of Livy's work survives only in his various excerptors. Of these Orosius (5. 20) and Eutropius (5. 7) have just one sentence (basically the same in each) on events in Italy between the death of Marius and Sulla's return. Florus has nothing at all. The *Periochae* of Livy, then, constitute our main source (*Per.* 80–4). But here we have the difficulty that Livy himself used two principal sources which occasionally contradict each other. These Badian has specified as a 'Sullan' source, the *Commentaries* of Sulla, and a 'senatorial source', the *Histories* of Sisenna. The bias in each, therefore, has to be taken into account.

Sallust's treatment of this period has been preserved in just twenty-six fragments—none of any great length. There are indications that he went into considerable detail. It is doubtful, however, even if this segment of his *Histories* had been preserved in its entirety, that it would have added much that was new. It is likely that in keeping with the viewpoint which controlled his narratives of the crisis of the Roman Republic, he would have expended detail on the aspects of ruthlessness, greed, and personal ambition which marked the activity of the period.

Four of the Sallustian fragments on this segment are preserved in *Adnotationes super Lucanum*—26, 30, 33, 35. E. Rawson, *CQ* 37 (1987), 163–80, has drawn our attention to the fact that the scholia to Lucan's *Bellum Civile* 2.70–233—*Commenta Bernensia* and *Adnotationes super Lucanum* —have preserved quite a deal of other material relating to civil strife in Rome during the eighties, chiefly on the return of Marius and Cinna to Rome in late 87 and on that of Sulla in 82. Errors of fact and confusion concerning events and personalities abound, especially in the *Commenta*, but the scholia are of interest in demonstrating the detail with which the source on which they are based has described these events. Rawson is of the view that much of the material for the comments goes back to the first book of Sallust's *Histories*. I find her conjecture attractive in that it supports the impression of a detailed treatment of some events which clearly emerges from some of the surviving Sallustian fragments—e.g. 21–2 on the flight of Marius; 29; 30 on the period of Sulla's return to Italy and the final campaign against the Marians. The fact that many of the comments stress the savagery with which Marius wreaked revenge and his use of slaves to carry out tasks of vengeance would not be a deterrent to accepting Sallustian authorship of the scholiast's source. As in the case of the Gracchi (1. 15), Sallust would have little sympathy with excesses committed in the allegedly good cause of resisting abuses of power in the case of generals or rulers. Nevertheless I confine myself here to referring to these scholia only where they are of relevance to the interpretation of the fragments of this section.

Modern works relevant to the civil strife of the eighties are: H. Bennett, *Cinna and his Times* (Menasha, Wis., 1923); E. Valgiglio, *Silla e la crisi repubblicana* (Florence 1956); T. F. Carney, *A Biography of C. Marius* (PACA suppl. 1: 1961); 'The Flight and Exile of Marius', *G&R* NS 8 (1961), 98–121; E. Badian, 'Waiting for Sulla', *JRS* 52 (1962) *Sulla the Deadly Reformer*, Seventh Todd Memorial Lecture (Sydney 1970); H. Bulst, 'Cinnianum Tempus', *Hist.* 13 (1964), 307–37; E. S. Gruen, *Roman Politics and the Criminal Courts 149–78 B.C.* (Cambridge, Mass., 1968); A. Passerini, *Studi su Caio Mario* (Milan 1971); E. Gabba, 'Mario e Silla', *ANRW* 1: 1 (1972), 765–805; A. Keaveney, *Sulla: The Last Republican* (London 1983).

**1. 21–2.**  By the end of 89 BC the military crisis of the Social War had been brought under control. There remained the task of dealing with the problems of restoration of concord within Italy and of countering the growing threats to Roman rule in the East. Because of the persistence of factional interest, however, the prospects for the maintenance of a fruitful peace were not bright.

Sulla, consul for 88, received the province of Asia and command against Mithridates, a commission coveted by Marius. The tribune P. Sulpicius Rufus took up the banner of Drusus and attempted to force the government to give reality to the concession of enfranchisement to the allies by distributing them over the thirty-five tribes (*Asc. Corn.* 64; App. *BC* 1. 55–6; cf. Liv. *Per.* 77) instead of confining them to, possibly, ten tribes (Taylor, *Vot. Dist.* 102–3 n. 6). To counter the opposition of the oligarchs, he proposed, among other measures, the transfer of the Mithridatic command from Sulla to Marius (Liv. *Per.* 77; Diod. 37. 29. 2; App. *BC* 1. 55–6) in order to secure the support for his programme.

Meeting opposition from the consuls, Sulpicius had them forcibly expelled from the city and carried out his measures. Sulla appealed to his troops who were mustering at Nola for the Mithridatic War and led them in the first march on Rome by a Roman army. He occupied the city, annulled the legislation of Sulpicius, who was executed, and exiled his main opponents, including Marius. (Plut. *Sull.* 7. 1–10. 2; App. *BC* 1. 57–60).

**1. 21.** Marius lost no time in getting out of Rome; he had need for speed since Sulla was quick to organize the pursuit of his fugitive enemies. Marius' goal was North Africa where his veterans were settled in great numbers. En route, his vessel was forced ashore near Circeii, close to Terracina, whose overlord, Geminius, was a bitter enemy of Marius. The latter decided to head inland to Minturnae, the inhabitants of which were kindly disposed towards him.

This fragment probably refers to an appeal he made to tenant farmers (Plutarch calls them 'herdsmen') in the region shortly after he landed, as Plut. *Mar.* 36. 3 reports. In his edition, *Granius Licinianus, Reliquiae* (Leipzig 1981), N. Criniti in the testimonia to 35. 8 made the very tentative suggestion that the fragment might refer to Marius' gathering of support in Etruria after his return in 87. This suggestion is recommended by Konrad (*AHB* 2. 13 n. 11) who refers to Plut. *Mar.* 41. 3–4 and App. *BC* 1. 67. Both of these passages do indeed refer to Marius' return in 87 but in neither of them is there any support for Criniti's suggestion concerning this fragment.

Carney, *G&R* 8 (1961), 98, noting Passerini's suggestion (*Caio Mario*, 183–4) that Marius sympathizers overdrew the picture of his suffering to explain the terrible revenge that he subsequently took on his adversaries and even to give him the excuse of mental imbalance brought about by hardship and exposure, adds the factor of artistic stylization where Marius is repeatedly plunged into dangers from which he escapes by the narrowest of margins and in most dramatic fashion. It is difficult, therefore to assess to what extent such factors have perverted the true history of the flight and exile.

On the problem of the book-number connected with

Nonius' citation of this fragment see Garbugino, *Stud. Non.* 5 (1978), 45–6.

**I. 22.**   The scholia to Lucan 2. 70 refer to a decision by the town councillors of Minturnae to carry out the execution of the fugitive Marius, while *Adnot. super Luc.* 2. 88 reports that a certain Fannia, who according to Plut. *Mar* 38. 3–4 had reason to be hostile to Marius, approved his escape when the authorities at Minturnae decided to assist his departure into exile. This fragment is a version of an incident reported elsewhere only in Appian. Leaving Minturnae, Marius headed back towards the sea; realizing that he was being pursued by Sullan cavalry, 'he rushed to the boat of an old fisherman which was on the beach, overpowered him, leaped into it, and although a storm was raging cut the painter, spread the sail, and committed himself to chance' (App. *BC* I. 62). He was subsequently driven on to an island where he found a ship manned by friends of his and from there sailed to Africa.

**I. 23–6.**   Even after the defeat of the Samnites under Pompaedius Silo by Metellus Pius in 88 the embers of the Social War still glowed in Samnium and Lucania.

Cinna, elected consul for 87, had sworn to maintain Sulla's measures (Plut. *Sull.* 10. 3–4; Dio. 30–5 fr. 102. 1; *Schol. Gronov.* 286 St.). When he entered into office as consul he attempted to carry a bill to enrol new citizens and freedmen in all the tribes (Cic. *Phil.* 8. 7; Vell. Pat. 2. 20. 2; App. *BC* I. 64; Exup. 4. 23) and one to recall Marius and the other exiles. Expelled from Rome by his consular colleague, Cn. Octavius, he secured the support of the troops of Appius Claudius, a Sullan commander at Nola, and was soon joined by Marius and his partisans. He easily overpowered Octavius and occupied Rome. In the ensuing conflict, sometimes called the *Bellum Octavianum*, the consul Octavius was killed and a reign of terror followed in which many senatorial opponents of Cinna and Marius were murdered. The impact of this reign of terror is indicated by the volume of the source material in which it receives a mention (*MMR* 2. 46). The victors repealed the laws of Sulla and re-enacted the laws of Sulpicius.

**1. 23.\*   that the war should come to an end.**   Q. Caecilius
Metellus, praetor in 89, legate in the Social War, who had
probably continued in command against the Samnites,
carrying on what was left of the Social War (App. *BC* 1. 68),
was instructed by the senate in 87 to negotiate a peace with
the Samnites. The words of the fragment convey Sallust's
version of part of these instructions. Dio, 30–5, fr. 102. 7,
reporting on the same incident, almost echoes Sallust's
words: 'bidding him to come to terms with the Samnites *as
best he might*'.

The Samnites put forward conditions which Metellus and
the senate would not accept. Marius and Cinna sent C.
Flavius Fimbria to the Samnites and accepted the terms they
demanded, thus winning Samnite support for their cause
(Gran. Lic. 35. 29–30C; cf. Liv. *Per.* 80; App. *BC* 1. 68).

**1. 24.   that nothing had been settled . . .**   Maurenbrecher,
agreeing with Kritz, interpreted these words as part of a
disavowal by Cinna of the oath he had taken to uphold
Sulla's measures of 88. Kritz is more specific in his
interpretation: Cinna 'had made no promises which were
inimical to the republic and the freedom of the Roman
people', that is, he was free to introduce legislation as he saw
fit, his oath notwithstanding. B. R. Katz, *RhM* 124 (1981),
332–8, refers the fragment to Sulla's negotiation of the
Peace of Dardanus with Mithridates. C. F. Konrad, 'Why
not Sallust on the Eighties?', *AHB* 2 (1988), 13 n. 12, points
out that Sallust does not use the verb *pacisci* (used in this
fragment) for formal agreements or treaties with foreign
powers; that the term is always *pactionem facere* or *agere*, as
in *Iug.* 29. 3, 38. 2, 40. 1, 62. 3. He therefore dismisses
Katz's conjecture as unconvincing and suggests that the
statement would fit in better at the end of 87, after the
capture of the city by Cinna and Marius: a retort by Marius
to some of his allies criticizing the carnage (e.g. Plut. *Sert.* 5.
6–7; *Mar.* 44. 10) or his and Cinna's assumption of the
consulship of 86 without proper election (Liv. *Per.* 80).

The cryptic nature of the fragment allows for a variety of
interpretations. I would interpret it in much the same way as
Kritz and suggest that a likely context is in the exchange of

statements in a meeting that took place when Metellus Pius
approached Cinna as an envoy of the Senate (Gran. Lic. 35.
48C; cf. Plut. *Mar*. 43. 1).

**1. 25. He tied . . . together . . .** Kritz attributes this
fragment to Marius' activity in the blockading of the Tiber
during the siege of Rome in 87. He does so on the basis of
App. 1. 67: 'the two latter [Sertorius and Marius] threw
bridges across the river in order to cut off the city's food-
supply'. Maurenbrecher relegated it to 'Fragments *incertae
sedis* ('of uncertain placement') of Book 1—i.e. fr. 1. 144M.
He objected that the Appian passage involves at least two
(possibly four) commanders in the carrying out of this
stratagem. Konrad, *AHB* 2 (1988), 14–15 points out that the
bulk of the food shipments will have come upstream from
Ostia, soon to be taken by Marius, and hence his blockade
to the south of the city would, at the outset, have been the
more important one. What is presented by Appian as a joint
effort need not have been simultaneous either in source or in
reality, or for that matter in Sallust. Maurenbrecher's other
objection that the resemblance between a bridge composed
of boats tied together and a chain is not an obvious one does
little to strengthen his point of view. La Penna, *SIFC* 35
(1963), 31, draws attention to a resemblance between this
fragment and Frontin. *Str*. 1. 21: 'The same Spartacus, when
besieged on the slopes of Vesuvius at the point where the
mountain was steepest and on that account unguarded,
plaited ropes of osiers from the woods. Letting himself down
by these, he . . . made his escape.' However, since it is firmly
allocated to Book 1 he would not recommend the transfer of
the fragment to Book 3 of the *Histories*.

**1. 26. unaccustomed to freedom.** Referred by Maurenbrecher to slaves running wild at Cinna's summons to
freedom during the siege of Rome. Marius, from the period
of his flight, frequently appealed to slaves; he enrolled them
in Africa and in Etruria after his return to Italy. Cinna also
called upon slaves before withdrawing from Rome in 87;
during the siege of Rome he was successful in summoning
the slaves to defection (App. *BC* 1. 69). The entry into
Rome of the Cinnan forces, comprising many runaway

slaves, led to five days of looting, rape, and murder. As Bennett, *Cinna*, 24, 30, 32, and Carney, *Marius*, 65 ff., have noted, the initial atrocities, committed without authorization by the lower ranks before military law was established, have been exaggerated by the sources. Specific cases of savage reprisal carried out by slaves are dealt with by the scholia to Lucan 2. 114, 119, 120, 121. La Penna (1963, 23), while acknowledging the acuteness of Maurenbrecher's suggestion, would prefer to place the fragment among those of uncertain placement on the grounds that one could think of several scenarios, e.g. placing it after 1.90M to illustrate Sertorius' character by alluding to the part he played in the punishment of the rampaging slaves (Plut. *Sert.* 5; *Mar.* 44. 6) or, less precisely, referring it to a barbarous people used to a despotic regime. Using this latter hint, Katz (1981, 338–40) suggested a reference to Cappadocians and Paphlagonians who, when granted their freedom by Rome in 96, unexpectedly rejected it (Iust. *Epit.* 38. 2. 3–8; Strabo, 12. 2. 11; see Badian, *Athenaeum* (1959) 286 ff. (= *Studies* 162 ff.), with sources cited, for Sulla's personal involvement. This fragment is securely allocated to Book 1 and even though Katz reminds us that Sallust discussed Cappadocia and Phrygia in Book 2 (2. 66), I do not find his conjecture convincing.

**1. 27–9.** (86–83 BC) During the Marian counter-coup of 87 Sulla, as proconsul in command of the war against Mithridates, was in Greece, occupied with the siege of Athens. The following triennium, called the *triennium sine armis* (i.e. without war) by Cic. *Brut.* 308, saw the continuation of Cinna in the consulship for each year and a period of comparative peace. But this was also the period of 'waiting for Sulla', so that the lack of overt hostile activity did not signify acquiescence in the settlement enforced by the counter-coup.

Marius died on 13 January 86 (Liv. *Per.* 80) and L. Valerius Flaccus was appointed consul *suffectus*. In the course of the year Sulla captured Athens and the Piraeus and had successful engagements against two Mithridatic armies, first at Chaeronea and later at Orchomenos (Liv.

*Per.* 81–2; Plut. *Sull.* 14. 1–21. 4; App. *Mith.* 33–51). In 85
Cinna shared the consulship with Cn. Papirius Carbo and
they began some preparations against Sulla's expected
return from the East (Liv. *Per.* 83; App. *BC* 1. 76–7).
Meanwhile in the East Sulla negotiated with Mithridates the
Peace of Dardanus on the basis of the situation before the
war (Liv. *Per.* 83; Plut. *Sull.* 22. 2–24. 4; App. *Mithr.* 54–8;
Gran. Lic. 35. 78C). Cinna and Carbo stayed in the
consulship for 84 but Cinna was killed early in the year by
mutinous troops at Ancona while arranging passage for his
army to Epirus (Liv. *Per.* 83; Vell. Pat. 2. 34. 5; Plut. *Sull.* 6.
1; *Pomp.* 5. 1–2; App. *BC* 1. 78). Carbo continued Cinna's
preparations against Sulla's return. Sulla returned from Asia
to Greece and, while negotiating with the senate in Rome
and recovering from an illness, prepared for his return with
his army to Italy.

The consuls for 83 were L. Cornelius Scipio Asiaticus
(Asiagenus) and C. Norbanus. In the course of the year
Sulla invaded Italy. Norbanus was defeated near Mt. Tifata
and retreated to Capua, where he maintained himself for a
time. Sulla won Scipio's army away from him at Teanum and
took him prisoner, but dismissed him unharmed.

**1. 27. Sulla having suspicions . . . opportune time.**
Donatus, Ter. *Phorm.* 464, reports the fragment from 'and
especially . . .'.

Editors before Maurenbrecher unanimously allocated this
fragment to 88 BC. Maurenbrecher rejected this on the
grounds that the future participle *bellaturi* ('would fight')
indicates that a war by Mithridates is in prospect, whereas
the expedition of Sulla to Asia in 88 was provoked by a
revolt of Mithridates already in progress. O. Pecere, *SIFC*
41 (1969), 61–7, points out that the emphasis on 'ferocious
temperament' places the fragment at a point at which, for
Sulla and for Rome, the unforeseen and bloody rebellion of
the Pontic king in 88 was already a sad and fearful memory.
The fragment therefore must refer to the period after the
signing of the Peace of Dardanus (Liv. *Per.* 85). Sulla had
long-standing problems to settle in Rome where his provisional constitution of 88 had been set aside. Given the

temperament of Mithridates the Dardanus peace was a fragile agreement; speed of decision and of action was imperative.

**suspicions concerning these matters.** Unfortunately the fragment gives no clue to the identity of 'these matters'. It is reasonable to assume that the reference is to developments in Italy and Rome during Sulla's absence.

**1. 28. at Dyrrhachium.** I have translated the Latin word *cogere* as 'muster at' (cf. Liv. 37. 10. 12). Kritz rejected Gerlach's suggestion that the fragment referred to the joint setting out of Appius Claudius (to his province) and Servilius (to the pirate war; see 1. 115) in 78 on the grounds that *cogere* has the force of 'collecting together' rather than 'transporting across'. While he relegated the fragment to *incertae sedis* of Book 1, he did provide the most likely explanation which I accept along with Maurenbrecher. Plut. *Sull.* 27. 1: 'And now Sulla, having passed through Thessaly and Macedonia down to the sea, was preparing to cross from Dyrrhachium to Brundisium with twelve hundred ships' provides convincing support for the assumption that we are here dealing with Sulla's preparations for his return to Italy and the showdown with the Roman government.

**1. 29.\* Thence arose a dialogue.** Refers to the desertion to Sulla of the army of the consul L. Cornelius Scipio Asiaticus at Teanum. Cicero, *Phil.* 12. 27, does not mention the part played by soldiers. Diod. 38. 16 speaks of Scipio's men being bribed and corrupted. Liv. *Per.* 85 talks of their being invited to desert by soldiers sent by Sulla; App. *BC* 1. 85 describes the consul's troops as dejected and susceptible to persuasion by Sulla's envoys. The Sallust fragment gives us more detail concerning the exchanges between the soldiers on both sides and confirms once again that in some aspects his treatment of this period was quite detailed.

**1. 30–4.** The campaigning season of 82 began on both sides with increased resources and a sharpened fierceness. Sulla had secured Apulia and Picenum and was hoping to extend his power by guaranteeing to the Italian communities that citizenship which they had won from his opponents. Two extreme Marians held the consulship, Cn. Papirius Carbo for the third time and C. Marius the younger, who attracted to his standard large numbers of the great Marius' veterans. Considerable forces were raised in Etruria and Cisalpine Gaul. Heavy fighting took place in three theatres of war—in Cisalpine Gaul, in Etruria and Umbria, and in Latium. The progress made by Sullan armies under Metellus Pius and Pompeius in Cisalpine Gaul aided the collapse of the Marian cause in Etruria and Umbria. Such successes enabled Sulla to maintain the blockade of Praeneste against the fury of the Lucanians and the Samnites.

**1. 30.\*** In Campania Sulla continued his march towards Rome. An army under the command of the younger Marius, swelled by the influx of veterans who had flocked to his support, had the task of halting this advance on Rome. A combination of fierce fighting by the Sullan forces and a lack of morale in their opponents brought about a total collapse of the resistance to Sulla's advance on Rome. With what remained of his forces after the terrible defeat at Sacriportus, Marius fled for refuge to Praeneste (Diod. 38. 12–15; Liv. *Per.* 87; Vell. Pat. 2. 26; Val. Max. 6. 8. 2; Plut. *Mar.* 46. 5–6; *Sull.* 28. 4–8; App. *BC* 1. 87–94; Flor. 2. 9. 21–5).

**Sacriportus.** Modern scholars have unanimously placed Sacriportus in the valley of the Trerus (Sacco) on the Via Latina, the inland route from Latium to Campania, and not far from Praeneste. Thus e.g. R. Gardner, *CAH* 9. 273 n. 1: 'The meaning and location cannot be determined. The *Torre Piombinara* or *Pimpinara* near Segni railway station is supposed (without good reason) to mark the site'; cf. E. Gabba, *Comm. App. BC 1* (Florence 1958), 396; E. T. Salmon, *Athenaeum* 42 (1964), 77, suggested Colleferro. These suggestions are based on Plutarch's description of the battle as περὶ Σίγνιον ('near Signion' (= Signia)) and the assumption of other sources that it took place near Praeneste (Plut. *Sull.* 28. 4; App. *BC* 1. 87).

However, as E. Rawson, *CQ* (1987), 171–2 reminds us, Appian says that shortly before the battle of Sacriportus Sulla had taken Setia. The capture of Setia would indicate that Sulla was coming up the Via Appia on the seaward side of the Monti Lepini. It is not inconceivable that, having been defeated somewhere north of Setia, Marius should have fled to the great fortress of Praeneste. Scholars have tried in various ways to combine the capture of Setia with a battle near Signia; Keaveney, *Sulla*, 137, for example, believes that Sulla's lieutenant, Dolabella, came up the Via Appia and took Setia, intending to rendezvous with Sulla near Signia; Plutarch (*Sull*. 28. 4) does in fact say that Sulla had difficulty joining up with Dolabella, since the Mariani held the roads.

Rawson notes that the scholiasts to Lucan 2. 134 present evidence to indicate that the main battle of Sacriportus must have been west of the mountains. However, the phrase used, 'between Circeium and the *ager Laurentinum*', is so vague as to be virtually useless. She therefore suggests some port on one of the rivers or canals of the Pomptine marshes as more likely than a place on the Sacco, hardly a navigable river.

**1. 31.\*   had enlarged the war.**   Refers to the necessity for Sulla to provide a force large enough to counter the several attempts made to raise the siege of Praeneste, and at the same time to contain his enemies in the other theatres of war. Appian, *BC* 1. 88, tells us that Sulla drew a line of circumvallation round the town a considerable distance from it and left the work in charge of Lucretius Ofella. Four unsuccessful attempts at relief were made: the first was when C. Marcius Censorinus was sent with eight legions by Papirius Carbo, but he was ambushed by Pompeius in Umbria and his army melted away (App. *BC* 1. 90); a more determined venture involving 70,000 troops, mostly Samnites and Lucanians under Lamponius, Pontius Telesinus, and Gutta of Capua, failed to break through, even though Marius tried to help by sallying forth and erecting a large fort between the city and Ofella's lines (ibid.). Next, Carbo sent two more legions from Etruria under Damasippus but they could not penetrate the lines (App. *BC* 1. 92). After Carbo's flight to Africa, Carrinas, Marcius Censorinus, and Damasippus, joining forces with Lamponius, Pontus Telesinus, and Gutta, made a last concerted effort to break through. Repulsed, they flung themselves into a final desperate attack on Rome and the battle of the Colline Gate.

**I. 32.**   Undoubtedly refers to Ofella, whom Sulla had left in command of the blockade of Praeneste. A Roman *eques* who had deserted from the Marians to Sulla, Ofella showed himself cool in a crisis when he refused the request of panic-stricken Sullan troops to raise the siege of Praeneste and allow them refuge inside that city from the Samnite troops who had demoralized them at the Colline Gate (Plut. *Sull.* 29. 8). Dio (30–5 fr. 108) paints him as a cynical manipulator of people for his own ends. However, he overreached himself. In 81 BC, relying on Sulla's gratitude for the services he had rendered at Praeneste and ignoring Sulla's law about the eligibility for official posts, he presented himself as candidate for the consulship even though he had not yet been quaestor. Sulla had him murdered by a centurion (Liv. *Per.* 89; Plut. *Sull.* 33. 4; App. *BC* I. 101).

**I. 33.\***   Adnot super Luc. 2. 548 has a slightly changed version ('deserted the army and Italy') of this fragment. Cn. Papirius Carbo, consul in 85, 84, and 82, played a leading part in opposing Sulla's rise to power. During the campaigns of 82 Carbo was commander of the Marian forces in Picenum, Umbria, and Etruria. When checked in Picenum by Metellus and Pompeius, he turned to face Sulla in Etruria but met reverses here also. He failed to relieve his lieutenant Carrinas in Spoletium, lost Cisalpine Gaul, and despite several attempts was unable to relieve Marius in Praeneste. Appian records the effect of all this on Carbo: 'although he still had 30,000 men around Clusium and the two legions of Damasippus and others under Carrinas and Marcius (Censorinus) besides a large force of Samnites . . . he fell into despair and weakly fled to Africa with his friends' (*BC* I. 92). Cf. Liv. *Per.* 88; Val. Max. 6. 2. 10; Plut. *Pomp.* 7. 3; 8. 4–6; Exup. 8. 53Z.

The condemnatory tone of Sallust's report here and in I. 44 indicates his even-handed attitude to both sides in the civil conflict, despite his desire to correct Sisenna's bias. This picture of Carbo is counterbalanced by the feelings concerning the *Sullani* implicit in 1. 35 and 36.

**1. 34.** Refers to a decision taken by Sullan commanders when the battle of the Colline Gate looked like turning into a disaster for the Sullan forces. Vell. Pat. 2. 27. 1 sums up the situation succinctly: 'Pontius [Telesinus] . . . fought with Sulla near the Colline Gate, a battle so critical as to bring Sulla and the city into the greatest peril.' Other detail pertinent to our fragment occurs in Plut. *Sull.* 29. 7: 'but at last his [Sulla's] left wing was shattered, and with the fugitives he sought refuge in his camp after losing many friends and acquaintances.' Appian (*BC* 1. 93) reports in much the same terms. He adds: 'the fighting continued through the night and a great many were slain'; the implication of this is revealed in Vell. Pat. 2. 27. 3: 'It was only after the first hour of the night that the Roman army was able to recover its breath and the enemy retired.'

**1. 35–7.** The victory at the Colline Gate sealed the fate of Praeneste. When the heads of Carrinas and other leaders were thrown into the city the garrison surrendered to Ofella. The younger Marius did not survive an escape attempt. Most of the survivors were herded together and executed, and the city was given over to pillage. This, however, was but the prelude to slaughter on a scale which Rome had never before witnessed. The execution of the captured Marian leaders and the butchering of the Samnite prisoners were followed by continual murders in Rome, clearly with the approval of Sulla. Nor were atrocities confined to Rome. Massacre followed by proscriptions which permitted legalized murder and confiscations occurred in the country towns of Italy. The communities which had resisted even at the Colline Gate were particularly savagely treated. Etruria and Samnium were devastated. This prosecution of bloody revenge persisted into the years 81–79. It was a reign of terror never forgotten in Rome. Mention of it occurs frequently in the speeches and letters of Cicero. Sallust also referred to it in an earlier work, *Cat.* 37. 6–9; 51. 32–4. It is highly probable that he spoke at greater length and with deeper feeling on the topic in his final work.

**1. 35.\*    that the domination which he had taken vengeance on . . .**    Maurenbrecher (1. 31M) accepted the passage as transmitted by the scholiast and interpreted it as follows: 'that the domination of Sulla which he [Marius or Cinna] had taken vengeance on was being longed for'. Such a formulation would take us back to the activity of Marius and Cinna in 87–86 and would give support to the impression that a very hostile picture of these leaders was to be found in Sallust's work. However, E. Figari, *Maia* 18 (1966), 167–9, has put forward a strong case for the view that the fragment as it stands in *Adnot. super Luc.* 2. 139 is corrupt. The English version I have given is based on my acceptance of his argument.

Figari noted that Exuperantius, in a closely parallel passage, probably based on Sallust, has the following: 'Then indeed Sulla after his victory cruelly hounded all traces of opposition remaining in the city; he did not restore the state, which he now claimed for his own, to the rule of law but showed himself to be such [a tyrant] that the Cinnan and Marian domination, which he had taken vengeance on, was being longed for' (32Z). Figari consequently held that the word *Sullae* ('of Sulla') which led to Maurenbrecher's interpretation was a marginal gloss which had crept into the text and had no business there.

Moreover the facts of the situation compel a rejection of Maurenbrecher's interpretation. The use of the word *dominatio* in the sense of tyranny as applied to Sulla is always in reference to the second domination of Sulla—to the true and proper tyranny installed after the battle of the Colline Gate—and not to the short period of Sullan power before his departure for Greece (87 BC) to which the name *Sullae dominatio* must apply if this fragment is read as it is currently presented in the text of *Adnot. super Luc.* Reference elsewhere in Sallust to the Sullan domination (*Cat.* 5. 6, 28. 4; *Hist.* 1. 48. 7, 1. 50) is always the period after 82 BC. It became a *topos* in the historical tradition—e.g. Lucan himself, *B. Civ.* 2. 139–44; Augustinus, *CD* 3. 27.

It is, therefore, as Figari remarks, more appropriate and in conformity with the historical tradition to take Sulla ('he') as the subject of 'take vengeance on' and to hold that the 'domination' referred to was that of Cinna and Marius.

**I. 36.** The Berne scholiast on the Lucan passage reports the last clause of this fragment.

The case of the execution of M. Marius Gratidianus after the battle of the Colline Gate is very probably one that Sallust developed in dramatic form in order to give point to general statements of revulsion and horror such as that in the preceding fragment.

Gratidianus was tribune in 87, twice praetor and a confirmed Marian. There are two versions of his death. The Ciceronian version is that his head was cut off by Catiline (Asc. *Tog. Cand.* 84. 8–9: cf. Plut. *Sull.* 32. 2). The other version started with Sallust and is partly preserved in this fragment. Sallust's version was followed by Livy (*Per.* 88), Valerius Maximus (9. 2. 1), Lucan (2. 173–93), Florus (2. 9. 26), with the details of torture and mutilation becoming progressively more gory. The two versions seem to have been subsequently combined (*Comm. Pet.* 10; Sen. *De Ira* 3. 18. 1–2; Firm. Mat. *Math* 1. 7. 31; Oros. 5. 21. 7–8).

The fragment as we have it does not state who carried out the execution nor give any indication of where it took place. For discussion on the possible executioner—Catiline or the younger Lutatius Catulus—and on the place—the tomb of the Lutatian family—see B. A. Marshall, *CQ* 35 (1985), 124–33 and *Hist. Commentary on Asconius* (Univ. Missouri 1985), 290–2.

**I. 37.** This fragment is repeated in Donatus, Ter. *Phorm.* 872.

As we have noted, the Ciceronian version specifically names Catiline as the murderer of Gratidianus. There is some evidence that Catiline was related to Gratidianus by marriage. The Berne scholiast, commenting on Luc. *B. Civ.* 2. 173, makes Gratidianus the brother of Catiline's wife at the time of his execution. The marriage is accepted by most scholars—e.g. M. Gelzer, *RE* 2A (1923), 1695, s.v. 'Sergius' no. 23; Syme, *Sallust*, 85–6; C. Nicolet, *REL* 45 (1965), 276–7 and 290; A. Kaplan, *Catiline*, (1968) 27; E. Manni,

*Lucio Sergio Catilina*[2] (1969), 205 n. 1; T. P. Wiseman, *New Men* (1971), 240. Marshall (1985) has attempted to show that Catiline never married a Gratidia and that he was not the executioner of Gratidianus. He admits that the argumentation for both propositions is mainly from silence. If, however, Catiline is the 'he' of this fragment, as being the uncle of Gratidianus' children, then the Ciceronian and Sallustian versions agree in indicating that Gratidianus' murderer was Catiline. Moreover, the friendship indicated by Catiline's letter to the younger Catulus (*Cat.* 35) could have arisen from Catiline's participation in an execution regarded as a ritual atonement to the ghost of Q. Lutatius Catulus, the victor of Vercellae.

**1. 38–43.** Following on the blood bath marked by the slaughter of captured and fleeing enemies immediately after the Colline Gate, Sulla issued a series of proscription lists by which he outlawed all who had in any public or private capacity aided the cause of his opponents. Rewards were offered to those who murdered or betrayed any of the outlaws and there were severe penalties for any who concealed or befriended them. Our major sources for this phase are Plut. *Sull.* 31–2 and App. *BC* 1. 95–6. The indelible mark imprinted on Roman minds and memories by these measures is clearly indicated by the bulk of the source material listed in *MRR* 2. 69.

**1. 38. the altars and other things set aside . . .** Sallust's description of the widespread impact of the proscriptions is echoed in Plut. *Sull.* 31. 5: 'Moroever, proscriptions were made not only in Rome, but also in every city in Italy, and neither temple of God nor hearth of hospitality, nor parental home was free from the stain of bloodshed . . .' and in Dio, 30–5 fr. 109. 18: 'Some were murdered while still ignorant of the fact that they were to die, and others, who knew it in advance, were slain anywhere that they happened to be; no place, either profane or sacred, was safe or inviolate for them.'

Kritz (1. 26) refers this fragment to the period of the domination of Cinna and Marius in 87. He relies heavily on Vell. Pat. 2. 22. 1 and Florus 3. 21. 16 and their recording of the blood-spattering suicide of L. Cornelius Merula, who replaced Cinna as consul in 87 when the latter was ejected from the city by his consular colleague, Octavius. Merula, the object of Cinna's vengeance, 'opened his veins and his blood drenched the altars . . .'.

**I. 39.*** Maurenbrecher is the first editor to have included this statement from Lydus, a 6th-cent. AD Greek writer. A *nomenclator*, in normal practice, was a slave who accompanied a candidate for a magistracy when he was on an electioneering promenade in the forum. The nomenclator's task was to remind him of the name of the electors. Sallust's mention of the official is connected with a less innocent use of his services by Sulla; Valerius Maximus, who probably derived his material from Sallust, provides us with more detail: 'nor was he content to vent his rage simply on those who had shown their disagreement with his policies through armed revolt, he even used a nomenclator to ferret out peaceful-minded citizens and added them to the number of the proscribed because of their great wealth' (9. 2. 1).

**I. 40.** Gellius, 15. 13. 8, gives a truncated version of this fragment.

**sold or simply given away.** Sulla's noble supporters were rewarded by the opportunity to acquire the goods of the proscribed for nothing or for a nominal sum. Confiscation of farms and public lands in Italy also led to the acquiring or the enlarging of *latifundia* ('large estates') by members of the nobility.

**I. 41. so generous a reward.** Refers to the methods used by Sulla to entrench his system and to give it a lasting bulwark of support and defence. He did so by placing colonies of his troops as garrisons among communities in different parts of Italy; he sequestered the lands and houses of local inhabitants and divided them among his soldiers 'whom he thus made true to him even after his death' (App. *BC* 1. 96). In Rome he added 10,000 slaves of proscribed persons to the body of the plebeians, granting them freedom and Roman citizenship, and he called them Cornelii after himself. 'In this way he made sure of having 10,000 men . . . always ready to obey his commands' (App. *BC* 1. 100).

**I. 42.   booty . . . restoration of freedom.**   With this picture
Sallust characterized the essence of the duplicity of Sulla's
claim that he was the restorer of the Republic. By way of
illustration Kritz (1. 39) quotes App. *BC* 1. 89 in which
Sulla, after defeating Marius at Sacriportus, advanced
towards Rome. By this time the opposing faction had fled
and their property was at once confiscated and put up for
public sale. Addressing the assembled people of the city,
Sulla 'lamented the necessity of his present actions and told
them to cheer up, as the troubles would soon be over and the
government go on as it ought'. The emptiness of such
promises of a secure and orderly *res publica* is indicated by
the words of Plutarch, probably drawn from Sallust, on the
occasion of the wholesale slaughter of 6,000 of Sulla's
enemies in the Circus Flaminius while Sulla was addressing
the senate in the nearby temple of Bellona: 'This gave even
the dullest Roman to understand that, in the matter of
tyranny, there had been an exchange, not a deliverance'
(*Sull.* 30. 4).

**I. 43.**   Maurenbrecher's allocation of this fragment to
Sallust's introduction to the *Histories* (1. 18M) is based on
the strong similarity of the wording with which Velleius
Paterculus describes the effect of the murder of Tiberius
Gracchus: (quoted in note on 1. 15, **an action . . . serious
political discord**). That statement, however, is a summary of
the age of revolution which was ushered in by the murder of
Tiberius Gracchus. With Dietsch and Kritz I would prefer to
view this fragment as part of the strongly condemnatory
judgement which Sallust expressed of the excesses and self-
seeking of factional fighting which in his view marked not
only Sulla's rise to personal domination but also the spirit of
the constitution which he set up to confirm his 'restoration'
of the Roman Republic.

**I. 44–6.**   (82–79 BC) In Rome, Sulla was by this time in
undisputed control. There were, however, forces with
Marian sympathies still at large in various regions of Italy.
Moreover, Africa and Sicily had provided refuge to large
numbers of fugitives from the vengeance of Sulla. Apart
from that factor, these provinces were the western granaries

of Rome and their recovery was a matter of urgency. Late in 82 (*MRR* 2. 72 n. 1) Pompey was given praetorian *imperium* and ordered to expel the enemy from Sicily. M. Perperna, governor of Sicily, had an army at his disposal; he had recently been reinforced by the fleet brought to Sicily from Africa by Carbo. Sicily offered no serious resistance to being taken over. Perperna disappeared, to be heard of next as a member of the retinue of M. Aemilius Lepidus, after the death of Sulla. His lieutenant, M. Brutus, surrounded by Pompeius' ships, fell on his sword, while Carbo, caught on the island of Cossura, was executed.

In Africa, too, Pompeius acted with great speed to put down the resistance of the Marians commanded by Cn. Domitius Ahenobarbus, a son-in-law of Cinna (Oros. 5. 24. 16) who had a considerable force to the east of the Gulf of Carthage and also drew some support from the Numidian region. Pompeius' army of six legions was swelled by 7,000 deserters from the enemy, but Domitius could still muster a force of 20,000. He was, however, defeated and killed. After establishing the authority of his government throughout the province, Pompeius moved eastward to Numidia.

There were also pockets of resistance to the Sullan regime inside Italy. Livy, *Per.* 89, tells us that Sulla retook Nola and received the surrender of Volaterrae, events which belong to the years 80–79 BC.

1. 44.* Cn. Papirius Carbo, as we noted in 1. 33, had abandoned Italy and his army and had fled to Africa. He then moved to join Perperna, the Marian governor of Sicily. He was captured at the island of Cossura by Pompeius and put to death at Lilybaeum, probably towards the end of 82 (*MRR* 2. 73 n. 1). Cf. Cic. *Fam.* 9. 21. 3, *Att.* 9. 14. 2; Liv. *Per.* 89; Val. Max. 5. 3. 5; 6. 2. 8; 9. 13. 2; Plut. *Pomp.* 10. 1–4; App. *BC* 1. 96. The attitude of Sallust to Carbo revealed in fr. 33 is also apparent here. The fact that Val. Max 9. 13. 2 gives graphic amplification of the Sallustian fragment combined with a condemnation of Pompeius' cruelty suggests that here, as in 1. 33, Sallust counterbalanced his picture with a criticism of the opposing side.

**I. 45.**  Nonius, 140. 29 has preserved this fragment down to 'Pompeius'. The reference is to Pompeius' activities in Africa in 81. The Marian leader, Cn. Domitius Ahenobarbus, had an ally in one Iarbas who had ejected Hiempsal, king of Numidia, from his kingdom. Disposing of Domitius, Pompeius moved to settle affairs in Numidia. He received some help from Mauretania whence Bogud, son of King Bocchus, led an expedition which caused Iarbas to take refuge in Bulla Regia. The town fell to Pompeius, who put Iarbas to death and restored Hiempsal to the Numidian throne. In a campaign lasting forty days Pompeius had won back Africa for Sulla. (Liv. *Per.* 89; Plut. *Pomp.* 11. 1–13. 5; App. *BC* 1. 80).

**I. 46.**  My rejection of Maurenbrecher's placement and interpretation of this fragment is based mainly on the arguments of A. Keaveney and J. C. G. Strachan in *CQ* 31 (1981), 363–6.

Maurenbrecher (I. 46M) presented the fragment as it appeared in Müller's edition of Festus (190M). This reads *obsidium cepit*, and Maurenbrecher took the fragment to mean that Lucretius Ofella, after the completion of the great siege-works at Praeneste (see note on I. 31) received reinforcements brought by Catiline, legate of Sulla. To arrive at this interpretation he took *obsidium* ('siege') to be the equivalent of *subsidium* ('help'), an extremely shaky assumption. The verb *cepit* ('receive', 'accept') does not appear in any manuscript; it is the reading of the Aldine edition of the work and may be an emendation or simply an error. Maurenbrecher's conjecture that the siege in question was that of Praeneste, which fell to Ofella in 82, is also based on a very shaky foundation. His connection of Praeneste with the career of Catiline was based on the report of Orosius (5. 21. 8) that the severed head of Gratidianus was sent to Praeneste, where its display to the besieged younger Marius was instrumental in hastening his suicide. Aware of the ample evidence concerning Catiline's part in the murder of Gratidianus, Maurenbrecher seems to have reasoned that if Catiline took reinforcements to a siege it might as well have been Praeneste. Keaveney–Strachan point out that it

was on the strength of Maurenbrecher's argument that
T. R. S. Broughton (*MRR* 2. 72) assigned the rank of *legatus*
to Catiline in 82 BC.

If, as I have done in my English version, we read *obsidium
coepit* ('began a siege') as in Lindsay's edition of Festus, it is
clear that the siege cannot be that of Praeneste: it was
Lucretius Ofella and no one else who was responsible for
that siege from the outset (App. *BC* 1. 94). There were, of
course, other sieges in later years, at which Catiline might
have been present as Sulla's lieutenant. We know of
operations at Nola and Volaterrae in 80–79 BC. From Livy,
*Per.* 89, we learn simply that Sulla retook Nola and received
the surrender of Volaterrae. Granius Licinianus, 36. 8–9C,
is more informative: he tells us that the besieged inhabitants
of Volaterrae stoned to death in ambush Carbo (brother of
Cn. Papirius Carbo), whom Sulla had put in charge of the
siege. They then surrendered to the Romans, expelling all
proscribed persons from their city. He reports that the
Samnites at Nola also surrenderd through fear of being put
through a siege.

Since it was Carbo who began the siege operations at
Volaterrae, even if he did not live to finish them in 79, this
fragment cannot be made to fit in with that operation. In the
case of Nola, the phrase *metu obsidionis* ('fear of a siege')
can indicate that the people of Nola either did not undergo a
siege before surrendering or at most that they had grounds
for supposing that they would be put under siege; in any case
the extensive siege preparations of which our fragment
speaks makes it clear that the siege in question was a present
fact, not a future probability.

With these considerations in mind, Keaveney–Strachan
decided that they should look elsewhere for a likely target
for a siege. After careful analysis of the manuscript of Livy,
*Per.* 89, they surmised that Aesernia, in 80 BC, might well
have been the scene of Catiline's siege activity. We know
that Aesernia had been captured by the rebels in 90 BC.
There is no record of its having been retaken, but the
probability is very strong that it was recovered at about the
same time as the other centres. The Keaveney–Strachan
textual argumentation for Aesernia may not meet with

universal acceptance, but there is no doubt that historically they are on the right track; Praeneste is out of the question.[1]

Two events of 79 had a marked influence on the history of the two following years: the abdication of Sulla and the election to the consulship of 78 of M. Aemilius Lepidus and Q. Lutatius Catulus.

The sources which refer to Sulla's abdication (Plut. *Sull.* 34. 3; Suet. *Iul.* 77; App. *BC* 1. 3 and 103–4; Oros. 5. 22. 1) do not give a precise dating. The assumption that it occurred after the consular elections of 79 for 78 (*MRR* 2. 82) is contradicted by those sources which refer to the timing. These indicate dates before the consular elections of 79. Syme (*Sallust*, 180) agrees with Gabba's assumption (*Comm. App. BC* 1. 480) that Sulla, who had shared the consulship of 80 with Metellus Pius, ceased to be dictator when he laid down the consulship on the last day of December of that year. The timing could have a bearing on the tone and content of Lepidus' speech. On the abdication see further A. Keaveney, *Klio* 65 (1983), 191–8.

**1. 47–72.**   (78–77 BC) The narrative proper of the *Histories* begins with the revolt of Lepidus. On the narrative structure of the work as a whole and on the content of each of its five books see Introd. section 5.

It is not unlikely that Sallust emphasized a Catilinarian aspect of this movement—the pursuit of reforms, necessary and admirable in themselves, by methods which were unacceptable and of danger to the state. Evidence concerning the antecedents to the revolt is provided in the speeches of Lepidus (1. 48) and of Philippus (1. 67). In the other fragments Sallust deals with the conflict between the consuls (1. 47), presents a fairly detailed picture of the character and habits of Sulla (1. 49–53), a report on measures taken by Lepidus, continuing his protest against the evils of the Sullan regime (1. 54–6), description of the peasants' revolt in Etruria and measures taken to deal with it (1. 57–8), Lepidus' activity in Etruria for the remainder of his consul-

---

[1] Maurenbrecher later accepted the view of Heraeus (*Arch. lat. Lex* (1896), 132) that *coepit* of the MSS had the meaning 'recaptured' and abandoned his attribution of the fragment to the siege of Praeneste. Cf. *Burs. Jahresb.* 113 (1893–8), 268.

ship and in the opening weeks of his proconsulship and the senate's reaction to this (1. 59–66), some aspects of the armed struggle in 77 down to Lepidus' departure for Sardinia (1. 68–72).

**1. 47. were competing against each other with great bitterness.** At the beginning of their year of office Roman consuls fixed the date of the *feriae Latinae*, a movable feast day (Macrob. *Sat.* 1. 16. 6). The attendance of the consuls of these celebrations necessitated their absence from Rome and a *praefectus urbi* had to be appointed to deputize for them.

This picture of hostile relations from the consuls' entry into office supports the assumption that Lepidus' speech was delivered in the early days of 78.

**1. 48.** On the function of speeches in Sallustian historiography see Introd. section 5.

Two aspects of this speech, the violence of Lepidus' attack on Sulla whom he depicts as still exercising his power, and the emphasis on Sulla as master of the Roman world, have raised such difficulty for some scholars as to give rise to the theory that it is a spurious speech, a later falsification by a rhetorician; thus C. Lanzani, *Roma* 10 (1934), 435–41. What we have here is a Sallustian formulation of a speech actually delivered by Lepidus early in his consulship. Lepidus' chief topic is an attack on the Sullan regime; Sallust expands this to present a programmatic introduction to the problems of the decade, some of which he introduces anachronistically. The material is governed by his constant theme: the moral and political degeneration of the basic Roman *virtus* which has brought to crisis point the future of the Roman Republic.

Sulla's rule is presented as a *tyrannis* which monopolizes all the powers and rights of the state, a *dominatio* which has reduced the Roman people to servitude (*servitium*). The attack is couched in terms with which we are already familiar from Sallust's descriptions of the power of the nobility in his monographs. Lepidus' protest relies on concepts which in his case recall the use of high-sounding slogans to excuse a desire to seize power, or, as in the case of the speech of L.

Marcius Philippus (1. 67) which presents the other side of this controversy, to hold on to power once achieved.

**1. 48. 1    fill me with the greatest fear.**   The tone is that of a patrician consul counselling the people, not that of a demagogue and revolutionary. The aim is to put the people on their guard against the enticements and deceits of the treacherous policy of Sulla, to which they are even more vulnerable because of their known qualities of clemency and honesty. He underlines aspects of Sulla's activity and of the people's reaction to his regime which he will bring up again in the course of the speech: Sulla had found safety and lack of opposition because of the fears aroused by the un-precedented extent of his violation of expected norms of political and personal behaviour; the citizens, with higher standards of ethical conduct, allow themselves to be deluded into the hope that Sulla's conduct will be modified by a return to traditional moral standards; this viewpoint presents the greatest danger to the citizen body: they must either throw off their torpor and resist the new regime or resign themselves to slavery.

**your concern for freedom.**   Freedom (*libertas*) is the principal slogan used (cf. §§ 2, 4, 6, 9, 26, 27). Other slogans: *imperium* ('rule over others'), *gloria* ('glory, fame'), *ius/iura* ('rights; principles of justice'), *virtus* ('courage') also play a part.

**1. 48. 2.    As for his satellites.**   Sulla's minions are mentioned again in §§ 12 and 21. In each case a specific section of his following is referred to. Here the concentration is on the pro-Sullan members of the ruling class.

**this state of affairs.**   Shared dominion over the people and government of Rome at the price of personal servitude to the will of Sulla.

**highest principles of justice.**   The slogan *ius*; the health of the Roman constitution depends on adherence to the rule of law (cf. *Cat.* 52. 21).

**1. 48. 3. Bruti.**   D. Junius Brutus, consul in 77. His wife Sempronia is said to have given some help to the associates of Catiline in 63 (*Cat.* 25).

**Aemilii.** Mam. Aemilius Lepidus Livianus, consul in 77 (cf. Cic. *Off.* 2. 58; *Cluent.* 99; Val. Max. 7. 7. 6). Possibly the Lepidus who captured Norba for Sulla in 82 (App. *BC* 1. 94; cf. Badian, JRS 52 (1962) = *Studies*, 217); but cf. note on 1. 69.

**Lutatii.** Q. Lutatius Catulus, consular colleague of Lepidus and his chief adversary. Nothing is preserved of Sallust concerning Catulus' energy in opposing Lepidus; his firm stand against the *Lex Gabinia* is praised in 5. 23. Despite his fierce and continuing hostility to Caesar (Cat. 49. 2; Vell. Pat. 2. 43. 3) Catulus' staid probity probably saved him from an accusation such as that levelled against another enemy of Caesar, C. Piso (4. 81M); nevertheless, laudatory notices from Sallust would be neither lengthy nor effusive.

**1. 48. 4. For what did these forefathers . . . Antiochus.** A small part of this sentence is preserved in the indirect transmission by Donatus, Ter. *Phorm.* 243. 'what, against Pyrrhus and Hannibal by sea and by land'. The names of the foreign generals listed refer respectively to the Pyrrhic War of 280–275 BC when Pyrrhus of Epirus aided Tarentum against the Romans; the Second Punic War of 218–201, referred to in 1. 10; the Macedonian War in which Philip V was defeated by Flamininus at Cynoscephalae; the Syrian War in which Antiochus III, the Great, was defeated at Magnesia in 190 by Scipio Asiaticus.

**our liberty . . . to nothing but the laws.** Slogans put into a context which justifies and illustrates their effectiveness. Reference to the prestige of ancient houses, to the exemplary merits of the forefathers makes it clear that the attack is not against the nobles as a caste. It isolates those members of the aristocracy who were pro-Sullan, traitors to the ethical and political traditions of their class.

**1. 48. 5. this caricature of a Romulus.** Servius, *Ecl.* 3. 13 reports this as *saevus iste Romulus* 'that savage Romulus', a derisory comment on Sulla's attempt to create a Romulean ideology inside his total reorganization of the state (cf. A. Alföldi, *Mus. Helv.* 8 (1951), 205; La Penna, *Athenaeum* 41 (1963), 214). Cicero, author of *De Republica*, is described as 'Romulus of Arpinum' in the Ps.-Sallustian *Invect. in Cic.* 7.

**as if they had been wrested from foreigners.** A useful line of attack, repeated in §§ 7, 17, and 18. Sulla has treated Roman citizens who opposed his legislation as *hostes*, foreign enemies.

**consuls, and other leading men.** Four consuls had fallen in the civil wars: L. Cornelius Cinna near Ancona in 89; L. Valerius Flaccus in Asia in 86; Marius the younger at Praeneste, and Cn. Papirius Carbo in Sicily in 82. For leading men, see note on 1. 67. 19, **the flower of this senatorial order.**

**1. 48. 6. for those yet unborn.** Sulla's law of proscription included the measure that the children of the proscribed 'were not only deprived of their fathers' property but were also debarred from the right of seeking public office' (Vell. Pat. 2. 28. 4; cf. Sall. *Cat.* 37. 9). This clause remained in force until its abrogation by Julius Caesar in 49 (Suet. *Iul.* 41).

**Worst of all.** Lepidus takes up two of the points raised in § 1 and uses them to launch into the first exhortation (§§ 7–15) of his speech.

**1. 48. 7. that your spoils.** Emphasizes once again the fact that Sulla treated Roman citizens as he used in former times to treat conquered external enemies (see note on § 5).

**may not be bestowed on him.** Cod. V has *illos* ('them'), which Hauler (*WS* 38 (1916), 172) defended with the argument that the spoils of the Roman people were available not only to Sulla but to the various types of satellite mentioned in the speech. Maurenbrecher accepted Corte's emendation *illum* ('him') as applying only to Sulla; the stress in the sentence is clearly concentrated on Sulla.

**looking for help . . . to the gods.** Cf. *Cat.* 52. 29 where Cato, castigating the timid inertia of the Roman senate against the threat of Catiline, warns: 'the help of the gods is not secured by prayers and womanish entreaties; it is through watchfulness, vigorous action, and wisdom in counsel that success comes.'

**1. 48. 8.   regards no position as illustrious unless it is safe . . .**
Another angle on the aspect of Sulla's outlook and activity
referred to in §§ 1 and 6.

**1. 48. 9.   that state of tranquillity and peace combined with
freedom.** A phrase of Cicero, *cum dignitate otium*, which
eventually became an Otimate party-slogan, is analysed
thoroughly by Wirszubski (*JRS* 44 (1954), 1–13). The
vagueness of the phrase facilitated its use for a variety of
political purposes: its specific meaning has to be deduced
from the context in which it is used. In general terms *otium*
('tranquillity') is identified with the preservation of the
established form of republican government; *dignitas*
('worthiness') embraces the political prestige and influence
of the preservers of the established order.

In this section Sallust, by putting in Lepidus' mouth the
variant *otium cum libertate* conveys his own judgement of
the Optimate position. The substitution of *libertate* ('freedom') is intended to recall times when men could elect to opt
out of public life and devote their time to other pursuits
profitable to the state. Thus the elder Cato defended his use
of *otium* for the writing of his *Origines* (Cic. *Planc.* 66).

**1. 48. 10.   must either be slave or master.** The opportunity
to make decisions such as those mentioned in § 9 can no
longer be taken for granted. It is now a case where 'you must
either submit to slavery or use force to maintain your
freedom' (*Iug.* 31. 22). In §§ 6, 20, 25, and 26 Lepidus
warns that the penalty for inaction is slavery. Instead of
peace with freedom (*otium cum libertate*) a peace combined
with servitude (*otium cum servitio*, § 25) will be their lot.

**1. 48. 11.   For what else is left to us?** For fierce emphasis
on the gap which divides the powerful few (*pauci potentes*—
applied to the ruling oligarchy) who have amassed power
and riches and the dispossessed classes see *Cat.* 20. 7–9; *Iug.*
31. 20.

**The Roman people . . . the ruler of nations.** Not the words
of a revolutionary but of a Roman aristocrat who resents the
degradation of Roman political life and imperial rule.

**stripped of power, repute, and rights.**   Applies not just to those affected by the proscriptions but to all levels of the citizenry affected by the Sullan constitution. The supreme magistrates of the state—consuls, praetors, and censors—all emerged from the Sullan restoration with diminished rights. The censorship, though not formally abolished, was for practical purposes dispensed with. New regulations governed the order, intervals, and probably the age limits for curule office. But it was the tribunate of the people that was most savagely treated: the tribunician veto was limited, the right to initiate legislation removed, and also the right to hold further office. For details of the Sullan legislation and the sources see *MRR* 2. 75.

**without the power to administer their affairs.**   The Latin phrase *inops agitandi*—which is also reported in Arusianus Messius, 480. 4, has been interpreted by some as 'without the means to live'. I agree with Mommsen and Gerlach in choosing another legitimate meaning of *agitandi*: 'to be occupied with', 'to administer'. Lepidus is referring to the chief problem facing the common people, his audience, namely the restriction on the tribunes of access to the people for the purpose of initiating legislation. Cf. Tac. *Ann*. 3. 27. 4.

**the rations of slaves.**   One of Sulla's enactments in 81 was the abolition of corn doles. The monthly rations which masters assigned to slaves for their maintenance were not always uniform. At the time when the younger Seneca was writing his *Epistles* (AD 64–5) the allotment was 5 *modii* and 5 *denarii* (*Ep*. 80. 7). In 3. 36. 19 the tribune Macer states that the ration allotted by the grain law of 73 amounted to five *modii* ('measures', equivalent to bushels) per month.

**1. 48. 12.   allies and people of Latium.**   See note on 1. 19, **allies.**

**debarred . . . from the citizenship.**   The grant of citizenship to the Latins and the Italian allies by the *Lex Iulia* of 90 had profound effect on the progress and outcome of the Social War (see note on 1. 20). Early in 82 Sulla undertook, in return for unspecified services, to maintain these rights (Liv. *Per*. 86). This promise was adhered to wherever it had been

followed by loyalty to the Sullan cause; those who held out
against Sulla paid the penalty: communities in Etruria,
Campania, and Latium were debarred from citizenship.
Notable examples were the Etruscan towns of Volaterrae
and Arretium (Gran. Lic. 36. 8C; Cic. *Caecin.* 102).

**debarred by this one man.** Underlines that it was not a
matter of legal abrogation but an exercise in despotism. The
validity of this act of disenfranchisement was open to
objection and was later admitted to be indefensible (Cic.
*Caecin.* 102).

**in return for their . . . services.** The law offered full
citizenship to Latins and to all communities in Italy which
had not revolted (see note on 1. 20). This reflects the
traditional Roman practice of granting citizenship to individuals for service to Rome, but even states which
persisted in the war received the citizenship in a similar
manner (Liv. *Per.* 75 and 76). Rome had in fact been forced
by military disasters early in the war to accede to Italian
demands. There could be the implication that the Julian law
was in a sense the outcome of the efforts of such tribunes as
C. Gracchus and M. Livius Drusus.

**a few of his underlings.** Thousands of landowners were
evicted from their homes to make room for Sullan veterans.
The confiscations were so extensive that even after all the
veterans had been provided for estates were granted to or
made available for purchase to owners who would uphold
the new regime. It is to this latter type of practice that the
'few' of this extract must refer. The notorious case of the
centurion L. Luscius, who acquired an estate valued at 10
million sesterces (Asc. 90. 25–6), provides an appropriate
example of this type of excess. (See notes on 1. 40 and 41.)

**1. 48. 13. The laws . . . in the hands of one man.** Com-
plaints of practically the same content concerning the
monopoly of power exercised by a few nobles (*pauci
potentes*) in *Cat.* 20. 7–8; *Iug.* 31. 9 and 20 are here heaped
on the head of one man.

**1. 48. 14. human sacrifices etc.** See notes on 1. 36 and
38.*

**1. 48. 15.   Is there anything left . . . or to die valiantly?**
The violent yet cautious condemnation of the Sullan regime
in §§ 7–14 is followed by an exhortation which is verbally
reminiscent of Catiline's military-type exhortation to a band
already primed for armed rebellion (*Cat*. 20. 9 and 13). But
this appeal is more akin in spirit and intent to that addressed
to Marcius Rex by Manlius, who felt himself being pushed
into a revolution from what in his view was simply a struggle
for *libertas*, the freedom to live without oppression from
magistrates and moneylenders (*Cat*. 33).

**1. 48. 16.   that I am a cause of political turmoil.**   The
insertion of a personal note in §§ 16–18 is undoubtedly the
response to Lepidus' feeling that, as a patrician consul who
had profited from the Sullan proscriptions, he had to justify
his stance as defender of the rights of ordinary citizens and
to dispose of the insinuations of Sulla's attack on him. He
does so with apparent conviction, but his defence has been
dismissed as a flimsy and derisory attempt to formulate a
revolutionary programme (Syme, 186; see note on 1. 67. 7).

The first charge (cause of political turmoil) is accepted and
defended with vigour in § 17; the second (love of war) is
dismissed as an empty accusation: Lepidus' activity aims at a
restoration of rights which apply in time of peace.

**1. 48. 17.   Vettius of Picenum.**   Acquired through Sulla a
villa which had once belonged to Catulus and later sold it to
Cicero (Cic. *Att*. 2. 24. 2 and 4; Suet. *Iul*. 17).

**the clerk Cornelius.**   One of the 10,000 slaves freed by
Sulla. Cicero identifies him with the Cornelius who was
elected quaestor in 44 (*Off*. 2. 29).

**the spoils of the Cimbri.**   A reference to the wars against
the invading Teutones and Cimbri of 104–101. Lepidus once
again attacks Sulla for treating citizens as foreign enemies.
(cf. §§ 5 and 7).

**1. 48. 18.   the very greatest of his crimes.**   A very neat
retort to Sulla's charge. Lepidus was no saint and probably
had no qualms about taking advantage of opportunity during
the proscriptions. He uses the theme of Sulla's attitude to
citizen property as the ethical norm which then prevailed

COMMENTARY                    121

and from which it would be dangerous to deviate. Uttered in
78 the excuse could nevertheless indicate a genuine attitude
of distaste for the type of action which the regime enforced
on otherwise upright citizens.

**Moreover the property . . . their rightful owners.** The Latin
version of this sentence has given rise to some disagreement.
Cod. V has *dominis* ('to the owners'); Dietsch emended to
*dominus* ('the owner') and put word *iure* ('rightfully') with
*dominus* to produce the meaning: 'That which I have
bought, paying the price and becoming the legitimate owner
of (*iure dominus*), I am nevertheless prepared to hand back.'
This version was accepted into their texts by Ernout and
Kurfess. Paladini, ad loc., points out that the stressing in
three different ways ('I bought'; 'I paid the price'; 'being the
legitimate owner') of a single concept is a tautology which is
non-Sallustian and of no particular efficacy. If one retains
*dominis* the sentence would read: 'The goods which I bought
at that time through fear, having paid the price I nevertheless return to their rightful owners.'

Maurenbrecher retains *dominis* of the codex but punctuates
in a peculiar way: *mercatus sum pretio, soluto iure dominis
tamen restituo* ('That which I brought for a price, having
given up my rights to the property, I am prepared
nevertheless to restore to its owners.' Paladini rightly points
out that to add *pretio* ('for a price') to *mercatus sum* ('I
bought') is pleonastic and breaks up a common ablative
absolute expression, *pretio soluto* ('having paid the price').
My translation agrees with Paladini's punctuation: *quae . . .
mercatus sum, pretio soluto iure dominis tamen restituo*. In
this way Lepidus makes clear that while he did hold
proscribed goods bought through fear, he recognized the
legitimate ownership of goods which Sulla had seized as if
they were the spoils of foreign enemies.

**1. 48. 20.    while I no longer have qualms.** Lepidus is sure
about the bad reputation which is now Sulla's lot, but there
remain other grounds for anxiety, notably the waiting for
someone to give a lead. Cf. Cato's words of reproach on the
senate's slowness to make a move: 'from slothfulness and

weakness of spirit you hesitate, waiting one for the other'
(Cat. 52. 28).

**and to appear fortunate in proportion to one's audacity.**    This
is a translation of Cod. V's *quam audeas tam videri felicem.* I
interpret the 2nd pers. sing. *audeas* as an impersonal 'you' =
'one'. With the opening statement of this section: 'I do have
fears about how far you are prepared to go (*quantum
audeatis*') Lepidus shows his concern about the measure of
courage he can expect from the people precisely because of
the general truth that fortune favours the bold.

   Maurenbrecher accepted Corte's emendation of *audeas* to
*audeat* ('his audacity'), relating it specifically to Sulla and
printing *Felicem* ('fortunate') with a capital letter as indicating Sulla's well-known nickname *Sulla Felix* (Sulla the
Fortunate) as in Vell. Pat. 2. 27. 5; Plut. *Sull.* 34. 2: cf. *Iug.*
95. 4.

   Lepidus undoubtedly did intend a reference to Sulla, but
as a more effective rhetorical device he cloaked it under the
impersonal nature of a *gnome* (maxim) as being applicable
to everyone, not just Sulla. The subtlety of the general
maxim is balanced by the sarcastic stress on the word
'appear' (*videri*). He proceeds with 'for' (*nam*) to stress this
aspect in the following sections.

**I. 48. 21.   crime-stained underlings.**    Satellites who owed
everything to Sulla, on whom they depended for their
continuing immunity from retribution.

**retaining only . . . victory?**    Kritz's emendation of V's
*praeter victoriam* ('except the victory') to *praeter victorem*
('except the victor') adopted by Dietsch and Maurenbrecher
is not acceptable in the context. *Praetor victorem* would have
to mean 'besides the victor', and would specify unnecessarily
what is meant by 'complete change'. Lepidus shrewdly
avoids the risk entailed in a total condemnation of Sulla's
activity, which included the victory of Roman arms. To cast
a slur on military victories even if attained under Sullan
leadership would alienate his hearers. However, he does go
on to stress that the fruits of such victories have been
squandered and demeaned.

**the soldiers at the cost of whose blood.** The Cornelii, slaves freed by Sulla, have gained more from the victory than the troops who risked their lives to attain it.

**Tarrula and Scirtus.** Nothing else is known about these slaves.

**1. 48. 22. Fufidius.** One of the more notorious minions of Sulla. In Oros. 5. 21. 3, where he is called L. Fursidius, he is named as the man who urged Sulla to publish a proscription list. He was elevated to high office—praetor in 81; propraetor in Spain in 80 (cf. 1. 95).

**a vile wench.** A description interpreted (Paladini, ad loc.) as indicating lowly birth and, presumably, lewd sexual conduct. The application of a feminine label to a man for the purpose of deriding effeminacy and shameful servility is met with elsewhere: thus *duce filiola Curionis* ('with little Miss Curio as leader' (Cic. *Att.* 1. 14. 5); *ut venefica haec* ('that this she-poisoner' (applied to D. Brutus in Cic. *Phil.* 13. 25). Cf. C. F. Konrad, *CP* 84 (1989), 128–9.

**the degradation of all honours.** This powerful expression of contempt (*omnium honorum dehonestamentum*) was imitated in later historiography, e.g. *Historia Augusta, Claud.* 5. 4; Amm. Marc. 26. 6. 16. At 1. 78 *dehonestamentum* is used to describe physical deformity.

**and so I place my greatest confidence in that victorious army.** The seekers for office would not necessarily be well disposed towards Lepidus and his point of view. His statement of preference has been interpreted as a subtle move to win over the support of Sullan veterans for the purpose of revolution. Reform not revolution is the objective at this stage. Further reasons for the preference are given in the following section.

**1. 48. 23. Unless perchance their mission.** Use is made in §§ 7, 23, 24 of *nisi forte* ('unless perchance', 'unless haply') and in §§ 17 and 21 of *scilicet* ('to be sure'; 'doubtless'; 'I ask you!') to put forward, for purposes of rejection, ideas which are impossible, absurd, far-fetched.

Here, with *nisi forte*, Lepidus, aware that the soldiers were descendants of those being levied in early Rome whose

protests forced the establishment of the tribunate, rejects
the notion of the army (veterans) continuing to support a
regime which had severely curtailed the rights and powers of
the representatives of the people (cf. § 11).

**by force of arms.**   In the Latin sentence *per arma* is placed
between the words *eversum* ('overthrow') and *conditam*
('established'). On the strength of such passages as *Cat.* 33.
3–4; *Iug.* 31. 6 and 17; *Hist.* 1. 11; 3. 48. 1 some
commentators (e.g. Fighiera) have referred *per arma* to the
act of the establishing of the tribunate. Paladini (ad. loc.)
prefers a reference to the possibility of overthrowing it by
the same means as it was founded. My rendering of the
passage conveys the notion that we have here a typical
example of Sallustian brevity: *per arma* applies to both
aspects.

**the power of the tribunes.**   See note on 1. 67. 14, **restore the
power of the tribunes.**

**Extraordinary indeed the reward.**  Lepidus picks up the
idea of delusion mentioned under § 1. There the point was
made that the people allow themselves to be deluded into
hopes of better times. Here, to alienate the veterans from
Sulla, he stresses the manner in which they have been duped
by their general. Cf. note on 1. 40, **sold or simply given
away.**

**1. 48. 24.  Because success is a wonderful screen.**   See
under §§ 1, 6, and 8 on the effect of success on Sulla's
immunity from opposition. The expression is cited, with
slight inversion of wording, by Porphyrion on Hor. *Epist.* 1.
18. 29 and by Seneca, *Controv.* 9. 1. 13; the maxim also
occurs in Isoc. *Archid.* 102; Dem. *Olynth.* 2. 20.

**under the pretext of maintaining peace and harmony.**   The
Latin expression *specie concordiae et pacis* is a play on the
slogan *pax et concordia* which was a basic element of
aristocratic propaganda down to the fall of the Republic.
The more precise application of these concepts as applied to
Sulla emerges from the next sentence: *pax*, as external
peace, goes with *belli finem* ('war be ended') and *concordia*
goes with *rem publicam* ('the republic').

**treason.** An interpretation of the Latin word *parricidium*. The fatherland (*patria*) is considered *parens omnium communis* ('common parent of all'); whoever seeks the ruin of the *patria* is a parricide. Cf. *Cat.* 14. 3, 51. 25, 52. 31.

**the citizens cruelly plundered.** Extension of the idea used in §§ 5, 7, 17, and 18 to describe the treatment of the people under the Sullan terror. Now, dispossessed, they face the continuing prospect of being the prey of those who provide maintenance and patronage only in return for political support.

**1. 48. 25. a peace combined with servitude.** See on §§ 1, 9, 10.

**1. 48. 26. the fame of my ancestors.** See note on 1. 67. 6, **the Aemilian clan.**

**my private interests.** That is, abuse of consular powers to increase personal wealth or to advance political ambitions.

**1. 48. 27. with the good help of the gods.** A ritual formula used to underline the seriousness of a plea, a warning, or a wish. Lepidus (Sallust) is more temperate in its use than Cicero in similar circumstances—e.g. Cic. *Cat.* 2. 15, 19, 29; 3. 4, 18, 21–3.

**1. 49–53.** The death of Sulla in March 78 was the occasion for the sharpening of the strife between the different factions in Rome, a disagreement which gave rise to significant changes in political alignments which in turn had important influence on Lepidus' programme of reform.

Catulus and the *Sullani* planned funeral honours of unprecedented magnificence and solemnity (App. *BC* 1. 105) designed to consecrate the regime as well as its founder and to demonstrate the strength of the military and political foundations on which it rested. It was a spectacle designed to be a warning to dissidents and would-be subverters (App. *BC* 1. 106; cf. Plut. *Sull.* 38). Lepidus and the *populares* strongly opposed these plans.

If Sallust did dwell on details of the funeral ceremonies, which he would probably have described in terms of derision and indignation (Syme, 181), no trace of his treatment has remained. But he did make his own comment by dwelling on aspects of Sulla's character and conduct which he had carefuly avoided in an earlier portrait (*Iug.* 95). In what appears to have been quite a detailed treatment of Sulla's sexual excesses, on which Plutarch's chapter on the same topic (*Sull.* 36) is probably based, Sallust provides his own counter to the mixture of adulation and superstitious fear aroused by the dictator's state funeral.

**1. 49.   dare to complain about the domination of Sulla.**   This fragment is also preserved in Donatus, Ter. *Phorm.* 371.

Kritz agreed with de Brosses's view that the reference is to Pompeius. Maurenbrecher rejected both Pompeius and Lepidus as candidates and suggested the far more likely alternative—the young Julius Caesar. Relations between Sulla and Caesar were never cordial (Suet. *Iul.* 20. 1) but the young politician was shrewd enough not to risk a head-on collision with the dictator. For this reason he left Italy early in 78, before the death of Sulla, as a military tribune under P. Servilius (Isauricus), proconsul of Cilicia (Suet. *Iul.* 3). He returned to Rome in 77 where he prosecuted Cn. Cornelius Dolabella, proconsul of Macedonia, for extortion (Vell. Pat. 2. 43. 3; Plut. *Caes.* 4. 1; Suet. *Iul.* 4).

**1. 50\*.**   The scholiast's introduction to this fragment identifies the 'prominent personage' beyond doubt: 'We know that Sulla in his boyhood was guilty of the most disgraceful behaviour.'

**1. 51.   flaunting his conduct before the eyes of all peoples.** The fragment is also cited in Donatus, Ter. *Adelph.* 93: *ut in ore gentibus agens.*

Kritz, giving the phrase *in ore . . . agens* a meaning which is acceptable in an appropriate context, 'alive on the lips of men', applies it to the senate, affirming that it could not be applied to any individual of the period. Maurenbrecher interpreted the phrase in the same way. He applied it to Sulla, even though the expression is normally used only of meritorious conduct, and justified his view by referring to the extract from Plutarch given under 1. 53.

Sallust uses *in ore agens* in *Hist.* 2. 47. 4: 'I have passed my life before your eyes', a meaning which is reflected in my translation of this fragment.

**I. 52.** The Charisius citation has a word missing and reads as follows: *insanum aliter sua sententia, atque aliarum mulierum . . .* with the genitive *aliarum mulierum* depending on a missing word. I accept Maurenbrecher's emendation to *aliorum mulierum* with *mulierum* depending on some such word as *cupidine* ('desire, lust') and *aliorum* as possessive genitive.

**I. 54. Octavius and Q. Caepio . . . requested to do so.** This is the only fragment which contains reference to legislative measures carried or proposed by Lepidus.

Kritz connected the names Octavius and Caepio with the consular elections of 77 in which a Cn. Octavius was successful; Dietsch even inserted *Gn[aeus]* before *Octavius* in his text. Sallust does, of course, use the word *ambiti* from the verb *ambire*, to solicit, canvass, a word often used in connection with elections. But the scholiast deliberately stresses that *ambiti* here simply means *rogati*, 'asked'. Moreover, there is no record of any activity by a Q. Caepio in those years.

Maurenbrecher considered that Octavius and Caepio were linked because of their participation in a similar activity, namely opposition to corn laws. The *lex frumentaria* of C. Gracchus was repealed at the urging of a certain M. Octavius (Cic. *Brut.* 222; *Off.* 2. 72). In 100 the tribune Saturninus proposed a grain law which set a low price for grain and was carried despite the veto of his colleagues and violence organized by the quaestor Q. Servilius Caepio (*Auct. ad Her.* 1. 21; *MRR* 1. 575 and 578 n. 3).

Licinianus (36. 34–5C) reports that Lepidus proposed a corn law which provided a dole of 5 measures (*modii*). It was passed without opposition. Sallust seems to have prefaced his report on this corn law with a history of previous legislation of the same type, in which he might also have included the grain law of M. Livius Drusus of 91, also attacked by Caepio. It is not unlikely that similarly detailed treatments of other measures proposed by Lepidus have also been lost to us.

**I. 55. Pimps and wine-merchants . . . organized for a price.** It was, perhaps, an increasing feeling of isolation

that prompted Lepidus to an action which could only serve
to alienate still more the noble group which had supported
him in the past and was not openly hostile to him down to
that time (cf. 1. 56). The attempt to secure for himself the
support of the commons with largesse expended flagrantly in
public and ominously in private (Exup. 36–7Z) was a
fruitless exercise. Whatever support the Roman plebs may
have given cannot have been great: the danger which civil
strife threatened to their already precarious way of life
would not generate noticeable enthusiasm (cf. *Cat.* 48. 1–2).

**1. 56.\*** **'tyrant' and 'Cinna'.** Presumably an element of
the aristocratic reaction to Lepidus' 'demagogic' activity. A
reaction, increasingly shared by his former noble supporters,
would be accusations of resurrecting the civil strife which
had marked Sulla's rise to power. Cf. 1. 67. 19; Appian, *BC*
1. 107.

Any room for manoeuvre left to Lepidus would arise not
from the inconsistent support from the urban plebs but from
the structural weaknesses of the restored oligarchy, the
enmities and partisanship of its leaders, the easily aroused
fears of the Optimates (Flor. 2. 11. 5), the ineptitude and
indecision of the senate (cf. 1. 67 *passim*). Above all it would
arise from the social and economic tensions which erupted
almost everywhere in Italy and in a more acute and dramatic
form in Etruria, a region particularly savagely treated by
Sulla. Cf. note on 1. 48. 12, **a few of his underlings**; L.
Labruna, *Il console 'sovversivo'* (Naples 1975), 46.

**1. 57.\*** **A large crowd . . . expelled from their city** Faesulae,
a town in northern Etruria was the target of an attack by
evicted citizens upon the veterans to whom Sulla had given
their property. The Faesulans attacked the various strongholds of the veterans and, after killing many of them,
restored the lands to their former owners (Gran. Lic. 36.
36–7C).

**1. 58.** **that Lepidus and Catulus . . . as early as possible**.
The Senate's reaction to the events at Faesulae receives a
slightly expanded treatment in Licinianus: the consuls with
an army which had been assigned to each of them marched,
in obedience to orders, into Etruria. Lepidus withdrew his

army into the mountains while Catulus kept to the coastal and lakeland regions (36. 38–41C). With the evidence as it stands one can assume either that this was part of a strategic plan agreed upon by the consuls, or more probably (Gran. Lic. 36. 42C) a division of zones in which one or the other sought mastery by following aims extraneous to the suppression of the revolt.

The decision to send the two consuls and the imposition on them after they had embarked on their separate ways in Etruria of a solemn oath not to attempt to resolve by force the differences between them (ibid.) were symptomatic of the grave state of uncertainty which existed among the senators. The oligarchy was not confident about sending Lepidus alone into Etruria or about keeping him, without his colleague, in Rome. The compromise masked their fear and impotence. All they achieved by such expedients was the putting off for a few months of a civil war that was swiftly becoming inevitable.

The uprising in Etruria, it seems, weakened rapidly and was contained, if not crushed, without serious difficulty. The reason for the swift collapse may have been lack of able leadership, as 1. 59 seems to imply. Catulus returned to Rome, Lepidus stayed on in Etruria.

**1. 59. Then the Etruscans . . . provoked war.** Appian states that Lepidus stayed on in Etruria, promising to restore the land that Sulla had taken from them (*BC* 1. 107). Licinianus comments on measures proposed by Lepidus: 'he promised many other measures: to recall the exiles, to rescind Sulla's legislation and to restore to their owners the farms on which Sulla's soldiers had been settled' (36. 35C). Exuperantius, an epitomizer of Sallust, records that Lepidus raised an army from those who had been dispossessed, promising, if they achieved victory, to restore their estates; he also won over the populace with private largesses and grants bestowed in the name of the government (36–7Z).

The measures proposed did answer the most pressing needs of those who had been impoverished, dispossessed, practically disenfranchised (1. 48. 12). Florus, who reflects the anti-*popularis* feelings of the period, recognized that the proposals of Lepidus might have been justified if they could have been realized *sine magna clade reipublicae*—'without great damage to the Republic' (2. 11. 2).

**1. 60.   having a good understanding . . . had recommended.** On receiving reports of the confusion caused in the senate by his refusal to respond to their instructions, Lepidus took up a more assured stance when dealing with the envoy sent by the senate, frr. 61 and 62.

**1. 61.\*   Was he therefore bound . . . decree of the senate?**   A fragment cited without book-number. La Penna advised relegation to Fragments of Uncertain Reference (Introd. section 8) on grounds of vagueness of content. Maurenbrecher accepted de Brosses's conjecture that the reference was to a senatorial decree commanding Lepidus to disband his army and return to Rome to oversee the elections for the consulships of 77. The use of the word *serviendum* ('to act in subservience to') might well reflect Lepidus' growing mood of defiance.

Appian explained Lepidus' refusal on the grounds that he would be released in the following year from his oath (binding only for his term of office) not to make war on the Sullani (*BC* 1. 107). This presupposes a decision by Lepidus to move from verbal protest and petition to demand by force. That was a later development.

To comply with the summons meant that Lepidus would forfeit his *provincia*; in an unresolved situation he chose to stay in Etruria. A more positive sign of future developments was his move towards Rome with his forces in 78, which evoked the senatorial response of sending an envoy to meet him en route (Gran. Lic. 36. 43C; Sall. *Hist.* 1. 67. 5). The irregularity which is the cause of our uncertainty concerning the real state of affairs is further illustrated by the fact that no attack was made on the proconsular *imperium* he assumed in 77 for the administration of the province which had been allotted to him in 78.

**1. 62.   the tribunician power, a prerogative of the people.** Maurenbrecher was the first to include this fragment. He rightly dismissed a common view that the fragment belonged to the speech of Philippus (cf. 1. 67. 14). He did so on the ground that the word *plebei* ('of the people') is not in Cod. V, on which the text of the speech is based. Moreover the form *plebei* is a normal dative sing. form, a rare genitive sing. form. Priscianus quotes this fragment precisely to illustrate the use of the rare genitive singular. In Philippus' speech a normal dative ('to the people') would have been required.

This forms part of the demands made by Lepidus to the senate's envoy. Earlier he had refused to raise the question of the restoration of full tribunician power (Gran. Lic. 36. 36C). Now, seeing that the senate was in disarray, he broached this crucial demand, one which might well have raised a body of support inside Rome.

This senate intervention did bring about a cessation of hostilities but we do not know on what terms.

On the expiry of his term as consul, Lepidus took up his *provincia* as a proconsul. In 78 he had been allotted the province of Gaul. Appian states that Lepidus' province was Gallia Transalpina (*BC* 1. 107) but it was probably both Transalpina and Cisalpina (Badian, *FC* 275–6; Syme, *Sallust* 186 n. 39). In any case, he did not himself go beyond Etruria, where he continued to base himself at Faesulae or thereabouts. His firm ally, M. Iunius Brutus, held Cisalpina for him with a strong army.

**1. 63. Lepidus, repenting of his decision.** Whatever promises were made by the envoy on behalf of the senate were either not ratified by that body or were not an adequate response to Lepidus' demands. He therefore regretted having allowed himself to be side-tracked by empty promises, and turned to the preparation of other forms of persuasion.

**1. 64. all of Etruria had joined the revolt.** Lepidus' preparations were now military. By combining his army with the many Italians who had flocked to his standard he headed a force of formidable size (cf. 1. 68). Ably led, such a force could present a serious threat to the ruling oligarchy; if, as it was feared, all of Etruria were to join in, Rome would face a danger as serious as that posed by Cinna and Marius in the eighties.

**1. 65.   enterprises of that kind . . . would bring ruin to the Republic.**   There is an abbreviated version of this thought in the opening sentence of Philippus' speech (1. 67. 1). It reflects the trend of thinking and debate that Lepidus' latest moves had aroused in Optimate circles. The conclusion that emerged from such thinking was that Philippus, who in age and wisdom surpassed the rest (1. 66) should attempt to instil enough resolution into the senate for the issuing of the ultimate decree (*senatus consultum ultimum*; 1. 67. 22) against Lepidus.

**1. 66.\*   [Philippus] who in age and wisdom surpassed the rest.**   The name was supplied by the scholiast so the identification is certain. L. Marcius Philippus was tribune of the people about 104, praetor by 96, consul in 91, censor in 86, and now *princeps senatus*. Sallust's evaluation may cause some surprise in view of the fact that Philippus was in his time a fierce opponent of M. Livius Drusus (Cic. *De Or.* 1. 24, 2. 220 and 255, 3. 2; *Prov. Cons.* 21; Val. Max. 6. 2. 2, 9. 5. 2; Flor. 2. 5. 8–9), a tribune killed in 91 because of his support of Italian rights. Philippus was a keen supporter of Sulla for whom as legate in 82 he recovered Sardinia (Liv. *Per.* 86) and was probably the 'most eloquent of the Romans then living' (App. *BC* 1. 105), who delivered the oration at Sulla's funeral.

**1. 67.**   In his *Cat.* 51 and 52 Sallust followed a Thucydidean practice of summing up the essential features of a situation —in this case the problem concerning the punishment of the arrested conspirators—by a pair of speeches reflecting the alternatives which governed motive and decision. The connection between the speeches of Lepidus and Philippus is not quite of the same nature: the general background is similar but Philippus concentrates mainly on the activity of Lepidus after his promise to play a leading part in righting the wrongs of the Sullan system. The principal thrust of his speech is to ensure the senate's support for his proposal that the ultimate decree, the *senatus consultum ultimum*, should be issued against Lepidus. To this end he presents a version of Lepidus' character, career, and more recent activity which highlights the danger, from the point of view of the ruling oligarchy, of the consul's promises and actions.

There is no doubt that at places Philippus' vehemence has produced exaggeration and distortion of the motives and actions attributed to Lepidus (e.g. §§ 3, 4, 7). This inaccuracy has given rise in modern research to an opinion that Lepidus has been unfairly treated by sources which are mainly biased in favour of the senatorial oligarchy; cf. N. Criniti, *M. Aimilius Q. f. M. Lepidus* (Milan 1969), 319 ff. 449–50. (summary), 345 and n. 66 (Lepidus' military capacity); L. Hayne, *Historia* 21 (1972), 661 ff.; Labruna, *Il console*, 133–4.

Sallust, however, who had no sympathy for the Sullan regime but would also have disapproved of Lepidus' method of seeking change, uses the speech to give a version of the oligarchic reaction to the threat which reveals both the innate weakness of the ruling clique (§§ 3, 12, 17) and its determination to cling to power.

**1. 67. 1. evil designs . . . to their contrivers** An abbreviation of the thought discussed in note 1. 65; here it is specifically applied to Lepidus' activity in Etruria.

**fomented by those . . . rather to suppress them.** Lepidus as a proconsul and those who actively or passively had deliberately chosen to add to the unrest (1. 63–4).

**1. 67. 2. unless perchance . . . of preserving peace . . . allowing aggression.** The irony of 'unless perchance' (*nisi forte*, see note on 1. 48, 23, **Unless perchance their mission**) is palpable: war would be the consequence of a foolish and timid love of peace (cf. Liv. 42. 13. 5).

**1. 67. 3. for the purpose of overthrowing our liberty.** Sallust was well acquainted with the slogans of political oratory which could be used in both directions. Lepidus had made use of the slogan *libertas* several times in a way which matched the aspirations of the *populares*. The *libertas* which Philippus refers to here and in §§ 6, 11 is the freedom of the senatorial nobility to continue without interference the control of the political and economic life of the Roman Republic which they considered their birthright.

**with words and the incantations of soothsayers.** Some
editors join 'with words' to 'mumbling and dithering'
(*mussantes et retractantes*); thus Ernout, Paladini, Pasoli. I
have assumed that the whole phrase refers to *pacem optatis*
('look for peace') on the analogy of *verbis arma temptabitis*
('will you . . . meet arms with words') in § 17. The suggestion
of Jacobs–Wirz–Kurfess, taken up by Pasoli ad loc., that
'incantations of soothsayers' was a sarcastic reference to the
oath imposed on both consuls in 78 (cf. note on 1. 58, **that
Lepidus and Catulus . . .**) presumably implies that the
reluctant senators were relying on the efficacy of this oath—
it had in fact long been broken. The notion that Philippus
was referring to consultations of the Sibylline books must
also be ruled out. The burning of the Capitol in 83 had
destroyed this store of oracles. New books were eventually
compiled but in the mean time unauthorized prophecies at
times leaked out to be freely interpreted by the fancy of the
people and were often used for political ends. Cf. Sall. *Cat.*
47. 2; Liv. 3. 10. 7, 38. 45. 3.

**1. 67. 4.   reached a consulship because of his robberies.**
Implying that Lepidus secured the consulship by bribery
financed by money allegedly extorted from the Sicilians
during his governorship of 80. The chief reference to
mismanagement in Sicily is that of Cicero, who is intent on
building up the reputation of C. Claudius Marcellus,
Lepidus' successor in Sicily (2 *Verr.* 2. 8; cf. ibid. 3. 212). We
are informed that the charges laid by the two Metelli, Celer
and Nepos, were dropped 'because of his popularity among
the people' (Ps.-Asc. 259 St.).

Those who find this reason unsatisfactory—e.g. E. S.
Gruen, *Roman Politics and the Criminal Courts* (Cambridge,
Mass., 1968), 275—have opted for the intervention of
Pompeius, who had a long-standing association with Lepidus
(cf. note on 1. 68.) No extant sources mention intervention
by Pompeius; furthermore, the probability that his marriage
to Mucia took place about this time also makes it unlikely.

The possibility that Lepidus had inherited wealth is not to
be overlooked. We know that his ancestor M. Aemilius
Lepidus Porcina, Augur in 125 was punished by the censors

for renting a house at 6,000 sesterces (Vell. Pat. 2. 10. 1) and for building too high a villa at Alsium (Val. Max. 8. 1 *damn.* 7). Lepidus' son, the future triumvir, used his own money to embellish the city and the monuments of his ancestors (Cic. *Phil.* 13. 8) and commemorated his father's embellishment of the Basilica Aemilia by issuing a coin around 65. Even if Cicero's remark concerning the son's wealth, 'a private fortune not only ample but pure of the stain of civil bloodshed' (ibid.), is part of special pleading, it is not likely to have been outrageously inaccurate.

**obtained a command . . . acts of sedition.** Some take the Latin word *provincia* literally and accept it as a reference to Lepidus' proconsular assignment in Gaul for 77. The province allotted to Lepidus in 78, according to the law formulated by Sulla, cannot be viewed as a reward for crime (see note on § 7, **Now he is a proconsul**). I have understood *provincia* in its other meaning, the special function or task assigned to a magistrate. The reference is to the commission given to Lepidus to put down the unrest in Etruria consequent upon the revolt of Faesulae (1. 57). Philippus distorts this normal constitutional procedure, alleging, in effect, that Lepidus engineered the rising in Etruria which he ultimately joined.

**1. 67. 5. have voted for embassies, for peace . . . and the like.** The only source which indicates that subsequent to Lepidus' decision to repudiate the agreement he had made in 78 (1. 63) the senate voted for the sending of envoys in order to maintain *pax et concordia.* The motive was the justifiable one of attempting to avert civil war. Philippus is stressing that civil war will ensue unless the senate firmly and promptly puts into effect the preventive measure provided by constitutional practice—the ultimate decree.

**1. 67. 6. when I saw Etruria conspiring.** The details are given at 1. 63–4.

**the proscribed being recalled.** An exaggeration. Lepidus had made a promise concerning the proscribed (note on 1. 59), and some of them may well have joined him in Etruria, but there was no formal legislation on the matter.

**the state rent asunder by bribery.**  A dramatization of Lepidus' activity described in notes on 1. 55 and 1. 59.

**with a few others I supported . . . of Catulus.**  The numbers of committed oligarchs must have been greater than Philippus implies here. Nevertheless, while a large number of senators were simply inactive, the number of noble supporters of Lepidus' programme up to this stage must also have been considerable.

**the Aemilian clan.**  Optimates who saw merit in Lepidus' reaction to the Sullan regime continued to support a fellow patrician down to the outbreak of the civil war. Lepidus' lineage was more impressive than that of the patrician Catiline, though both houses had by now fallen into decay. Cicero, speaking of Lepidus' son M. Aemilius Lepidus, the consul of 46 and later triumvir, spoke of the fame of Lepidus' grandfather, twice consul, censor, *pontifex maximus* and *princeps senatus* over a long period (*Phil.* 13. 15; Syme, *Sallust*, 183).

**by taking a lenient view.**  A form of the clemency expressed as an admirable trait of the Roman people in *Cat.* 9. 5; cf. 1. 48. 1.

**in spite of the fact . . . to overthrow freedom.**  To pinpoint the disastrous effects of the indulgence and indecision of the senate, Philippus distinguishes between two phases in the conduct of Lepidus: the period (78) in which he was consul and that (77) in which he was proconsul. Here with the emphasis on *privata arma* ('had taken up arms on his own responsibility') the reference is to Lepidus' acceptance in Etruria of the support of the dispossessed and discontented, an illegal action by a legally appointed official. Lack of appropriate counter-measures by the senate allowed support to grow to the stage where Lepidus in the course of the second phase posed a serious threat to Rome. Philippus picks the point up again as a clinching argument for his demand for the issuing of the *senatus consultum ultimum* (§ 22). There the crucial phrase is *privato consilio* which I discuss ad loc.

**seeking power or protection for themselves.** An accusation analogous to that levelled by Cato against the senate of 63 (*Cat.* 52. 5, 21–3).

**has suborned the deliberations of the senate.** Given the circumstances and thrust of this speech I have given a meaning to *consilium publicum* here which frequently occurs in other writers. Cicero, e.g., uses the phrase to mean 'senate' in *Fam.* 3. 8. 4 ('in the council chamber of the world—the senate') and as 'deliberations of the senate' in *Cat.* 1. 1. 2. Cf. Vell. Pat. 1. 8; Liv. 2. 23. 11; Tac. 6. 15. 6, and see Mommsen, *Staatsrecht* 2. 1028 n. 1 for further examples.

**1. 67. 7. At that time . . . a brigand.** By referring to Lepidus as a brigand (*latro*) with meagre support Philippus is emphasizing that prompt counter-action at the time would have been totally effective.

The original meaning of *latro* was 'mercenary soldier' (Festus 105. 27L; cf. Servius, *Aen.* 12. 7), which later because of the method of fighting came to denote brigand, assassin, and also those who fought without rules, without legitimate cause as distinct from *hostes iusti*, legitimate enemies (Liv. 35. 7. 7, 40. 27. 10). The word came to be used as a bitter insult: thus Cic. *Cat.* 2. 1 calls the activity of Catiline *apertum latrocinium* ('open robbery',) and in *Phil.* 14. 8 calls Antonius *latro*.

**camp-followers.** Soldiers' servants, baggage carriers, slaves who accompanied *patroni* to war. Usually remained close to the baggage-train; sometimes incorporated as light-armed troops, but were poor fighters, and always first to pillage. The use of the term here is not so much technical as derogatory.

**could have got a day's pay for his life.** My translation of the Latin phrase *diurna mercede vitam mutaverit*. It has been interpreted as indicating the extreme wretchedness of existence caused by Sulla's handiwork. Philippus is emphasizing rather the individual worthlessness of those who flocked to Lepidus' banner.

**Now he is a proconsul.** The first opportunity to quell the Lepidan threat having been missed, Philippus now concentrates on the second phase: Lepidus' decision not to return to Rome, to join the Etruscan rebels, and to build up a force strong enough to bend a weak Roman government to his will.

**The most vicious characters of every social class.** The discontented, dispossessed, impoverished, and exiled are depicted as a band of 'professional' rebels. Not all were the dregs of society: there were men of substance and breeding who remained with Lepidus. Only a few of these receive mention in the sources. M. Junius Brutus, father of the tyrannicide, was Lepidus' legate in Cisalpine Gaul. He surrendered to Pompeius at Mutina (1. 69) and was put to death on the orders of Pompeius [Liv. *Per.* 90; Val. Max. 6. 2. 8; Plut. *Pomp.* 16. 2–5; Oros. 5. 22. 17]. Marcus Perperna Veiento, Marian governor of Sicily, member of an important Etruscan family, was probably also a legate under Lepidus (App. *BC* 1. 108; Exup. 42Z). He escaped first to Sardinia and then to Spain, where he joined Sertorius with a large force (Plut. *Sert.* 15. 1; App. *BC* 1. 107–8; Oros. 5. 23. 12). See note to 1. 44–6. L. Cornelius Cinna, son of the consul of 87–84, brother-in-law of J. Caesar, son-in-law of Pompeius, also took part in the revolt; he later joined Sertorius in Spain and returned to Rome under the *Lex Plautia de reditu Lepidanorum* (Suet. *Iul.* 5. 2; cf. G. Rotondi, *Leges Publicae Populi Romani* (Milan 1912), 366).

**driven by the consciousness of their crimes.** Almost a cliché; cf. Sall. *Cat.* 5. 7; Cic. *Sex. Rosc.* 67; *Pis.* 46. There is a rhetorical motive in the description of the perpetual restlessness he ascribes to the following of Lepidus in that it anticipates the portrait of their leader which will follow in § 11.

**Saturninus.** L. Appuleius Saturninus embarked on programmes of legislation in each of his tribunates. In 103 he introduced a law allotting land in Africa to Marius' veterans, a law on treason, and a corn law. In 100 he proposed a measure for founding colonies in Sicily, Greece, and Macedonia, and one for settling veterans on allotments in

Gaul. An illegal seizure of the tribunate for 99 cost him his popularity and the support of Marius. He was murdered in the Curia Hostilia while awaiting trial. (Liv. *Per.* 69; Vell. Pat. 2. 12. 6; Val. Max. 9. 7. 1 and 3; Plut. *Mar.* 29–30; App. *BC* 1. 29–30 Flor. 2. 4. 1–6; Oros. 5. 17. 4–10; cf. Rotondi, *Leges Publicae* 329–32).

**Sulpicius.** Tribune in 88. See note on 1. 21–2.

**Marius.** The son of the great Marius, as the linking with Damasippus indicates. See notes on 1. 30 and 1. 35–7.

**Damasippus.** L. Iunius Brutus Damasippus, praetor in 82, chiefly remembered for the carrying out, under the orders of the consul Marius, of the execution of Mucius Scaevola, the *pontifex maximus*, Carbo Arvina, L. Domitius, P. Antistius, and other opposing leaders (Liv. *Per.* 86; Vell. Pat. 2. 26. 2; Val. Max. 9. 2. 3; App. *BC* 1. 88; Oros. 5. 20. 4). Attempted to relieve Marius at Praeneste (1. 33) and was killed at Sulla's command after the battle of the Colline Gate (Sall. *Cat.* 51. 32; App. *BC* 1. 92; Dio 30–5, fr. 109. 4.)

**1. 67. 8. the Spanish provinces.** Since 80 Sertorius had waged a series of victorious engagements in Spain against generals sent out by the senate to subdue him. See further in note on 1. 93–114.

**Mithridates . . . looking for an opportunity for war.** The policy of expansion of control over neighbouring kingdoms followed by Mithridates VI Eupator of Pontus had brought him into conflict with Roman interests in that region and for over twenty years constituted a serious problem of foreign policy for the Roman government. Already the first Mithridatic War of 88 had been brought to a close with the Peace of Dardanus mainly on terms laid down by Sulla in 84. The second Mithridatic War of 81 saw the defeat of the Roman army under L. Murena and a termination of hostilities again imposed by Sulla on terms which were inconclusive and allowed Mithridates ample opportunity to plan other attempts. The third Mithridates War did in fact break out in 74 and is dealt with by Sallust in Books 3–5 of his *Histories*.

**in close proximity to . . . tributary peoples.** The people likely to be affected and influenced by a fresh outbreak of

the Mithridatic War. The clearest description of the extent
and importance of the revenue of the eastern provinces is
that of Cicero: 'For while the revenues of our other
provinces are barely sufficient to make it worth our while to
defend them, Asia is ro rich and fertile as easily to surpass all
other countries in the productiveness of her soil, the variety
of her crops, the extent of her pastures, and the volume of
her exports. This province, gentlemen, if you wish to retain
what makes either war possible or peace honourable, it is
your duty to defend not only from disaster but from the fear
of disaster' (*Leg. Man.* 14).

**1. 67. 9.   just for virtue's sake.**   My paraphrase for *gratuito*
('for nothing'). The idea emerges more clearly in Ps.-Sall.
*Ep. ad Caes.* 2. 8. 3: 'Wickedness is practised for gain; take
that away, and no one at all is wicked for nothing.'

**1. 67. 10.   to come again with an army.**   The first march
towards Rome was that dealt with in notes on 1. 61–2.
Several passages in this speech seem to support the
assumption that such a confrontation did indeed take place
in 78: thus § 3 'has transformed himself into an object to be
feared'; § 6 'in spite of the fact that he had taken up arms'
etc.

**than is civil war to peace and concord.**   The strongly
elliptical Latin sentence needs amplification to provide a
meaning such as 'He who dared to move from peace and
concord to war and rebellion will the more easily dare to
attack the city now that he is a rebel and has an army.'

**peace and concord.**   See note on 1. 48. 24, **under the
pretext . . .**

**1. 67. 11.   to overthrow our laws and our liberty.**   See note
on § 3, **for the purpose of overthrowing our liberty.**

**driven and tormented in mind etc.**   A portrait which
probably owes more to Sallust's reading of Plato's *Republic*
579 D–E than to Philippus and which no doubt influenced the
depiction of Lepidus in later historiography, e.g. Licinianius'
'turbulent and restless by nature' (36. 45C). The accumulation
of negative qualities fits in with the description of Lepidus'
satellites in § 7. Sallust had drawn a very similar picture of

Catiline in *Cat* 5. 1–5 (cf. ibid. 15. 4), and both portraits convey the fierceness of feeling with which the historian viewed attempts to destroy the structure and institutions of the republic. The Catiline portrait received significant amelioration at the hands of Cicero even taking into account that it formed part of special pleading (*Cael.* 12–14).

**he takes advantage of your indolence.** The lazy indifference of many senators is encouraging or at least not preventing Lepidus' activity. Lepidus himself had used the same line of attack against the indifferent attitude of the people (1. 48. 20).

**1. 67. 13. public mischief.** A translation of *malum publicum*, a phrase used in *Cat.* 37. 8 with the meaning 'corruption of the state'. Here it refers to the plans made to overthrow the state.

**peace and harmony.** The *pax et concordia* slogan of aristrocratic propaganda; the threat is to the assets and privileges of the ruling oligarchy. See § 10 and note on 1. 48. 24.

**unless perchance.** Another instance of the ironic *nisi forte*; see note on 1. 48. 23, **unless perchance . . .**

**1. 67. 14. to render to each his own.** Florus, 2. 11. 3, maintains that the goods of proscribed citizens assigned to others by Sulla, though wrongfully seized, were yet held under a form of law (*iure belli*). He does not explain what he means by this; the point he is making is that demands for their return tended to disturb the peace and harmony restored by the Sullan regime. Lepidus had in fact clearly stated what he considered the legal position to be (1. 48. 18). Philippus totally ignores the legal aspect, adding just a personal jibe.

**and keeps the property . . . others.** A reference to Lepidus' statement in 1. 48. 18; see notes on this. This accusation has provided many commentators with 'ample proof' of Lepidus' worthlessness.

**the laws set up in time of war.** Refers to Lepidus' rebuttal of Sulla's accusation that he was a lover of war. See note on 1. 48. 16.

**to validate the citizenship . . . he denies it has been taken.**   A cheap rhetorical trick which confirms the weakness of Philippus' argument: he says, in effect, that Lepidus is asking for the return of something which he says has not been taken away. For Lepidus' more impressive handling of this topic see 1. 48. 12 and notes on it.

**restore the power of the tribunes.**   The phrase *tribuniciam potestatem restitui* ('to restore the power of the tribunes') is the part of this speech referred to in the note on 1. 62, **the tribunician power . . .** where it is pointed out that the word *plebei* does not occur in the manuscripts.

It appears from the above statement that Lepidus, who had broached the topic at his first confrontation with senatorial envoys (1. 62), had placed this demand firmly on the agenda of subsequent discussions (§ 5).

**from which all our discords have been kindled.**   A blanket condemnation of the office, which formed part of oligarchic thinking from the time of the Gracchi. Cf. Cic. *Leg.* 3. 20, 26; *De Or.* 2. 124. Sallust, speaking of the period after the restoration of tribunician rights in 70, points out that the nobles' opposition to the tribunate was really to protect their own privileges. The same, he felt, applied to many who sought the tribunate in the closing decades of the Republic (*Cat.* 38).

**1. 67. 15.   You ask for a second consulship.**   If Lepidus did ask for a second consulship it was certainly a demand as unconstitutional as the act of Pompeius Strabo (consul in 89) in taking over command of his former consular army when the soldiers, whom he was suspected of inciting to mutiny, killed Pompeius Rufus (consul in 88). Continuous consulships, after the experience with Marius, were regarded as a serious threat to good order. See further in note on 1. 68.

**as if you had ever given up your first!**   Recalling the stubborness with which Lepidus, probably repeatedly, had refused to return to the city to conduct the consular elections (see note on 1. 60). In similar fashion he had without ceremony changed over to the exercise of proconsular power by virtue of the province allotted to him in 79 (see note on 1. 62).

**enemy of all good men.** The Latin form, *hostis omnium bonorum*, sharpens the meaning of this statement. *Hostis* as distinct from *inimicus* indicates a public enemy; Philippus is in a sense anticipating the passing of the ultimate decree (*SCU*) which he recommends in his summing up (§ 22) but the declaration as *hostis* was not part of the *SCU*; it was the result of the declaration that a *tumultus* ('insurrection') was in progress. Thus in 63 this judgement was applied to Catiline and Manlius after their departure from Rome. According to Florus, 2. 11, Lepidus was not declared *hostis* until after his defeat at Rome in 77. See A. W. Lintott, *Violence in Republican Rome* (Oxford 1968), 155–6.

*Boni*, a word regularly used of those who agreed with the views of the ruling oligarchy, but sometimes, for political purposes, expanded to embrace supporters of the government from every social class (see note on 1. 12, **was considered 'good'**). Paladini considers that it was used to designate all the good and honest citizens who had no part in Lepidus' movement. But it is the exclusive *boni* who are being addressed.

**perjury.** Refers to Lepidus' decision to ignore the terms of the oath he had shared with Catulus soon after their arrival in Etruria to deal with the troubles caused by the rebellion at Faesulae (see note on 1. 58).

**1. 67. 16. Neither the provinces . . . laws . . . gods tolerate you as a citizen.** The first leg of this tripartite sentence (*neque te provinciae*) has been subjected to repeated emendation. The manuscript transmission, which I have translated, can be retained in all three of its parts if we take the idea *civis* (citizen) as a contrast to *hostis* (public enemy) of the preceding segment (see G. Perl, *WZ Rostock* 18 (1969), 382).

**1. 67. 17. how long . . . will you allow . . . ?** A phrase which recalls Cicero's words to Catiline: 'how long will you abuse our patience, Catiline?' (*Cat.* 1. 1) and Catiline's own words to his accomplices: 'how long will ye endure this?' (Sall. *Cat.* 20. 9). The similarity of the two rebellions is once again implied.

**money extorted . . . individuals . . . treasury.** Rhetorical
balance at the expense of the truth. The only reference we
have to Lepidus' money-dealings with individuals is that of
1. 55 and there it is Lepidus who is dispensing money. The
reference to the treasury is an oligarchic view of the costs
involved in administering the provisions of Lepidus' corn
law (see note on 1. 54).

**garrisons removed . . . and stationed in others.** According
to whether the cities with which Lepidus dealt were
favourably disposed towards his cause or not.

**sending envoys and making decrees.** See note on § 5.

**since he finds . . . more by your fear . . .** The version of
Cod. V has *cum intelliget* ('when he finds out'). Steup, on the
grounds that what is required here is motive or reason, not
undefined expectation in the future, emended *intelliget* to
*intelligat* to the meaning translated above (*RRM* 58 (1903),
536–7). Lepidus, who had turned himself into something to
be feared (§ 3), had come to understand the significance of
the fear factor (§ 5; cf. §§ 12 and 13).

**1. 67. 19. If this is what you want . . . upon your
spirits.** These words are also cited by Nonius 229. 3.

**the crimes of Cinna.** See note on 1. 23–6.

**the flower of this senatorial order perished.** Livy provides a
fuller picture: 'Cinna and Marius were received into the city
and proceeded to ravage it with slaughter and plundering as
if they had captured it. Consul Gnaeus Octavius was killed
and all of the outstanding men of the opposing party were
slaughtered' (*Per.* 80). He goes on to name Marcus
Antonius, a leading orator, grandfather of Marcus Antonius
the triumvir and of the C. Antonius mentioned in Sall. *Cat.*
21. 3; L. Iulius Caesar, consul in 90 and responsible for the
*Lex Iulia* which influenced the outcome of the Social War
(see notes on 1. 20; 1. 48. 12), his brother C. Iulius Caesar
Strabo, an orator and poet of some ability. The heads of
these three men and that of the consul Octavius were
exhibited on the rostra in the Forum. P. Licinius Crassus,
father of the more notable M. Licinius Crassus, ran on his
sword. L. Cornelius Merula, priest of Jupiter and victor over

the Crimbri, and Q. Lutatius Catulus, father of Lepidus' consular colleague, were also driven to suicide (Cic. *Cat.* 3. 24; Diod. 38. 4; Vell. Pat. 2. 22. 1–4; Val. Max. 2. 8. 7, 4. 3. 14, 5. 3. 3, and 6. 4; Tac. *Hist.* 3. 83; Plut. *Mar.* 43–5; Sert. 5. 6; App. *BC* 1. 72–4; Flor. 2. 9. 13–16).

The fact that Philippus himself was politically skilful enough to avoid slaughter in this crisis and to attain the censorship in 86 contains an element of irony.

**1. 67. 20. Cethegus.** Publius Cornelius Cethegus, proscribed in 88 by Sulla, but later a follower of the dictator. After Sulla's death Cethegus, by astuteness and ability, acquired a reputation and great influence in senatorial circles but never attained office (Cic. *Cluent.* 31; *Parad.* 5. 40).

**1. 67. 21. all the nobles.** I take this to be a reference to the *domi nobiles*, members of the local aristocracies of Italian cities. Such men were members of the upper voting classes that determined the elections in the *comitia centuriata*, the Roman assembly responsible for important legislation and the election of magistrates with *imperium*. Many had close personal ties with leading Roman politicians.

**soon the forces . . . our negligence . . . will melt away.** The Latin reads: *iam illa quae socordia nostra collecta sunt*: 'soon those things which our negligence etc.', a general expression open to interpretation. Some have interpreted: 'those calamities which our negligence has brought about'. The thrust of the narrative would seem to support the interpretation I have chosen.

**our negligence.** In § 11 Philippus had used *vestra socordia* ('your indolence'); here, to win support for his proposal, he presents himself and his faction as sharing the responsibility.

**1. 67. 22. Therefore this is what I recommend.** A sentence also cited in Donatus, Ter. *Eun.* 1072. This is a formal motion, containing words and phrases of a formulaic character: the sentence, 'let it be resolved . . .' is one version of the wording of the ultimate decree, the *senatus consultum ultimum*.

# 146

SALLUST, *HISTORIES* I

**the authority of this body.** *Senatus auctoritas*, the symbol
and slogan of the aristocratic conservative regime (J.
Hellegouarc'h, *Le Vocabulaire Latin des relations et des
partis politiques sous la République* (Paris 1963), 311–12).
At the time of speaking it meant the political influence and
real power of the ruling class made up of what had survived
of the authentic patriciate. This is what Philippus was
referring to in § 19 when he connected Lepidus with the
spectre of Cinna, responsible for the rapid eclipse of
senatorial rule in the course of his tyranny. So even those of
the senatorial order who were hesitant and alarmed, perhaps
even tempted by opportunism or through resignation to
come to an understanding with one whom they thought
might become their new master, now made up their minds.

**on his own authority.** See note on 1. 67. 6 **in spite of the fact
. . . to overthrow freedom.** Here with the phrase *privato
consilio* Philippus picks up the point about illegal activity on
the part of Lepidus. The latter did indeed accept the support
of discontented people of every social class (§ 7), but
Philippus' statement, *exercitum privato consilio paratum*, is
not an accurate description of Lepidus' force; it is contradicted by Philippus' own words on Lepidus' legal standing in
§§ 4 and 7.

Parallels between the *tumultus Lepidi* and the civil war
which broke out in the winter of 44 have long been noted—
e.g. C. Morawski, *Eos* 17 (1911), 135–40; J. Gagé, *REL* 30
(1952), 66–8; Syme *Sallust* (1964); G. Perl, *Philol.* 113
(1989), 213–15. It has been justifiably assumed that the train
of thought, tenor, and phrasing of the Philippus speech owes
much to Cicero's *Philippics*. Cicero used the expression
*privato consilio* to describe the action of Octavianus who late
in 44 levied an army against the consul Antonius although he
had no legal right to do so (Cic. *Phil.* 3. 5 and 14; cf.
Augustus, *Res gestae* 1. 1: 'I raised an army on my own
initiative and at my own expense'). With this army, for
which Cicero subsequently engineered legal cover (*Phil.* 5.
43–6), Octavianus marched on Rome in August 43 and
extorted a consulship from the senate (Tac. *Ann.* 1. 10. 1–2;
Suet. *Aug.* 26).

COMMENTARY 147

Philippus' apparent inaccuracy may well be a deliberate reference by Sallust to the illegal activity of Octavian on that occasion. E. Pasoli (*GIF* 22: 3 (1970), 65–70) rejects this parallel mainly on the ground that Lepidus' legal position in 78–77 more nearly corresponds to that of Marcus Antonius in 44–3. But Sallust is not so much interested in exactness of parallel as in stressing the constitutional behaviour of so-called preservers of the Republic constitution.

**Appius Claudius [Pulcher].** Praetor in 89; after some political side-stepping in the eighties (Liv. *Per.* 79; Vell. Pat. 2. 20. 4) he returned to the Sullan fold and with the dictator's help reached the consulship in 79 (App. *BC* 1. 103). Allotted the province of Macedonia for 78, he did not reach his province, having been struck by illness in Tarentum (Sall. *Hist.* 1. 115). After the death of Sulla he returned to Rome and was appointed *interrex*. Early in 77 he finally arived in Macedonia, where he successfully defended the province from the attacks of the Thracians; he died there in 76.

**the interrex.** Because of the difficulties of 78 and in particular Lepidus' refusal to return to Rome to hold the elections, 77 opened without consuls and an *interrex* was appointed. Under the Republic the *interrex* was a magistrate appointed by and from the senate to exercise provisional power in the absence of a consul or other supreme magistrate. An *interrex* was successively appointed from each of the senatorial *decuriae* (panels) for five days, until new consuls were elected. Certainly at the time that the command against Sertorius in Spain was being discussed the consuls D. Iunius Brutus and Mam. Aemilius Lepidus Livianus had taken up office (Cic. *Phil.* 11. 18; cf. Dio 36. 25, 27. 4; Cic. *Leg. Man.* 62; Plut. *Pomp.* 17. 4). Mention of the *interrex* would indicate that Philippus' speech was delivered early in 77.

**others who have *imperium*.** Praetors and proconsuls (cf. Caesar, *B.Civ.* 1. 5. 3). Those to whom the *SCU* is addressed already have *imperium* by virtue of their office; the decree instructs them on how to exercise that *imperium* and by implication promises the senate's backing for their performance (Lintott, *Violence*, 156). This did not include Pompeius, who was later given a command against Lepidus, probably as legate to the proconsul Lutatius Catulus.

**see to it that the Republic comes to no harm.**    The wording of the *SCU* has come down to us in three forms with discrepancies which may be due to carelessness in citing. These forms occur in Cic. *Cat.* 1. 4; *Phil.* 8. 14, and Sall. *Cat.* 29. 2. From this evidence it is likely that the full formula was: *ut consules rem publicam defendant operamque dent ne quid res publica detrimenti capiat* ('that the consuls defend the republic and take steps to see that the state comes to no harm'). Philippus' paraphrase comes close to the full formula. The title *senatus consultum ultimum* is not found before Caesar (*BCiv.* 1. 5. 3).

**1. 68–72.**    The five fragments which have survived from the section dealing with events after the issuing of the *SCU* can be interpreted to show agreement with the other evidence we have in indicating that initially there were two theatres of war, Rome and Cisalpine Gaul; that the force commanded by Lepidus was defeated outside the walls of Rome; that in Cisalpine Gaul the troops under the command of Lepidus' legate, Brutus, capitulated on Brutus' surrender to Pompeius and the fall of Mutina; that the remnants of Lepidus' army mustered at Cosa on the Etrurian coast.

**1. 68.    he was hastening his flight.**    Plutarch's statement, 'Lepidus had made a hasty rush on Rome, and sitting down before it, was demanding a second consulship' (Plut. *Pomp.* 16. 3), can mean only one of two things: either he was demanding the office by force or he was seeking exemption from Sulla's law of iteration of office and from the compulsory biennium between curule offices (which had applied in pre-Sullan legislation). Even if exemption were granted he would have to be elected. However, the terms of the *SCU* were adhered to and Lepidus was defeated, but not routed completely. Florus says that the government forces were commanded by Catulus and Pompeius (2. 11. 6); Appian implies that Catulus was in sole command in Rome (*BC* 1. 107) while other sources, Plut. *Pomp.* 16. 3–5; Liv.

*Per.* 90; Oros. 5. 22. 17 show clearly that Pompeius commanded the government forces in Cisalpine Gaul.

On receipt of news that Pompeius had effectively disposed of the rebel troops in Gaul, Lepidus hastened his departure from Rome for the comparative safety of Etruria, where he might reorganize and yet salvage his cause.

**1. 69. superior in numbers . . . devoid of military experience.** Maurenbrecher's ascription of these words to Lepidus has been accepted by later commentators. While he based his identification on the size of the army collected by Lepidus, founded on such statements as 'terrifying the citizens with a vast throng of followers' (Plut. *Pomp.* 16. 3), and on his evaluation of Lepidus' military skill as deduced from the fact that he suffered defeat, two scholars who explicitly agree with his view have relied mainly on the phrase *privus militiae* ('being himself devoid of military experience').

Badian views Sallust's comment as implying lack of experience of command and adduces what is known of Lepidus' military experience as proof of this. The presence of Lepidus' name on a list of Pompeius Strabo's staff at Asculum in 89 (*CIL* I². 709 = *ILS* 8888), men whom Cichorius, *Röm. Stud.* 147, suggested were military tribunes, is considered irrelevant; Badian lumps Lepidus with Cicero, who also served under Strabo, as sufficient indication of Lepidus' lack of military experience. But Lepidus could have acquired considerable experience in the course of the Social War. Badian's case, however, is largely based on his view that the legate Aemilius Lepidus who captured Norba for Sulla in 82 (App. *BC* I. 94) could only have been the consul for 77, Mamercus Aemilius Lepidus Livianus. The evidence he cites for Mamercus' military exploits is beset with problems; see the report of Broughton, whom Badian quotes in a carefully selective way, on the Aemilii Lepidi, *MRR* 2. 71; on Mamercus, ibid. 43 and 45 n. 10; on Metellus Pius, conqueror of Pompaedius Silo, ibid. 42. There are few firm facts about Mamercus' career apart from his election to the consulship for 77. On the other hand, M. Aemilius Lepidus' praetorship of 81 and his governorship of Sicily in

80 might well have been the reward for military service to
Sulla at Norba and elsewhere. Syme (184 and n. 25) bases
himself on Badian.

The criteria of size of army and lack of military experience
would far more convincingly apply to M. Iunius Brutus,
opposed by an army under the young, experienced general,
Pompeius. As *legatus pro praetore* to the proconsul Q.
Lutatius Catulus (H. Last, *CAH* 9. 295, 316; cf. R. E. Smith,
*Phoenix* 14 (1960), 9), and entrusted with the task of holding
the Lepidan army under Brutus in check, Pompeius very
probably had to confine his recruiting to the old Pompeian
stamping-ground of Picenum. His army would therefore be
smaller than that of the rebels, but this was counterbalanced
by the disparity in military experience of the opposed
generals. Very little is known of M. Iunius Brutus before his
emergence as legatus to Lepidus in 77. He was tribune of the
plebs in 83 and his activity was in civil and administrative
affairs. He carried a bill to colonize Capua (Cic. *Leg. Agr.* 2.
89, 92, and 98), and he induced the litigants in the case of
Quinctius to delay proceedings (Cic. *Quinct.* 29, 63, 65).
There is no evidence of military experience before 77.

**I. 70.   near Mutina.**   Pompeius besieged Brutus in Mutina,
accepted his surrender on conditions, gave him safe conduct
but had him done to death on the following day. He then
turned to Etruria (Liv. *Per.* 90; Plut. *Pomp.* 16. 2–5; *Brut.* 4.
1–2; Val. Max. 6. 2. 8; Frontin. *Str.* 1. 9. 3; Oros. 5. 22. 17).

**I. 71.\*   Cosa.**   The remnants of Lepidus' defeated army
(1. 68) were forced to retire from Rome towards Etruria as
far as Cosa on the coast. Here they halted, probably aware
of the Pompeian menace looming from the north, wishing to
reorganize their ranks and attempt a desperate victory over
the government forces or, if need be, to abandon Italy as
their base. They could not afford to allow the two
government forces to unite. A second battle took place and
once again Lepidus was defeated. The majority of the
sources (Liv. *Per.* 90; Val. Max. 2. 8. 7; Plut. *Pomp.* 16. 3
and 6, 17. 3; App. *BC* 1. 107; Oros. 5. 22. 16–18; Rut.
Namat. 295–8) indicate that the defeat at Cosa was at the
hands of Catulus alone—Pompeius took no decisive part in

the last encounter in Italy of this revolt. This was not,
however, the view of the anonymous Auct. *Vir. Ill.* 77. 3
who, disregarding Catulus, bestowed on Pompeius the merit
of 'having put the subversive one to flight from Italy'.
Exuperantius offers a reconstruction of the final events
which completely overturns the canonical version in an even
more crude and obvious exercise in pro-Pompeius propaganda
(36. 39Z).

The only source which specifically connects Cosa—on
which see E. T. Salmon, *Roman Colonization* (London,
1969), 29–39—with the encounter in Etruria and the flight
to Sardinia is Rutilius Namatianus. The point of embarkation
could have been *Portus Cosanus* or *Portus Herculis* on the
peninsula Monte Argentario or a combination of these.
Both harbours provided the best anchorage along that part
of the coast. The name has been transmitted without book-
number among the Sallustian fragments, but its placement
here seems secure.

**1. 72.   speeding up their departure.**   A report in Exuperantius 39Z of Lepidus' second defeat contains the sentence:
*fugientes eius copias ac se implicantes festinatione formidinis
ita prostravit* ('he [Pompeius] so utterly defeated his [Lepi-
dus'] forces who were in flight and entangling themselves in
the haste occasioned by their fear'). Maurenbrecher, noting
a slight similarity between *se implicantes festinatione* of
Exuperantius and the Latin wording of this fragment
(*profectionem festinantes*), referred this fragment to a defeat
and flight of the Lepidan forces.

*Profectionem* ('departure') points rather to the decision
taken by Lepidus to embark the remainder of his forces on
board ship and transport them to a new base in Sardinia.
The speeding up was occasioned by the fear that the
government forces would reorganize and, perhaps supplemented by the arrival of Pompeius' contingent, succeed in
thwarting this design.

**1. 73.*   After the expulsion . . . from Italy.**   Sacerdos, 458.
1, has: 'After the expulsion of Marcus Lepidus . . . Italy';
Servius, *Aen.* 1. 630 reports: 'a less urgent but by no means
less serious and complex anxiety'.

Sallust's treatment of the *tumultus Lepidi* in Book 1 came to a close with the defeated proconsul's flight to Sardinia; the final stage of the episode is narrated at the beginning of Book 2. Maurenbrecher's ordering of the rest of the material of Book 1—an introduction to the Sertorian War with a treatment of Sertorius' career from 105 to 80 BC, when he was summoned back to Spain by the Lusitanians to take command of their forces in their struggle against the oligarchic government in Rome (frr. 73–92); a description of the early stages of the Sertorian War, marked by repeated victories over the Roman general Metellus Pius, prior to Pompeius' arrival in Spain with a fresh army in 77 (frr. 92–114); a treatment of operations in Cilicia and Macedonia (frr. 115–21) follows the sequence preserved in Livy's *Per.* 90 and seems, most probably, to have been the order followed by Sallust.

**an anxiety less urgent but by no means less serious.** Refers to the critical phase of the Sertorian War, to be dealt with in detail in Book 2, marked by the entry of Pompeius as a Roman commander in 77. It was 'less urgent' to the extent that it involved conflict outside the confines of Italy and that Pompeius' success against Lepidus gave promise that the threat posed by Sertorius would also be contained. It remained 'serious and complex' because it involved the granting to Pompeius of an extraordinary command which had in effect been extorted by threatening conduct; the fragility of the senate's position is starkly illustrated by the content and tone of the letter sent by Pompeius to the governing body in the winter of 75/74 (2. 82).

**1. 74.\*   Hither Spain was in turmoil.** Victorinus, 158. 26, quotes this fragment in full but does not specifically allocate it to Sallust. It forms a general picture of the situation of stress and danger, the result of ineffectual leadership of Metellus Pius, which made Pompeius' appointment inevitable.

Of the twenty fragments allocated to this segment (frr. 73–92) fifteen have been transmitted without book-number. The content of the majority of these and evidence from other sources justify their placement. Of the remaining few, such as this one, it could be said that the content is general enough to fit into any one of several scenarios. However, they do retain sufficient relevance to the career and character of Sertorius to make their collocation reasonably probable.

**1. 75. He requested Curio . . . to concede priority to Mamercus . . . .** The context is the long-delayed consular elections for 77. The successful candidates were D. Iunius Brutus and Mamercus Aemilius Lepidus Livianus. A senior member of the ruling oligarchy persuaded one of the candidates, C. Scribonius Curio, to stand aside in favour of the patrician Mam. Aemilius Lepidus, who had failed in a previous election—perhaps that for the consulship of 78 (Cic. *Off.* 2. 58)—and was in danger of repeating that experience. Curio was subsequently elected consul for 76 and showed himself an active supporter of the Sullan regime (cf. 2. 23–6).

The consuls for 77 were singularly undistinguished; H. Last (*CAH* 9. 317) described them as nonentities whose only claim to fame was that they gave their names to a year which was a turning-point for the worse in constitutional development. The witticism of M. Philippus (Plut. *Pomp.* 17. 4) that Pompeius was sent to command in Spain not with proconsular *imperium*, but *pro consulibus* ('in place of the consuls') incidentally reveals the beginning of the breakdown of the traditional Roman constitutional practice in military matters marked by the entrenchment of the device of extraordinary commands. (Cf. Cic. *Leg. Man.* 62; *Phil.* 11. 18).

Badian's view (*FC* 277 and n. 6) that the consuls were unwilling to take the command against Sertorius out of sympathy with the attitude of their kinsmen Aemilius Lepidus (consul in 78) and his chief lieutenant M. Iunius Brutus has rightly been questioned by Sumner, *JRS* 54 (1964), 45–6, and Spann, 196–7 n. 158; cf. B. Twyman, *Aufsteig und Niedergang der Römischer Welt*, 1 (Berlin/New York 1972), 844–5, 848–9).

**1. 76\*–77.\* toga . . . military cloak.** Servius Dan. does not mention Sallust in connection with this fragment, but he

is quoted as the source of the same phrase by Schol. *In Iuv.*
6. 400 and Isid. *Orig.* 19. 24. 9.

The generally accepted date for Sertorius' birth is *c*.123
(Schulten, 26; Ehrenberg, 180; L. Wickert, 'Sertorius', in
*Ratloses Schaffen*: Festschrift für Friedrich Lammert (Stuttgart 1954), 97; J. van Ooteghem, *Pompée le Grand,
bâtisseur d'empire* (Brussels 1954), 96). B. R. Katz (*RhM*
126 (1983), 44–50 defends this canonical date against
Spann's proposal of *c*.126 (pp. 2–3);[1] Konrad suggests *c*.125
(p. 31). Sertorius' first attested military experience is
reported as having taken place in 105 (Plut. *Sert.* 3. 1) and
would fit in with the commonly accepted birth date since
Sertorius would have reached the required age of 17 years.

The surviving Sallustian fragments on Sertorius' early
career indicate an emphasis on the young Sabine's capacity
as a soldier and an eventual leader of men. Plutarch's
description of his service under the proconsul Q. Servilius
Caepio, whose refusal in 105 to co-operate with the consul
Cn. Mallius Maximus brought about the Roman defeat at
Arausio at the hands of the Cimbri, concentrates on one act
of courage and endurance: the young Sertorius' feat of
swimming, although wounded, across the Rhône with
armour and weaponry intact. Despite Scardigli's doubts
(*SIFC* 43 (1971), 43–4), it is not unlikely that this story
received mention at a similar point in Sallust's narrative, as
it probably did in Posidonius and certainly in Livy (*Per.* 67).

Sertorius' service against the Germans from 105 to 102
was, however, chiefly under the command of Marius, from
whom he undoubtedly learnt valuable lessons in tactics and
strategy (Plut. *Sert.* 3. 2–4).

We have no firm evidence as to where Sertorius spent the
period 101–98. If he continued to serve in the army,
Macedonia, under Didius' command, and Sicily, under M.
Aquillius (consul in 101), are likely theatres (*MRR* 1. 571,
577; 2. 2–3; cf. Konrad, 39). Spann suggests that he saw
service in Gallia Cisalpina in connection with the founding

---

[1] Spann's book *Quintus Sertorius*, a condensed version of his dissertation,
appeared in 1987. I have stayed with his dissertation, noting instances where the
book reports a change of mind on specific points.

of Eporedia in 100 (Spann, 15; cf. Strabo 4. 6. 7; Vell. Pat. 1. 15. 5).

The summarizing nature of fr. 77, the most lengthy of the fragments providing a characterization of Sertorius, was probably also a feature of the first segment of the introductory material (73–92) to Sallust's treatment of the Sertorian War. In many cases the brevity of the surviving fragments of this section can be amplified fairly securely by similar material in Plutarch's *Life of Sertorius*, where Plutarch has presumably used a source other than or in addition to Sallust. Gellius introduces this fragment with: 'Sallust wrote as follows concerning the general Sertorius in his *Historiae*.' Donatus, Ter. *Eun.* 482, has the sentence, 'He took the greatest delight in these disfigurements.'

**Titus Didius.** Praetor no later than 101 and governor of Macedonia until *c*.99 when he returned to Rome to celebrate a triumph for his defeat of the Scordisci in Thrace (sources in *MRR* 1. 571). Consul in 98, he held proconsular *imperium* in hither Spain from 97 to 93. It is likely that he began campaigning in Spain in 98 while still consul (Obseq. 47). Sertorius may have served under him from the outset, but certainly did from 97 to 93. After a series of successful encounters against the Spaniards he was awarded his second triumph in June 93 (Liv. *Per.* 70; Obseq. 47–8; Frontin. *Str.* 1. 85, 2. 10. 1; Plut. *Sert.* 3. 5; App. *Hisp.* 99–100).

**covered himself in glory.** The only attested military exploit in which Sertorius was involved in Spain is the Castulo incident described by Plutarch in *Sert.* 3. 6–10. There are no grounds for rejecting this colourful episode as a Plutarchan fabrication, but the narrative does contain difficulties concerning the timing of incidents and the distances between towns which inhibit its acceptance at face value. Konrad suggests misunderstanding or mispresentation by Plutarch of a brief original report on this incident in Sallust (Konrad, 44). Schulten, 31, on the basis of Pliny *NH* 22. 12, suggested that for this action Sertorius was awarded the *corona graminea*, a decoration bestowed on a general for saving his troops from capture or dishonourable capitulation. This conjecture has been convincingly refuted by B. Scardigli (*A&R* 15 (1970), 174–7).

**as a military tribune.** In this period the people elected 24 tribunes for the first four legions of the Roman army; these were referred to as *tribuni a populo* (Sall. *Iug.* 63. 4; Frontin. *Str.* 2. 4. 4) or as *comitiati* (Ps.-Asc. 126. 26). The much more numerous officers (referred to as *rufili*) of the rest of the troops were appointed by the commanders; their number varied in accordance with the varying number of extra legions. It seems likely that Sertorius belonged to the latter group; cf. R. E. Smith, *Service in the Post-Marian Roman Army* (Manchester 1958), 60; Plut. *Sert.* 3. 5. On this topic see discussion and sources in J. Suolahti, *The Junior Officers of the Roman Army in the Republican Period* (Helsinki 1955), 35–42; Wiseman, *New Men*, 143–7.

**In the Marsic War.** For the Marsic or Social War see note on 1. 18 etc. It is generally accepted that Sertorius returned to Rome with his commander Didius by 93, and that he stood for the quaestorship of Cisalpine Gaul for 90. This chronology has to take into account the statement in Plutarch (*Sert.* 4. 1): 'As soon as he [Sertorius] returned to Rome he was appointed as quaestor of Cisalpine Gaul at the opportune time (ἐν δέοντι).' On the basis of this Spann (pp. 19 ff.) has argued for Sertorius' return to Rome in 92, his election for the quaestorship of 91. Katz *RhM* 126 (1983), 53–6 and Konrad, 44–7, have argued against the finality of Spann's conclusions.

The phrase ἐν δέοντι is explained by the following statement: τοῦ γὰρ πολέμου συνισταμένου (*Sert.* 4. 2) 'for the Marsic War was breaking out'. It is well established that the Social War was breaking out late in 91; Sertorius would have entered on his quaestorship for 90 late in 91, an opportune time to take part in Roman preparations for the emergency. Spann's chronology depends on his interpretation of συνισταμένου as 'threatening', 'about to break out'.

**in the preparation of troops and weaponry.** Although quaestors' functions were mainly financial, they were in all other respects the administrative deputies of magistrates with *imperium*. We do not know the identity of the magistrate concerned here, but under the immediate threat of war Sertorius' duties became military rather than financial —Plutarch, *Sert*. 4. 2 is more explicit: 'He was ordered to levy troops and procure arms'. Cisalpine Gaul was one of the most important Roman recruiting areas during the late Republic. Gabba, *Comm. App. Lib.* 1. 777 suggests that it was mostly Roman citizens that were levied in Cisalpina, but it is not unlikely that many of the numerous Gallic forces fighting for Rome (*CIL* 1². 864; App. *BC* 1. 41) were also raised by Sertorius; cf. Konrad, 48.

**many achievements carried out under his command.** If attached to magistrates or pro-magistrates quaestors were expected to serve until their commanders gave up office. Besides attending to the commander's *fiscus* ('finances') they undertook other responsibilities (see Cic. *2 Verr*. 1. 40). They often commanded military forces and might even take over supreme command (*pro praetore*) in the absence of their superior. Given Sertorius' experience and natural talent for warfare it is certain that in his quaestorship of 90 and 89 he distinguished himself in military affairs. We have no explicit testimony to show in what area of Italy or under what general he saw active service. Conjectures have not been lacking. Schulten, 32, suggested a senior post under his former commander, T. Didius, in the south (cf. Cic. *Font*. 43; Ovid, *Fasti* 6. 567–8; Vell. Pat. 2. 16. 2; App. *BC* 1. 40), a view supported by Katz, *RhM* 126 (1983), 57. Spann, 22–4 conjectured a command under Q. Servilius Caepio (Liv. *Per*. 73; App. *BC* 1. 40) and Marius in 90; then, during 89, successively under the consuls L. Porcius Cato and Cn. Pompeius Strabo, all in central and northern Italy (sources *MRR* 2. 32). Konrad, 49–50, argues that, since three of the men listed on the staff of Pompeius Strabo (*CIL* 1². 709; cf. 1. 69), namely, Q. Hirtuleius, brother of Sertorius' principal lieutenant L. Hirtuleius, L. Insteius, and C. Tarquitius, are later found as officers under Sertorius in Spain, ties of *amicitia* must have been forged between these three and Sertorius while he served as a senior officer in Strabo's army.

**were left unrecorded . . . spite of historians.** Sallust's emphasis on Sertorius' *ignobilitas* ('lack of noble status') justifies the general conclusion that the reference is to the inherent bias against all that was non-noble, characteristic of the 'senatorial' interpretation of Roman history. Explicit reference to Sisenna, a leading proponent of such an outlook, has been assumed (Schulten, 15; Badian, *JRS* 52 (1962), 51 (= *Studies*, 214); La Penna, *Athenaeum* 41 (1963), 272). It is very likely that the career of Sertorius down to 78 would have been dealt with in Sisenna's *Historiae*, but Sallust, who speaks of historians (*scriptorum*) would also have had other writers in mind. Posidonius may have said something about Sertorius, especially when he dealt with the Cinnan regime. Sulla's *Commentarii* would almost certainly have had unfriendly references to Sertorius. Varro, who had served in Spain with Pompeius (Sall. *Hist.* 2. 69), and wrote a *De Pompeio* in three books (see Cichorius, *Röm. Stud.* 193 ff.) is also a possibility. Orosius, 5. 23. 9, names Galba as a source for his account of Pompeius' arrival in Spain; this Gaius Sulpicius Galba, grandfather of the emperor, wrote a historical work (Peter *HRR* 2. 41) cited by Juba II king of Mauretania, who himself wrote a history of Rome (see Plutarch, *Romulus* 17. 5). Strabo, 17. 3. 8, reports that Tanusius Geminus dealt with an incident from Sertorius' experiences in Africa. Plutarch mentions Theophanes of Mytilene as a source for his *Pompeius* (37) while Cicero (*Arch.* 24) refers to Theophanes as Pompeius' '*scriptor rerum suarum*' (the recorder of his exploits). There may have been others.

**numerous battle scars and an empty eye-socket.** Marks of his prowess in the engagements participated in during the Social War. Plutarch expands: 'He did not remit the activities of a daring soldier after he had advanced to the dignity of a commander, but displayed astonishing deeds of prowess and exposed his person unsparingly in battle, in consequence of which he got a blow that cost him one of his eyes' (*Sert.* 4. 3).

**the greatest delight in these disfigurements.** An element here of the attitude of the non-noble aspirant to office and power—the path to glory was through character rather than ancestry, *moribus non maioribus*, which is a leading motif of

Marius' speech (*Iug.* 85). The noble careerist buttressed his claim to distinction by the war trophies and portraits (*imagines*) of his ancestors; Marius can point to his battle scars with these words: 'These are my portraits, these my badge of nobility, not left me by inheritance as theirs were, but won by my own innumerable efforts and perils' (ibid. 85. 30; cf. G. M. Paul, *Historical Commentary on Sallust's Bellum Jugurthinum* (ARCA 13; Liverpool 1984), on ch. 85). For the non-noble, war wounds were a political asset; the fact that Sertorius was very probably canvassing for the tribuneship about the time he was uttering these sentiments may have some relevance. Note the Plutarchan version of this attitude (*Sert.* 4. 3–4) and the remarks of F. Caviglia (*Maia*, 18 (1966), 156–8).

**1. 78.\* and they were greeting . . . shouts of congratulation.** Plutarch, still referring to Sertorius' feats in the Social War, continues: 'The people also paid him fitting honours. For when he came into the theatre they received him with clapping of hands and shouts of welcome, testimonials which even those who were advanced in years and honours could not easily obtain' (*Sert.* 4. 5).

Such popularity was not sufficient to secure Sertorius' election to the tribunate. His candidacy, usually dated to 88 for the tribunate of 87 (Schulten, 32; Scardigli, *Athenaeum*, 49 (1971), 229–37; Sumner, *Orators*, 108) was blocked through Sulla's influence (Plut. *Sert.* 4. 6) and as a result he became an enemy of the future dictator. What caused Sulla's enmity remains obscure.

**1. 79.\* In the midst of civil war.** On Sallust's general survey of the civil war of 87–83 BC see notes on 1. 23–6, 27–9. Sertorius' part in the defeat of the Sullan party was as a member of a triumvirate of commanders, the other members being Cinna and Marius (Plut. *Sert.* 5. 5). The other sources, Liv. *Per.* 79, 80; App. *BC* 1. 67, 69; Flor. 2. 9. 13; Gran. Lic. 35. 9C; Oros. 5. 19. 9–13, give the impression that Papirius Carbo (consul in 85, 84, 82) was also a principal commander. From Appian, *BC* 1. 67, it appears that Carbo's force operated jointly with Cinna's; there are no reports of independent operations by him; cf. Konrad, 58.

Only three corps, those of Marius, Cinna and Carbo, and Sertorius were deployed in the siege of Rome (Bennett, *Cinna*, 13).

**a reputation for justice and virtue.**   Plutarch contrasts the savagery with which Cinna and Marius conducted a purge against the defeated followers of Sulla after the surrender of Rome at the end of 87 and the moderation of Sertorius, who neither killed to gratify his anger nor grew arrogant with victory. He actually rebuked Marius for the barbarity of his revenge and prevailed upon Cinna to act more moderately (*Sert.* 5. 6).

There is no need to doubt this picture. Sertorius' principal enemy was overseas. He was astute enough to realize that brutal arrogance in victory could quickly erase the benefits acquired by hard fighting. Diodorus (fr. 38. 4), however, states that the purge was decided upon by a meeting of the 'most eminent leaders', summoned by Cinna and Marius, a procedure analogous to that followed forty-four years later in the triumviral proscriptions. Sertorius was undoubtedly present at this meeting; it may well mean that he, while not taking personal vengeance, supported the joint decision and the choice of victims. He would not have foreseen the savagery with which the decision was put into effect.

It is clear that the atrocities committed at this time by armed slaves against private citizens and their families were not sanctioned by the meeting of generals. After the ordeal of the siege of Rome sanction of such activity would have destroyed whatever remained of goodwill towards the Cinnan regime: Sertorius' massacre of the slaves (Plut. *Sert.* 5. 7) revealed his own feelings on this incident and would undoubtedly have increased his popularity among the common people, probably more than compensating for his failure in the tribunician elections.

He did succeed in being elected to a praetorship. His year of office is generally agreed to have been 83 (e.g. P. R. v. Bieńkowski, 'Kritische Studien über Chronologie . . .', *WS* 13 (1891), 135; Broughton, *MRR* 2. 63; Wiseman, *New Men*, 260, no. 394). Spann's proposal to shift the date to 85 or 84 (pp. 39, 43–8) is supported by Konrad, who goes on to give reasons for preferring 85 (pp. 68–9). His reasons are plausible but not compelling.

**1. 80.\* unless counteraction . . . in concert.** Sertorius had good reason to fear both the military skills of Sulla and the probable effects of his persuasive personality. He therefore counselled strong concerted opposition to Sulla's march from Brundisium along the Via Appia in the summer of 83. But his warnings went unheeded: Norbanus, Carbo, and Scipio provided no determined resistance to Sulla's advance on Rome (Plut. *Sert.* 6. 1).

**1. 81.\* a conference was granted . . . against his will.** Sallust also referred to this incident in his general survey of the civil war: see note on 1. 29\*, **thence arose a dialogue**.

On his march towards Rome Sulla defeated the army of the consul Norbanus near Capua; he then met up with the army of the other consul, L. Cornelius Scipio Asiaticus, and offered to negotiate. Scipio agreed to an armistice and handed over hostages. The two commanders next met between Cales and Teanum Sidicinum and apparently reached an agreement. To obtain the opinion of his colleague Norbanus, Scipio sent Sertorius to Capua. En route Sertorius captured Suessa, a town which had sided with Sulla. The negotiations consequently broke down, but the situation was eventually decided by the decision of Scipio's force of 40 cohorts to desert to Sulla (App. *BC* 1. 85).

Sertorius' opposition to these negotiations is clearly attested: Plut. *Sert.* 6. 3; Exup. 45Z. There is little doubt that he deliberately sabotaged the armistice: Gabba points out that he did not take the direct route to Capua, since Suessa was to the west of Teanum (*Comm. App. Lib.* 1. 385) and Spann has shrewdly argued that Sertorius had reason to fear that his head might be the price of a compromise between Sulla and the Cinnan regime (p. 44).

The Teanum fiasco influenced Sertorius' subsequent activity in two ways: he spent the remainder of 83 mostly in Etruria, where he levied forty new cohorts to replace the loss through desertion of Scipio's force (Exup. 47–8Z); he continued to criticize the conduct of the war (ibid. 49Z),

which now involved the newly elected consuls Papirius
Carbo and Marius the younger. He had objected to Marius'
election not only because it was illegal but also because he
had serious doubts concerning the competence of the new
consuls—deservedly so. Exuperantius recounts the outcome
of Sertorius' criticism: 'Then the consuls and other leaders of
the faction, engulfed in such a torrent of reprimands, sent
him off to hither Spain, either to remove from their sight a
rival, and a vehement critic of their heedlessness, or to put a
suitable governor in charge of a warlike province concerning
whose loyalty they had doubts' (50Z). On the basis of this
evidence most scholars assume that Sertorius' province was
hither Spain (e.g. Mommsen, *Hist.* 3. 361; Maurenbrecher,
*Proleg.* 21; Stahl, 37; Schulten, 39, Broughton, *MRR* 2. 63;
Spann, 50). Badian (*PACA* 1 (1958), 1–18 = *Studies*, 71–
104) points to an acute shortage of governors throughout the
empire during the eighties and argues that Sertorius was in
charge of both hither and farther Spain. Konrad, (73–4),
suggested that Badian's view may have support in Sertorius'
statement: *quantum Hispaniae provinciae interesset suas
partes superiores esse* ('how advantageous it would be to the
province of Spain if his side had the upper hand'; Liv. 91 fr.
22W–M), and added that Exuperantius' statement is not
reliable because of the errors inherent in his summarizing
narrative. Neither argument is compelling enough to give
authority to an extension of Sertorius' sphere of responsibility.
See Maurenbrecher, *Proleg.* 21.

**1. 82\*–92.**   Deal with Sertorius' Spanish governorship, 82–
81 BC. It is a very curtailed treatment of a multifaceted
segment of Sertorius' career. Several important episodes are
either just fleetingly referred to or omitted entirely.
   Sertorius arrived in Spain either late in 83 or early in 82;
the only sources which refer to timing—Plut. *Sert.* 6. 1;
App. *BC* 1. 86, 108—do not provide a precise date. At the
time of his departure fighting troops could not be spared
from the war with Sulla and it is likely that he was
accompanied by a very small force (P. A. Brunt, *Italian
Manpower 225 BC–AD 14* (Oxford 1971), 470). Plutarch
implies that this contingent was so weak that he was forced

to pay dues to 'pestilent Barbarians' for safe passage through the mountains (*Sert.* 6. 5). After his arrival in Spain he had command of a legion from Italy (App. *BC* I. 108), which may either have remained in Spain throughout the Social War or have been sent out there on its conclusion (Brunt, *Manpower*, 470).

**I. 82.\* Spain was his ancient motherland.** The fragment is repeated by Servius at *Aen.* 3. 297 without *antiquam* ('ancient'). A conciliatory approach to a people alienated by the arrogant rapacity of earlier Roman officials was imperative. Thus Maurenbrecher, following Kritz, Dietsch, and de Brosses, is correct in assuming that this statement was part of such an approach by Sertorius.

The objection that only a Spanish nobleman could justifiably have uttered such a sentiment is countered by Servius' observation: *sed illic ad laudem pertinet, non ad veritatem* ('in that context its object was praise not a statement of fact'). A context in which Sertorius points to his former service in Spain (I. 77) and is affirming love of Spain persisting from that experience is the attractive conjecture of de Brosses (I. 582).

**I. 83.\* He was greatly loved . . . exercised command.** Plutarch provides details of Sertorius' approach: 'He tried to win them over, the chiefs by his personal intercourse with them, the masses by a remission of taxes. His greatest popularity, however, was won by ridding them of the necessity of furnishing quarters for soldiers' (*Sert.* 6. 7–8). Plutarch goes on to add that Sertorius did not rely on the goodwill of the Spaniards; he made himself formidable by the measures he took to establish and maintain a stance of military preparedness. Sallust's epitomator Exuperantius also mentions this twofold aspect of his approach (51Z).

**I. 84\*–86.** (spring of 81) The news that, consequent upon the victory at the Colline Gate on I November 82 (Vell. Pat. 2. 27. I), Sulla was practically master of Rome would have reached Sertorius about early February 81. Suspecting that an army would be dispatched from Rome to settle affairs in Spain, Sertorius took precautions which turned out to be ineffectual.

**1. 84.\*   Salinator is killed while on the march.**   Livius
Salinator (see Cichorius, *Röm. Stud.* 256) was commissioned
by Sertorius to hold the passes of the Pyrenees with 6,000
men (Plut. *Sert.* 7. 1). This force was probably Sertorius'
regular legion (Brunt, *Manpower*). As a result the Roman
army under C. Annius sent against Sertorius was forced to
wait in frustration at the foot of the mountains until the
passes could be cleared. The impasse was solved by the
killing of Salinator by 'Calpurnius surnamed Lanarius' (1.
85). Plutarch (*Sert.* 73) uses the word δολοφονήσαντος
('slaying by treachery'), which has led to an assumption by
some (e.g. Stahl, 42; Schulten, 45) that this Calpurnius was a
Sertorian who betrayed or murdered his commanding
officer, Salinator. Syme's conclusion (*Historia*, 4 (1955), 58–
9) that Calpurnius, an officer of Annius (cf. *MRR* Suppl.
12), caused Salinator's death through a tactical manoeuvre
or ruse is supported by the words 'while on the march'.

**1. 86.   a few men . . . occupying the pass.**   Plutarch states
that Annius crossed the Pyrenees 'routing all opposition'.
This fragment could be taken to signify either that a few
Sertorian troops were overtaken in the course of a disorderly
retreat or that some groups from Salinator's force did not
join in a headlong flight.

**1. 87–92.**   (81 BC) After Sulla's victory there would be a
considerable number of troops available for overseas duty.
Annius' army would have amounted to three or four legions,
and once he had crossed the Pyrenees Sertorius did not have
the resources to meet him in the field. Sertorius' whereabouts
at the time of the rout of Salinator's army are unknown. In
the absence of information from other sources we can only
deduce that he was near enough to New Carthage (Cartagena)
to arrange the embarkation of his remaining force of 3,000
men for a voyage to Mauretania (Plut. *Sert.* 7. 4).
    The Moroccans attacked the Romans, inflicting serious
losses and forcing Sertorius to sail back to Spain. He was
prevented from landing there and after being joined by some
Cilician pirate ships he attacked the larger of the Pityussian
Islands, Ebesus (Ibiza) (Plut. *Sert.* 7. 4–5; cf. Schulten, 47 n.

237; Strabo, 3. 5. 1), organized a landing and overpowered the garrison which Annius had established there.

**1. 87. Some . . . began to sink.** A fragment reported with slightly different wording by Nonius (453. 6). After a short time Annius came to Ebesus with numerous ships and 5,000 men-at-arms (Plut. *Sert.* 7. 5) Sertorius, who knew that his chances in a land battle were negligible against a superior force, decided on a naval engagement which would also be one-sided but at least offered the possibility of escape. During the naval battle in the Gulf of Valencia a fierce storm arose 'and the greater part of the vessels of Sertorius, owing to their lightness, were drawn aslant the rocky shore' (ibid. 7. 6).

**1. 88.\* unable to make a sortie.** The extant version of this fragment is corrupt. The translation is based on a version corrected by scholarly conjecture.

Plutarch's report continues: 'while he himself, with a few ships, excluded from the open sea by the storm and from the land by the enemy, was tossed about for ten days'. When the storm abated Sertorius headed back towards Spain, passed through the straits of Gibraltar, and anchored a little north of the mouths of the Baetis (Guadalquiver).

**1. 89.\* with the natural desire . . . unknown places.** Nonius, 129. 9, introduces this fragment with *Sallustius in Jugurthino*; since he depends on Gellius, this can be dismissed as an error on Nonius' part, arising from the recollection of a phrase in *Iug.* 93. 3: 'the natural desire of mankind to overcome difficulties'; cf. Maurenbrecher on 1. 103\*M where, however, he refers this statement to Sertorius.

I take it to refer to a voyage of some sailors from Cadiz who had recently returned from the Atlantic Islands (Plut. *Sert.* 8. 2). Sertorius, anchored off the western coast of the peninsula, met up with them on their return home. The sailors' description of what they believed to be the Isles of the Blest must have aroused in Sertorius a longing for the peace and comfort which was a prospect rendered remote by his existing status as an outcast.

**1. 90. that the two islands . . . distant from Cadiz.** Maurenbrecher obelized this fragment because the codices

of Nonius have *Sallustius hist. lib. XI*; this has justifiably
been corrected to Book 1, and is part of Sallust's treatment
of the Isles of the Blest. Originally identified with Madeira
and Porto Santo, the name was subsequently transferred to
the Canary Islands, which are dealt with in detail by Pliny,
*NH* 6. 201–5. As C. Th. Fischer, *RE* 7. 42–3 and Schulten,
49 n. 242 have noted, Plutarch's description, which is almost
certainly based on the Sallustian original, strongly suggests
Madeira/Porto Santo. Spann, 253 n.103, prefers the Canaries.
On this topic see R. Rebuffat in *Mélanges Heurgon* (Paris
1976), 877–902.

**spontaneously produce food for their inhabitants.**   Plutarch
enlarges: 'They enjoy moderate rains at long intervals, and
winds which for the most part are soft and precipitate dews
so that the islands not only have a rich soil which is excellent
for ploughing and planting, but also produce a natural fruit
that is plentiful and wholesome enough to feed, without toil
or trouble, a leisured folk' (*Sert.* 8. 3).

**1. 91.\*   have been celebrated in the songs of Homer.**   The
mythical Elysian plain at the world's end 'where life is
easiest for men' (Hom. *Od.* 4. 563–8; cf. ibid. 15. 403–12;
Hes. *Op.* 167–73) had by Plato's time become the abode of
the just in the life of the hereafter (*Grg.* 523). It was a
doctrine inculcated by Greek philosophers resident in Rome
and became part of Roman poetic thought (*Aen.* 6. 637 ff.)
It was probably the scholarly Posidonius, who had himself
voyaged in the western Ocean, that first gave an actuality to
this mythical concept (Ehrenberg, 186) and it is not unlikely
that Sallust found a description of the Isles of the Blest in
Posidonius.

**1. 92.   a flight to distant stretches of Ocean.**   Cf. Plut *Sert.*
8. 2–9. 1; Flor. 2. 10. 2. Given the low ebb of Sertorius'
fortunes at this time, it would not really be surprising if he
had indeed thought of 'getting away from it all'. Action
based on such a feeling was contemplated or carried out by
several notables in the last decades of the Republic (e.g.
Sulla, Lucullus, Cicero, M. Antony). Cf. Schulten, 51–2.
Sallust himself had acted on such feelings and his attribution
of similar thoughts to Sertorius could well be simply

rationalizing on his part even though the scholiast on
Horace, *Epod.* 16 states that Sallust put Sertorius' decision
to 'get away' in a context of dejection about his defeat.

In any case Sertorius did not translate thought into action.
This has been explained as a result of the refusal of the
Cilician pirates to accompany him on such a voyage (Plut.
*Sert.* 9. 2) but, as a Sabine whose future was centred on
Roman affairs, Sertorius realized that departure would
involve abandonment of his political and military expectations
and the disintegration of the armed band which formed the
nucleus of the force which he must create to achieve his
aims. Such a line of thought seems to be confirmed by his
subsequent activity. He headed with his remaining troops
for Mauretania, the land of the Moors, and took part in the
defeat of Ascalis, the deposed king of Mauretania; he also
posted a victory over Pacciaecus, sent by Sulla to help
Ascalis. The soldiers of Pacciaecus he won over to his cause
and then forced the surrender of Tingis, the town in which
Ascalis had taken refuge (ibid. 9. 3–5). It was at this
juncture that he received the invitation from the Lusitanians
to take over command of their forces in their struggle against
Rome.

**I. 93–114.** (80–77 BC) This segment deals with the return
of Sertorius to Spain in 80 and the early years of the
Sertorian War, fought chiefly against Metellus Pius, down to
and including part of 77. Maurenbrecher assigned to it
twenty-three fragments (104–26M). Two of these fragments
(123 and 125M) I have transferred to Book 2; I have
consigned fr. 109 to 'Fragments of Uncertain Reference' and
fr. 117M to Fragments *incertae sedis* of Book 1 (Introd.
section 8). I have added to this group two fragments placed
by Maurenbrecher in the segment which follows this one
(i.e. 1. 135 and 136M) and one (139M) which he placed in
fragments of uncertain allocation of Book 1.

The decipherment of the parchment leaf (P. Vindob.
Lat. 117) published by Bernhardt Bischoff in *WS* 13 (1979),
116–22 and its historical interpretation by Herbert Bloch
(ibid. 122–9) has added significant detail to the fragments
published by Maurenbrecher as 107 and 136. This affects the

chronological order of the fragments assigned to this section. On the Codex P. Vindob. Lat. see Introd. section 4 (*a*).

This period to which I have assigned twenty-two fragments involves a number of events, military, diplomatic, political, which occupy eight of the twenty-seven chapters of Plutarch's *Life of Sertorius*. It emerges that only a handful of haphazard references to just a few of the events have survived from the Sallustian treatment of the same period. There are, however, signs that this treatment was far more detailed than the Plutarchan version.

**1. 93.   a small garrison in Mauretania.**   We are told that Sertorius, in his flight from Annius, took with him from Spain 3,000 men; he must, however, have lost many of these at the Pityussian Islands together with a large number of ships (Plut. *Sert.* 7. 4–6; cf. notes on 1. 87 and 88). He landed back in Spain with 2,600 men 'whom he called Romans' (ibid. 12. 2). This group must have included remnants of Pacciaecus' force (ibid. 9. 5; see note on 1. 92), the majority of whom were probably *Hispanienses*, i.e. Roman or Italian settlers in Spain (see B. Scardigli *A&R* 15 (1970), 180–1; id. *Athenaeum* 49 (1971), 250–1; Spann, 66–7). They were Romanized 'but hardly for the most part citizens' (Brunt, *Manpower*, 470).

The small garrison could have consisted of about 700 Roman and *Hispanienses* troops. To make up the numbers he enlisted the force of 700 Moors he took with him to Spain.

**and tried . . . to avoid a battle.**   The wording implies that Sertorius' precautions were fruitless; he did in fact encounter Roman naval opposition somewhere in the straits near Mellaria (Plut. *Sert.* 12. 3), about 43 miles SE of Cadiz (A. Schulten, *FHA* vi. 145). The Roman fleet, commanded by a certain Cotta, was decisively defeated. Given Sertorius' serious losses at the battle of the Pityussian Islands, the force commanded by Cotta cannot have been a large one.

**1. 94.   a mountain . . . gave them all shelter.**   Nonius, 453. 4, records this fragment in the form given by Gellius. Servius, *Aen.* 1. 518, records that when they had crossed, a mountain, Belleia, gave them all shelter. This proper name has been included by some editors, including Kritz and Maurenbrecher. The latter, misunderstanding the Servius passage, considered that the grammarian had confused the name of the mountain Belleia with a city of the same name in the Tarraconnensis region. G. Garbugino (*Stud. Non.* 5 (1978), 73) provides a more satisfactory explanation: very close to Mellaria there was a town called Baelo, which corresponds to modern Silla del Papa (see Schulten, 54 and n. 274) and which also gave the name to the river close by. This locality was the landfall for whoever sailed from Tingis in Mauretania. Servius' identification is a correct one, but the grammarian, probably copying it from Asper's commentary, has erroneously inserted it as part of the Sallustian text.

**seized in advance by the Lusitanians.** Presumably the 4,000 light-armed infantry and 700 cavalry which Plutarch implies (*Sert.* 12. 2) joined Sertorius immediately upon his arrival.

**1. 95. And soon Fufidius . . . to his own troops.** Part of the description preliminary to an account of Sertorius' second engagement on Spanish soil, the battle against the Roman force led by Fufidius. Plutarch summarizes the outcome: 'He routed Fufidius, the governor of Baetica on the banks of the Baetis, with the slaughter of two thousand soldiers' (*Sert.* 12. 4). This latter figure is undoubtedly exaggerated (cf. Brunt, *Manpower*, 694–7) a feature, however, which should not cast doubt on the crushing nature of Fufidius' defeat; his subsequent action (1.96) confirms it.

**And soon.** Indicates that this battle took place not long after the victory over Cotta near Mellaria.

**Fufidius.** See note on 1. 48. 22. A former senior centurion (*primipilaris*, Oros. 5. 2. 3), Fufidius became praetor in 81, and propraetor in farther Spain in 80. Both his identity and his career have been topics of exhaustive and somewhat fruitless debate (e.g. Spann, 73–6; Konrad, 222–31; C. F. Konrad, *CP* 84 (1989), 122–9).

**with his legions.** At least two, amounting to perhaps 10,000 men. Sertorius' choice of battleground was dictated by the disparity in numbers and the mixed nature of the troops under his command. He would not necessarily have known of the general worthlessness of the opposing general (1. 48. 23).

**such steep banks.** Nonius' version of this fragment has *tantas spiras* ('such great formations') which Dietsch, accepting it as a reference to enemy forces, changed to *tantas copias* ('such great forces'). Maurenbrecher more perceptively, since the point at issue is the nature of the terrain and the topographical disadvantage it presented to Fufidius, emended to *tantas ripas* ('such steep banks').

**just one ford.** The Nonius version also omits *unum* ('one') which, although present only in Codex C of Charisius, 37. 21, should be included for the same reason.

**1. 96. He summoned Domitius the proconsul . . . had assembled.** Maurenbrecher, unaware of the existence of the Vienna fragment (P. Vindob. Lat. 117), assumed that it was Metellus who in 79 summoned Domitius from hither Spain. The mention of Domitius in close connection with the consternation caused by the presence of Moorish troops in Sertorius' army (1. 98) makes it definite that the summoning was done by Fufidius and that the year was 80 BC.

**Domitius.** M. Domitius Calvinus, now generally accepted as the otherwise unattested father of the consul of 53, Cn. Domitius Calvinus.

**the proconsul.** The dates of the governorship of Domitius and of his defeat and death at the hands of Sertorius' *legatus* L. Hirtuleius have been matters of dispute. The evidence of the Vienna fragment now makes it clear that he was governor of hither Spain in 80. As praetor (Eutropius, 6. 2) he was sent *pro consule* to govern that province. Other sources—Liv. *Per.* 90; Plut. *Sert.* 12. 3–4; Flor. 2. 10. 7; Oros. 5. 23. 3—offer no guidance.

On his way to help Fufidius, Domitius was intercepted by L. Hirtuleius, the most capable of Sertorius' generals, defeated, and killed on the River Anas (Guadiana). See 1. 100. This action may also have occurred in 80, although 79 (*MRR* 2. 84) remains a possibility, since we have no indication as to how quickly Domitius responded to the call for help.

**with all the forces that he had assembled.** Could indicate that Domitius had earlier been requested or had decided on his own initiative to raise sufficient forces to meet the threat posed by Sertorius. The equipping and organizing of those troops might well have caused a delay to his response to Fufidius' summons.

**1. 97. A people . . . borders of their own region.** Maurenbrecher applied this description to the Lusitanians; he assumed that they reacted in an extreme way to the sight of Sertorius' mixed force, especially the Moorish contingent, largely because of their isolation from contact with the appearance and customs of people of other regions. Kritz agreed with de Brosses's surmise that the fragment referred to a Thracian tribe and hence to the war conducted in 77 by Appius Claudius Pulcher against the Macedonians and Thracians. Given the revised interpretation of the next fragment, I take this fragment to refer to the Moors who fought as a cavalry contingent under Sertorius against the Roman army commanded by Fufidius.

**1. 98. and throughout the whole province . . . by Domitius.** The Vienna fragment, Cod. P. Vindob. Lat. 117, provides a mutilated version of 'were alleging that they were eaters of human flesh' and follows with a corrupted passage which has been conjectured as containing 'by Domitius'.

**the whole province.** Farther Spain, of which Fufidius was governor.

**fifty thousand or more enemy troops.** Probably the type of exaggeration not uncommon from soldiers who have suffered an unexpected and decisive defeat. The figure may also owe something to the impression that the Moorish cavalrymen were, because of their speed of movement and their enthusiasm for slaughter, in all quarters of the battle arena.

**men of strange and monstrous aspect.** The major impact was the terror inspired by the colour and demeanour of the Moorish cavalry and by the savagery of their fighting methods.

**fetched from the confines of Ocean.**   Confirms the impression conveyed by I. 97: this was the first time within living memory that Moors had been seen on Iberian soil.

**by Domitius.**   There is no doubt about Domitius' close connection with the above passage. It confirms the judgement that the passage deals with the widespread panic which followed the decisive defeat of the Roman army on the Baetis, the very first land battle fought by Sertorius' polyglot army.

**I. 99.   The horses . . . are throwing . . . into confusion . . . .** Maurenbrecher placed this among the fragments *incertae sedis* (of uncertain placement) of Book I i.e. I. 139M. Kritz drew attention to Priscianus' warning that the Latin verb *consternantur* was deponent, not passive ('the horses were throwing the combatants into confusion') and points to a Tacitean passage probably modelled on the Sallustian description: 'repeatedly also straggling chariots, the horses terror-stricken and driverless, at the casual prompting of panic made oblique or frontal charges' (*Agr.* 36).

The first sentence of fr. I. 100 suggests that both fragments belong to the same context.

**I. 100.   they were in favour . . . four days.**   The words 'as if paralysed . . . hearing or speaking' are reported by Nonius, 276. 15, which Maurenbrecher reports as his fr. 136. Donatus, Ter. *Adelph.* 310, reports 'was not sufficiently in control . . . hearing or speaking' and adds an indication of the context: 'since he was speaking of Septimius who was in a state of distraction'. This explanation led Maurenbrecher, who knew only of the Nonius–Donatus transmission, to accept Kritz's view that the Septimius in question was the orator L. Septimius mentioned in Cic. *pro Vareno* fr. 8 (Priscianus, 2. 112. 20) and to hypothesize some form of crisis in a court case or public meeting. The fuller form of the fragment makes the context much clearer, even if not totally secure.

**in favour of submitting . . . killed.**   The validity of the interpretation of this segment depends on accepting the conjecture that from the mutilated . . . INTERFECER . R . . S we are correct in detecting the word *interfecere* ('they

killed'). Four sources affirm that Domitius was defeated on
the Anas by Hirtuleius (Liv. *Per.* 90; Plut. *Sert.* 12. 4; Flor.
2. 10. 7; Oros. 5. 23. 3); possibly two, (Eutrop. 6. 12 and this
fragment) state that he was also killed. As it stands, the
subject of the verb 'killed' remains unclear, and we are left
with the alternatives: either Domitius was captured by the
enemy and then put to death, or he was killed by his own
troops in a bid to save their own skins.

**the legatus Septimius.** Apparently a legionary legate and
therefore compelled to take over command on the death of
his superior officer. The conjecture *percu⟨ss⟩it* ('struck') at
lines 11–12 of the fragment is attractive, in spite of the fact
that the verb does not occur elsewhere in Sallust: a wound,
in addition to the loss of Domitius, would account for the
intensity of the confusion attributed to Septimius.

**1. 101.    and Metellus . . . by letter.** After the victory over
Fufidius, Sertorius apparently turned to the task for which
he had been commissioned by the Lusitanians in preparation
for their coming struggle against the government of Rome.
The Lusitanians 'he proceeded to organize at once, acting as
their general with full powers, and he brought the neighbouring parts of Spain into subjection' (Plut. *Sert.* 11. 1).

**Metellus.** Q. Caecilius Metellus Pius, son of Q. Metellus
Numidicus (consul in 109). He was praetor in 89, proconsul
in Apulia in 88, where he defeated Q. Pompaedius Silo,
general of the northern group of rebels in the Social War.
Recalled to Rome to support the senate in the civil war
against Marius and Cinna, he abandoned Italy for Africa
when negotiations broke down, and stayed there till 84.
Joining Sulla in Italy after the latter's return in 83, he played
a leading part in Sulla's victory and he was his colleague in
the consulship of 80. As proconsul in farther Spain 79–71 he
was at first unable to cope with Sertorius' guerrilla tactics
(Plut. *Sert.* 12. 6–7); in 75, however, he annihilated
Hirtuleius' army in Lusitania, effectively ending Sertorius'
power in farther Spain and facilitating the combining of his
own force with that of Pompeius in hither Spain. Later in the
same year his victory in the triple battle of Segontia over
Perperna and Sertorius effectively destroyed Sertorius'

capability to meet the enemy in pitched battles. In 74 Metellus operated with Pompeius in the highlands of Celtiberia, where he captured several towns; at the end of the year both Metellus and Pompeius were forced to withdraw from Calagurris with the loss of 3,000 men. Metellus took no part in the 73 campaign against Sertorius.

**informed of their numbers.**   Presumably refers to the size of the forces which Sertorius had been building up and training from the time of his arrival in Lusitania after the defeat of Fufidius. News of Sertorius' re-emergence in the Iberian peninsula will have reached Rome by the late summner of 80; his activities were undoubtedly monitored.

**by letter.**   The departure of Metellus for farther Spain is not clearly indicated in the sources. He was consul in 80; Auct. *Vir. Ill.* 63. 2 says that Metellus operated in Spain as consul. There was nothing in the constitution to prevent consuls from going out to the provinces in their year of office (Balsdon, *JRS* 29 (1939), 58–65) although it was not normally done in this period. Metellus could have left Rome late in 80, arriving in Spain in early 79.

**1. 102–5.**   Metellus' troop strength and details of his strategy after his arrival in Iberia are not mentioned in the sources. Brunt surmised (*Manpower*, 471) that his army, which Appian described as large (*Hisp.* 101) consisted probably of four legions. It must have been fairly soon after his arrival that Metellus dispatched L. Thorius Balbus with an army (probably one legion) against Sertorius (Plut. *Sert.* 12. 4; Flor. 2. 10. 7). The defeat of Balbus probably involved the destruction of his army. Thus Metellus, with a force of three Roman legions, now faced Sertorius who commanded an army larger than the 8,000 men he had brought with him to Spain in 80. It was, however, composed largely of volatile native troops. It was not until he was reinforced in 77 by an Italian army of fifty-three cohorts under Perperna that Sertorius was able to think in terms of pitched battles.

These and other factors conditioned the strategy and tactics of the Spanish campaigns of 79–77. The defeats of Fufidius and Domitius in 80, the loss of Balbus and his army in 79 motivated the methods adopted subsequently by

Metellus. To counter these Sertorius had recourse to the skills of troops knowledgeable in the methods of guerrilla warfare.

Chronology is the besetting problem of the Sertorian War as a whole. However, for the first three years, from Sertorius' return to Spain in 80 down to Pompeius' Spanish command in 77, so little has survived of the Sallustian version that no serious scholarly controversy has been aroused. There is no reason to suppose that the sequence of events given in Plutarch's *Life of Sertorius*, ch. 12, which I have adhered to, is in any way erroneous; the items listed are found in the same order in Orosius and Eutropius. Florus arranges material for its rhetorical effect and is no proper guide to chronology, while Appian ignores nearly all of the events before Pompeius' arrival. In chs. 13–14 of Plutarch's *Life of Sertorius*, which does provide details of the war in Lusitania, there is no satisfactory evidence for the dating of the various episodes.

**1. 102. Setting out . . . the laying of ambushes.** Frontinus provides a clue to the context of this activity and to the identity of the protagonist. Reporting on an incident in the Sertorian War (*Str.* 5. 2. 31), he speaks of *Hispani aptissimi ad furta belli* ('Spaniards best suited to the tricks of war'). The protagonist therefore is Metellus and not, as La Penna suggested (*SIFC* 35 (1963), 28), P. Servilius in his expedition against the pirates.

**for that region.** The strategy now adopted by Metellus was a cautious one, aiming above all at striking the enemy at the sources of their support. He therefore headed for Lusitania. The fragment is part of a general description of the tactics he adopted.

**neither wide-ranging . . . any great speed.** A descriptive statement which emerges from emendation of two corruptions in the Latin version. 'Wide-ranging' arises from Gerlach's emendation of *elate* (the result of dittography *neque (e)late*) to *late*. 'Nor with any great speed' renders Garbugino's *festinus nimis*, his emendation of the meaningless ‡*fetustissimus*‡ (*Stud. Non.* 5 (1978), 79). In 1962 P. Frassinetti produced a conjecture which was palaeographically and contextually appealing—*fretus suis nimis*, 'nor relying too much on his own troops' (*Athenaeum* 40 (1962), 94). I accept G. Garbugino's view that *neque late aut festinus nimis* forms a typically Sallustian *variatio*. It also fits in with Plutarch's description of the distinctly different quality of the opposed armies, a significant factor especially in the reliance by Metellus on tactics appropriate to heavily armed and slow-moving formations, tactics inappropriate against an enemy which relied on speed and surprise (*Sert.* 12. 6–7).

Research into the building activities of Metellus reveals that he built a series of fortified positions north (e.g. Castra Caecilia and Caecilius Vicus) and west (Caeciliana) of Metellinum, which was probably his headquarters in Lusitania (Schulten, 66–9). The sources reveal little concerning the marches undertaken by Metellus. I have more or less followed Schulten's proposal that in 79 Metellus concentrated on campaigns to the north and in 78 on expeditions to the west and south-west; I am not, however, prepared to assert that such an orderly procedure was in fact maintained.

**I. 103. the Tagus was seen to subside.** Refers to a phenomenon not uncommon in Spain. The onset of sudden rainstorms causes immediate flooding of rivers (cf. Caes. *BCiv.* I. 48) which very quickly subside to their normal levels after the rainstorm has passed. Although this fragment is transmitted without book-number, it seems reasonable to assign it to Metellus' northern campaigns, where either the Roman general or Sertorius was at first hindered by a flood but was soon able to proceed with the crossing.

**I. 104.\* He took up a position . . . low trees.** Maurenbrecher accepted de Brosses's view that this probably referred to an ambush set by Sertorius for Aquinus, legatus of Metellus: 'He set an ambush of three thousand men in the road by which Aquinus was to return. These sallied forth from a shady ravine and attacked Aquinus in the rear while Sertorius himself assailed him in front' (Plut. *Sert.* 13. 11).

**I. 105. they did not have time to withdraw.** The Roman troops were taken completely by surprise; some were slain, some taken prisoner, while Aquinus escaped to join Metellus in an ignominious withdrawal.

This ambush was connected with Metellus' attempt to capture the town of Langobriga (Plut. *Sert.* 13. 7–10). This town is in Callaecia, south of the Duris River, near Portus Cale and close to Averro (*Itin. Ant.* 421. 7; A. Tovar, *Iber. Landeskunde* 2. 257–8). Earlier identifications of Langobriga with a Lac(c)obriga on the site of modern Lagos in the extreme south of Portugal (Maurenbrecher on 1. 119M; Schulten, 71) or with the Lac(c)obriga near Olisipo, modern Lisbon (Mommsen, *Hist.* 4. 20; Bieńkowski, *Chronologie*, 156) have been shown to be untenable (P. O. Spann, *TAPA* 111 (1981), 229–35). I have therefore connected these fragments (Maurenbrecher's 120* and 121) with the northern theatre of Metellus' campaigns.

**1. 106. Dipo.** A town about 45 km. west of Emerita on the route to Lisbon. It was probably the first town to be captured in Metellus' campaign in the west and south-west of the peninsula.

**1. 107.\* a heavily fortified town of Lusitania.** The fact that Caeciliana, a fortified position built by Metellus, as the name suggests, was less than 2 km. south-east of Olisipo (modern Lisbon) would support the assumption that the object of Metellus' march was an attack on Olisipo, which had played a leading role in the earlier Spanish wars (Strabo, 3. 3. 1).

**1. 108.\* He came to Conisturgis.** Named by Appian as a large town of the Cunei, Roman citizens who dwelt in the Algarve region of Portugal (*Hisp.* 57, 58); its exact location is not known.

**the leading town of the region.** This fragment, in the form: *ille Conisturgim apud legionis venit* ('he came to Conisturgis to the legions'), was recorded by the grammarian Pompeius to illustrate a solecism—the use of *apud* ('near') with the meaning of *ad* ('to' motion). He also quoted an explanation of the solecism by Asper, a late 2nd-cent. AD commentator on Sallust's *Catiline* and *Histories*. Oronzo Pecere in a detailed treatment (*Omaggio a E. Fraenkel* (1968), 194–9) rejected both Asper's explanation and that of Kritz (fr. *incertae sedis* 70) and maintained that as it stands *apud legionis* cannot be satisfactorily explained. He therefore suggested that *apud legionis* was a corruption of *caput regionis*, a phrase in apposition to Conisturgis. The correction seems acceptable on the grounds of palaeography, Sallustian usage (which Pecere illustrates), and its relevance to the general context.

**1. 109.   At the command . . . a call.**   Maurenbrecher presented this fragment, as 1. 135M, as follows: *Iussu Metelli Celeris cornicines occanuere tubis* ('at the order of Metellus Celer the trumpeters blew on their trumpets'). The grammarians Diomedes and Priscianus do not have *Celeris* or *tubis* in their versions. The *cognomen* is present in a Vatican glossary published by Angelo Mai (*Classici Auctores* (Rome 1828–38) 8. 86). For some reason Maurenbrecher placed more trust in the glossator and accepted Metellus Celer as the commander referred to. Since nothing is known of operations conducted by this Metellus in 78 or 77, Maurenbrecher supposed that this man as quaestor or proquaestor conducted an operation in 78 in some minor war in Macedonia or Asia. Broughton (*MRR* 1. 87) recorded this but with some reservations.

We now know that the glossary published by Mai is that, with the title *Panormia*, composed by Osbern (cf. G. Goetz in *CGL*, 1. 196 ff.). It is practically certain (La Penna, *SIFC* 35 (1963), 29) that these additions are inventions of Osbern, as Goetz, 209, suspected.

The fragment therefore refers to an action which took place during the campaigns of Metellus Pius in Lusitania.

**1. 110–12.**   Plutarch (*Sert.* 12. 6–13. 6) prefaced his narrative of the war waged in Lusitania between Sertorius and Metellus Pius with a short excursus on the character and military expertise of the generals involved. I have assumed that these fragments formed part of a similar exercise by Sallust, on which that of Plutarch was probably based. The brevity and the vagueness of these extant reports make identification of protagonist and action extremely difficult. I hazard possible scenarios since all three have been transmitted with book-number.

**1. 110.   irreproachable in other respects.**   The phrasing indicates that some form of reproach follows. Maurenbrecher assumed censure of Metellus' attitude to and conduct of his unproductive attempt to destroy Sertorius' power base in Lusitania. La Penna (*SFIC* 35 (1963), 29) insinuates that praises such as those of Cicero (*Arch.* 9; *Balb.* 50) are unreliable indicators of Metellus' true worth; moreover there is the difficulty of reconciling the praise expressed in the fragment with the censures against Metellus in 2. 59. K. Büchner, *Sallust* (Heidelberg 1982), 268, maintains that the reservation implied in *alias* ('in other respects') applies to Sertorius; he refers to 1. 88 which he interprets as boasting and glory-seeking on Sertorius' part, and to the charges against which Plutarch defends Sertorius in his *Life of Sertorius*, 10. 5. Spann's rejection of the arguments used by Büchner to support the theory that Sallust, despite his admiration of Sertorius, had grave reservations about his personality and conduct (pp. 221–7) forms a strong argument against the view that this fragment refers to Sertorius. In the absence of clinching evidence it seems that we have to resign ourselves to ignorance.

**1. 111. although driven off . . . lose his confidence.** Despite the caution counselled by La Penna, I agree with Maurenbrecher's attribution of this description to Sertorius: it could refer to his determination to persist with his guerrilla tactics despite the odd setback.

**1. 112. While the gates . . . on the top of the wall.** This fragment is reported in two places by Nonius—282. 22 and 530. 26. Servius, *Aen.* 9. 555, testifies that 'Sertorius raised on shoulders climbed the walls.'

The Nonian citations are corrupt in several places; the translated version is based on a Latin version emended chiefly by Mercier, whose *dein superstantium* ('of those [soldiers] who were by then standing on the top . . .') gives a clearer picture than the jumbled and corrupt *deinsuper adstantium* (282) and *deinsuper stantium* (530) of Nonius.

Plutarch (*Sert.* 14. 6) provides a paraphrase of this action which does little to clarify the technique of the rescue operation (cf. Konrad, 112 ff.). His description does, however, help to decide to what part of Book 1 the fragment is to be assigned. In Plutarch the *calones* (soldiers' servants) of the Sallustian version are specifically identified as Iberians, and he is also using the incident to illustrate the love and admiration aroused in the Lusitanians by the exploits and demeanour of Sertorius.

The campaigns of 79/78 in Lusitania produced little by way of results. Metellus was able to undertake offensive operations along limited and fortified lines of march but Sertorius and his force remained largely intact. On the other hand the guerrilla tactics used by Sertorious were not sufficient permanently to remove the threat posed to his allied cities. The real success story of the period was that of Hirtuleius. After his defeat of Domitius he had advanced into the hither province to consolidate the effects of his victory. In 78 the new governor of hither Spain, Q. Calidius, was more interested in exploiting the provincials than in resisting Hirtuleius' incursions. On his return to Rome Calidius was convicted of extortion (Cic. *Verr*. 1. 38; 2 *Verr*. 3. 63; Ps.-Asc. 219 St.)

**1. 113. A very high hill . . . many defensive works.** Priscianus 3. 66 has 'near Ilerda and . . . defensive works'. As a consequence of Calidius' inertia in dealing with Hirtuleius, the governor of Gallia Transalpina for 78, L. Manlius, intervened in Spain (Liv. *Per*. 90; Plut. *Sert*. 12. 4). Orosius provides the fullest account of this action (5. 23. 4): Manlius brought an army of three legions and 1,500 cavalry—a total estimated at 13,500 (Spann, 86). Nevertheless he was soundly defeated and forced to take refuge in Ilerda. From Sallust's brief description it can be deduced that Hirtuleius had made skilful use of terrain in his victory over an enemy probably superior in numbers; (cf. Caes. *BCiv*. 1. 43).

The whereabouts of Metellus in 77 are unknown to us. Information concerning Sertorius' activity at this time is provided by a fragment of Livy's Book 91 (fr. 22W–M) which covers events of 77 and the winter of 77/76. Sertorius was in a position to extend his authority into hither Spain and win over Celtiberian cities to his alliance, to increase his forces for the coming struggle with Pompeius. Hirtuleius he sent south to protect the allied cities there and, presumably, to keep an eye on Metellus' movements. In Celtiberia he subdued many cities (Liv. *Per.* 91), was joined some time during the summer by M. Perperna and his army, and after a successful siege of Contrebia retired into winter-quarters.

**1. 114. Sertorius had transformed ... naval base.** Nonius, 206. 19, has 'that pirate emporium'. Sertorius' strategy for the spring of 76 included sending M. Perperna to patrol the southern part of the east coast of the peninsula (Liv. fr. 22W–M). The most important port on this part of the coast was Dianium; this fragment may form part of Sallust's description of Sertorius' intention in 77 to use this port for reception of supplies and reinforcements. His use of Dianium goes back to 81, when he teamed up with Cilician pirates after his expulsion from Spain (see note on 1. 82–92). The work of adaptation and fortification may have extended over a long period in 78.

**1. 115\*–121.** (78–77 BC) The final narrative section of Book 1 deals with the expedition of P. Servilius Vatia against the Cilician pirates (1. 115–19) and the Thracian War waged by Appius Claudius (1. 120–1). This would have been quite a short section since both generals were not actively engaged until the campaigning season of 77. The active service of Appius Claudius was brief; the war conducted by Servilius covered three years, so that the narrative of his campaigns is resumed in Book 2 (2. 63–9).

**1. 115.\* Servilius.** P. Servilius Vatia (Isauricus), consul in 79, was appointed proconsul of Cilicia in 78 with the task of bringing under control southern Asia Minor, the coasts of which were infested by pirates whose fleets posed a threat to Roman supremacy. (Cic. *2 Verr.* 3. 210–11; Liv. *Per.* 90 and 93; Suet. *Iul.* 3; Eutrop. 6. 3; Oros. 5. 23. 21–2). Eutropius and Orosius refer to his campaigns as a three-year war; H. A. Ormerod (*JRS* 12 (1922), 38) was probably correct in assuming that the year 78 was given over to preparations (cf. Flor. 1. 41. 4), while the main operations were carried out in 77–75. Cf. Magie, 1. 287–90; 2. 1167–73 nn. 17–25.

**sick colleague.** Appius Claudius Pulcher, colleague of Servilius in the consulship of 79. See note on 1. 67. 22, **App. Claudius.** He did not arrive in Macedonia until sometime in 77. He carried out a successful war against the Thracian

tribes who were threatening the security of the province of
Macedonia. In 76 he fell ill and died. (Liv. *Per.* 91; Flor. 1.
39. 6; Eutrop. 6. 2. 1; Oros. 5. 23. 17–19).

**1. 116.\*  overlooking the lands of Lycia and Pisidia.**
Servilius' campaign in 77 opened with a naval victory near
the Chelidonian Islands (Strabo 14. 3. 3; Flor. 1. 41. 4;
*OGIS* 552). He then turned his efforts to the suppression of
Zenicetes, robber chieftain of eastern Lycia. The fragment
refers to the mountain fortress from which Zenicetes
dominated the adjacent coasts and plains.

A mountain near the town Olympus which Maurenbrecher
maintained as the one being referred to is described by
Strabo as 'a mountain of the same name which . . . is also
called Phoenicus' (14. 3. 8) and evidently refers to modern
Musa Dagh south of the city. In his description of the
stronghold of Zenicetes (14. 5. 7) Strabo says: 'I mean
Olympus, both mountain and fortress, whence are visible all
Lydia and Pamphylia and Pisidia and Milyas.' This description
cannot apply to Musa Dagh (1000 m.) but rather to Tachtali
Dagh (2,400 m.) near the coast further north, from which
there would be a more panoramic view, a mountain more
likely to have been given the venerated name Olympus
(Ormerod *JRS* 12 (1922), 40–1; H. A. Ormerod, *Piracy in
the Ancient World* (Liverpool 1969), 271; cf. Magie, 2. 1169
n. 19). This latter identification has been regarded as
probable by W. Ruge, *RE* 18. 319–20.

**1. 117.  towards Olympus and Phaselis.**   The operation on
Tachtali Dagh which ended with the capture of the fortress
and suicide of Zenicetes (Strabo, 14. 5. 7) was followed by
the capture of the coastal towns Olympus, Phaselis, Corycus
(Cic. *2 Verr.* 1. 56, 4. 21; Eutropius 6. 3 (where *Ciliciae*
should be deleted); Oros. 5. 23. 22; Ps.-Asc. 237 St.). The
wavering regions of Pamphylia were recovered and the
people of Attaleia were punished by confiscation of territory
(Cic. *Leg. Agr.* 1. 5, 2. 50).

**1. 118–19.  Corycus.**   In both fragments *Corycus* is part of
the same context in Priscianus' citation and is probably part
of the same segment of narrative. La Penna, *SIFC* 35 (1963),
mentions the possibility of duplication on Priscianus' part or

a dittography in the tradition of his text. Maurenbrecher's note ad loc. has more relevance to his 2. 81M (see note on my 2. 63).

**1. 120–1. the town of Lete.** In Macedonia. The reference is to Appius Claudius' activity in defending his province from incursions by Thracian tribes. There is no way of determining which of the leaders had suffered the repulse (121).

**1. 122–38.** The brevity and the repetitive technical nature of the majority of these fragments *incertae sedis* of Book 1 justify their relegation to this section. I comment only on the few for which a more definite location has been suggested by earlier editors.

**1. 122. rejected those ⟨practices⟩.** The Latin version simply has *ea* ('those things') which I have rendered as 'practices'. Maurenbrecher thought in terms either of a speech of the *Histories* or an opinion expressed by Sallust himself; he preferred the former. La Penna advances the attractive conjecture that Sallust was speaking of specific vices in contemporary oratorical and historiographical practice from which only a few people were exempt. To this he added the fragment reported by van den Hout in his edition of Fronto's *Epistulae*, 143. 19 ff. which I have included as fr. 1 of Fragments of Uncertain Reference (Vol. 2). La Penna suggested that both might well have been part of the prologue in which Sallust, praising and defining the function of historiography, compares it against an eloquence which is gloomy and degenerate (*SFIC* 35 (1963) 21).

**1. 123. ⟨city⟩ . . . devoid of men of military age.** The Latin original is corrupt: *vacuum istum urbibus aetate*. The version I have translated is Lindemann's correction of the above to: *vacuam istam urbem hominibus militari aetate*. Keil suggested *vacuum istum laboribus militaris aetatis*: '[that] the man in question was exempt from the burden of military service'.

Most editors have accepted reference to a city. Gerlach suggested an opinion of Lepidus as he was about to attack Rome; Kritz, an attack on the Spanish town of Castulo.

Maurenbrecher, who put the fragment into his text as
1. 40M, offered the more attractive conjecture, based on
App. *BC* 1. 92, that it was an opinion expressed by Samnites
to the commanders Damasippus, Carrinas, and Marcius
Censorinus before their desperate attack on Rome in 82
(see note on 1. 32). The suggestion also justified Maurenbrecher's placing of the fragment *Samnitium*, transmitted
without book-number, as 1. 39* of the text; I have relegated
this latter fragment to Fragments of Uncertain Reference in
Vol. 2.

The corrupt state of the Latin version, the fact that we
cannot even be certain if a city is the topic under discussion
would support the transferring of the fragment to this
section.

**1. 124. in two minds.** This is fragment 1. 41 in Maurenbrecher's edition; he couples it with his 1. 42 which refers to
the panic exhibited by the Sullan troops during the battle
of the Colline Gate (see note on 1. 31). An attractive
suggestion, but in its existing form the fragment could apply
to any one of several military crises in Book 1.

**1. 126. chose a location.** Servius Aen. 8. 127 has also
preserved this fragment, but without 'chose'. Neither transmission gives compelling support to de Brosses's view that
the reference was to Catulus after his victory over Lepidus at
Cosa (see note on 1. 71).

**1. 128. without pausing . . . against the town.** Kritz rightly
dismissed the contention of de Brosses and Gerlach that this
referred to Metellus hastening to attack Lacobriga (see note
on 1. 105). Plutarch's *Sert.* 13. 7, on which this view was
based, is not precise enough to support its acceptance.

**1. 135. deserted tracks.** Relying on the quite generalized
description of Plutarch's *Sert.* 13, Maurenbrecher daringly
put this into his text as 1. 117M, as part of Sallust's treatment
of Sertorius' character.

**1. 136. immoderate . . . feelings.** Attributed by Büchner
(*Sallust*, n. 184) to Sertorius on the basis of the Sabine's
unrestrained expressions of grief over his mother's death
(Plut. *Sert.* 22. 10–11). But, as Spann, 226, points out, this

identification could be countered with several alternative candidates, e.g. Sulla or Marius, known to be of such a temperament.

**I. 139. the defective forms.** 'Archaic' or 'earlier' forms might be more precise. Phocas, 436. 5, has 'One may read *quaesere* in Sallust and Tullius [Cicero].' The form *quaeso* appears in *Hist.* 1. 67. 13, 2. 98. 8, and 3. 48. 13; *quaesit* in *Hist.* 1. 86; *quaesitur* in *Hist.* 4. 69. 1. Apart from this reference the infinitive *quaesere* has not been preserved in any extant fragment. The normal forms *quaero, quaerere*, etc. occur about twice as often as the rarer forms.

## BOOK 2

**2. 1–20.** (77 BC) Sallust begins by taking up the narrative of the events of 77 which were left unfinished in Book 1. He precedes his treatment of Lepidus' failure and death in Sardinia with an excursus on the geography, ethnography, and mythical history of the Roman province Sardinia–Corsica (2. 1–13). Only one fragment with probable reference to the last phase of the Lepidan insurrection has been preserved (2. 14); the remaining fragments (2. 15–20) have to do with Pompeius' appointment to take over from Metellus Pius as supreme commander of the Roman forces in hither Spain.

**2. 1.\* the geography of the island.** Transmitted without book-number. Editors have referred it to Sardinia. Dietsch mentioned the possibility of a reference to Crete on which there is an excursus in Book 3. La Penna (*SIFC* 35 (1962), 31) considered Dietsch's alternative suggestion the more likely but his argument is not a compelling one.

**2. 2. the African Sea** Separating Africa from Sicily and Sardinia.

**the shape of a human foot.** Nonius, 53. 1, gives a garbled version of this description. It occurs also in other sources which deal with Sardinia—Sil. *Pun.* 12. 357; Paus. 10. 17. 2; Isid. *Etym.* 14. 6. 39; Claudian, *Bell. Gild.* 507.

**2. 3.\*    Sandaliotis in Timaeus.**    Sandaliotis, a name derived from the Greek σάνδαλον a wooden sole. Timaeus (*c.*356–260 BC) wrote a book primarily concerned with the origins and history of Sicily. Maurenbrecher (2. 59 n.) accepted Müllenhoff's conclusions that Timaeus was an important source of Sallust's ethnographical narrative. This view has been contested, e.g. by E. Lepore, *Athenaeum* 28 (1950), 289 ff.

**Ichnusa in Crispus.**    Silius Italicus (*Pun.* 12. 357–8) gives a fuller account: 'The land within its borders is irregular in shape, resembling the sole of a naked foot. Hence it was called Ichnusa ⟨from ἴχνος, footprint⟩ by the first colonists from Greece.' Cf. Paus. 10. 172; Isid. *Etym.* 14. 6. 39; Pliny, *NH* 3. 85, attributes the first reporting of this name to Myrsilus, a historian of Lesbos interested in early migrations.

Silius goes on to provide material which is no longer extant in Sallust's treatment: 'But afterwards Sardus, proud of his descent from the Libyan Hercules, named it afresh after himself.' (*Pun.* 12. 359–60). Pausanias and Isidorus make it clear that Sardus was the leader of a colonizing mission from Libya.

**2. 4.\*    one cause of invasions was sea-voyaging.**    Influenced by the context within which Servius made this statement, Kritz and Gerlach tied it exclusively to the Trojans' wanderings after the fall of their city. Maurenbrecher, without comment, places it, as 2. 9M, in close conjunction with 2. 8M which deals with the Trojan wanderings.

My placement of 2. 4 and 2. 5 assumes a general application to the various immigrations which Sardinia and Corsica experienced. There is no definitive version of the sequence of the colonizing process. The sources which deal with ethnography agree in general on the ethnic origins of the immigrants, but their order of narration differs.

**2. 6.\*    of Geryon.**    Solinus (4. 1) puts the order of colonization as follows: 'When Sardus, son of Hercules, and Norax, son of Mercury, the former from Libya, the latter from as far as Tartessus in Spain (fr. 2. 7), passed over into these lands, Sardus gave his name to the island, Norax his name to the town of Nora.' Pausanias (10. 17. 4) elucidates:

'They say Norax was the son of Hermes [Mercury] by Eurytheia daughter of Geryon.'

**2. 8.\* the son of Apollo and Cyrene.** That this was Aristaeus is confirmed by Servius, *G.* 1. 14 and the scholiast (Schol. Bern.) on *G.* 4. 238. Servius goes on to say that, according to Sallust, Aristaeus left Thebes after the death of his son Actaeon and first landed on the island of Ceos and subsequently crossed over to Sardinia with Daedalus. On the colonizing expedition to Sardinia see Sil. *Pun.* 12. 367–9; Paus. 10. 17. 3; Solin. 4. 2. Solinus adds that Aristaeus founded the city of Coralis and ruled peaceably over a mixed population.

**2. 9. to Iolaus.** This is from fragment (2) of the Rylands Papyrus 473, published in 1938. I have consulted C. H. Roberts's notes to the text. Strabo's account of the settlement of Sardinia states that Iolaus led to the island Thespians, descendants of Hercules, who were consequently called Ioläes. They were identified with the Ilienses, the people of Ilium (Troy)—*RE* 9. 1062 and 1846. In Sardinia they built Olbia and other Greek towns (Paus. 10. 17. 4; Solin. 1. 61).

**The Balari . . . the Corsicans.** Pausanias (10. 17. 4) explains: 'Not far from Sardinia lies an island the Greeks call Cyrnos, but the Libyans who live there call it Corsica. Quite a large number left there for political reasons and came to Sardinia, where they took over part of the mountains as their home. The Sardinians call them by their home name, Corsicans. When the Carthaginians were very strong at sea they reduced everyone in Sardinia except the Ilians and the Corsicans . . . Some Libyans or Iberians from the Carthaginian allied forces got into a quarrel about spoils of war and marched off in a fury; they too went to live among the island heights. In the Cyrnian language they are called the Balari, which is the Cyrnian word for fugitives.'

**Pallantians.** From Pallantia in Hispania Tarraconnensis, one of the towns of the Vaccaei. Since an alternative identification of the Balari with Spaniards also occurs in the fragment, Roberts could find no satisfactory explanation as to why the Pallantians should be distinguished from other Spaniards. Moreover ⟨*Pa*⟩*llanteos* in the Latin version is conjectural. Roberts suggested that the scribe wrote ⟨*At*⟩*llanteos* for *Atlanteos*, referring to tribes living in the neighbourhood of the Atlas Mountains. Lepore, *Athenaeum* 28 (1950), takes the view that Sallust's source deliberately used *Pallanteos* and not the blanket term Iberians as in Pausanias precisely because they were Celtiberians and because he knew of a version according to which the Balari were fugitives from Pallantia. Lepore produces this detail as proof of his main thesis that Posidonius and not Timaeus was the principal source of Sallust's version.

**in the Celtiberian war . . .** Could be part of a reference to Pallantia's participation in the Celtiberian War (151–133) against Rome; if so, it would strengthen Lepore's interpretation.

**Daedalus . . . ⟨and power⟩ of Minos.** The citation from Priscianus, 2. 255, used by Maurenbrecher for his 2. 7M, provides the full version of this sentence. The words ⟨and power⟩ are missing from the Latin text of the papyrus fragment.

The myth of Daedalus includes the story of his stay in Crete where his skill as a craftsman won him the friendship of Minos. But he fell foul of the king, was imprisoned, and managed to escape by fashioning wings for himself and his son Icarus. Pausanias (10. 17. 3) maintains that on chronological grounds Daedalus could not have participated in Aristaeus' Sardinian settlement.

**2. 10.\* others . . . settled in Sardinia.** The influx of Trojan refugees into Sardinia is mentioned also in Sil. *Pun.* 12. 361–2 and Paus. 10. 17. 4.

**2. 11. country rich in crops and fodder.** This fragment is repeated in Servius, *Aen.* 1. 441; Servius Dan. *Aen.* 11. 338. Maurenbrecher placed it, as 2. 83M, in the context of Servilius Vatia's campaign against the Isaurians and suggested a reference to one of the lands adjacent to the Taurus mountain range. My placement of it is influenced by La Penna's observations in *RFIC* 99 (1971), 61–2. He points to a hitherto unnoticed passage in Claudius Claudianus (*Bell. Gild.* 507–24) which (509) describes Sardinia as *dives ager frugum* ('a land rich in crops') a description very similar to that of Sallust in this fragment (*frugum pabulique laetus ager*) and in the description of Numidia in *Iug.* 17. 5: *ager frugum fertilis, bonus pecori*. That Claudianus almost certainly imitated Sallust's description of Sardinia seems to be confirmed by his description of the configuration of the island as a footprint (507) and an indication that in contrast to the fertility of the land the climate was unhealthy and pestiferous (514–15; cf. Sil. *Pun.* 12. 371 ff.; Pompon. 2. 123).

**2. 12.*   a plant similar to balm.**   Receives mention also in Paus. 10. 17.7; Solin. 4. 3; Isid. *Etym.* 14. 6. 10.

**2. 13.   a bull . . . Corsa used to tend.**   Isidorus supports his statement that inhabitants of Liguria were the first settlers of Corsica by quoting the legend of Corsa and the bull (*Etym.* 14. 6. 41). This animal was in the habit of swimming away from the herd and returning after an interval, obviously much better nourished than the rest of the herd. Corsa followed the bull on one of his trips and discovered the island that was the bull's feeding ground. She reported on its fertility; the Ligurians settled there and called the island Corsica in her honour.

Corsica receives mention in Solinus and the younger Seneca. Solinus simply confirms Isidorus' statement that Ligurians were the first settlers on the island. Seneca, *Helv.* 6. 5, paints a grim picture of the harshness of the topography and climate of the island and the barrenness of its soil. The fact that he lived in exile on Corsica may have some bearing on his description of it. His treatment of the ethnography (*Helv.* 7. 8–10) deals with (i) a temporary settlement of Phocaeans on the way to found Massilia (Marseilles); (ii) an immigration by Ligurians; (iii) an immigration by Spaniards; (iv) the effect on the language of the islanders of their intercourse with the Greeks and Ligurians; (v) the foundation of two Roman colonies, one by Marius, the other by Sulla. In a third passage (9. 1) he gives detail of the paucity of agricultural produce and mineral deposits.

**2. 14.   to Tarrhi.**   A town on the west coast of Sardinia (Tharros). The fragment is repeated by Probus at 27 and by Sacerdos, 473. de Brosses identified it as the port to which

Lepidus sailed on his voyage from Cosa. Kritz conjectured that the town received mention in the geographical excursus. I follow Maurenbrecher in assuming that it played some part in the fighting between Lepidus and C. Valerius Triarius, the governor of Sardinia.

The final phase of the Lepidan revolt receives scant notice in most of the sources. The most extensive is that of Exuperantius (40. 41Z): 'and there he fought in several fierce battles against the propraetor Triarius. The latter, by skilfully protecting his province, brought Lepidus' plan to naught; for, prevented by defensive works from sacking towns, Lepidus was unable to carry out his strategy and while he was in the midst of alternative measures he was affected by a fatal disease and died.' The other sources merely report his death (Liv. *Per.* 90; Plin. *NH* 7. 122 and 186; Plut. *Pomp.* 16. 9; App. *BC* 1. 107; Flor. 2. 11. 7), the only point of interest being the differences in the alleged cause of death. Despite the general agreement of the sources, M. E. Deutsch (*U. Calif. Publ. Class. Phil.* 5 (1918), 59–68) on flimsy evidence deduced from Cic. *Cat.* 3. 24 and Suet. *Iul.* 5. 2 argued that Lepidus met a violent end. Cf. Criniti, *Lepidus*, 445 ff. with notes.

**2. 15.   banished from the [Roman] world.**   Undoubtedly refers to the proscribed adherents of the *popularis* cause. It may have been applied to the followers of Lepidus in general or, more probably, to the quite large contingent which, on the death of Lepidus, accompanied Perperna on his flight from Sardinia to Spain (Plut. *Sert.* 15. 1; App. *BC* 1. 107–8; Exup. 42Z).

**2. 16–22.**   (77 BC) This segment deals with the transfer of the command against Sertorius in Spain from Metellus Pius to Pompeius Magnus. The narrative of Pompeius' subsequent career is preceded by a character-sketch of the young general. For a general statement on Sallust's treatment of Pompeius see Introd. section 6.

**2. 16.   in their gossip . . . they were destroying.**   Comparing this statement with the content of Plut. *Sert.* 25. 4 which deals with a conspiracy against Sertorius, de Brosses suggested that the target of denigration was Sertorius. This identification was accepted by later commentators, but Maurenbrecher maintained that since the fragment is transmitted with book-number and the material in *Sert.* 25 refers to events dealt with by Sallust in his Book 3 the person under attack must be Metellus Pius. The fragment is thus part of an introduction to the portrait of Pompeius; Metellus, victim of pro-Pompeian propaganda, becomes the object of negative evaluation in Rome.

Modern critics have rejected Maurenbrecher's solution; they have not, however, been able satisfactorily to dispose of two problems: the clear transmission of book-number and what that entails; the style and emphasis of the content of the fragment.

It has been shown (A. K. Frihagen, *SO* 50 (1975), 149–53; G. Maggiulli, *Stud. Non.* 6 (1981), 117–22) that 6–7 per cent of Nonian citations have been transmitted with incorrect book-number. Careful research has stressed that the judgement that an error is present can be accepted only where other writers have cited the fragment with a different book-number. Moreover, Maurenbrecher's conviction that Book 2 dealt only with events which did not extend much beyond the year 75 is confirmed by the Fleury MS (Introd. section 4 (*a*)). It is highly unlikely, therefore, that reference was made at this point to events dealt with in 3. 79–81. Kritz's view that Sertorius was the object of attack led him to supply an object for the verb 'destroyed'. He proposed 'the army' or 'the good reputation of Sertorius'. Because of the transmitted book-number both he and La Penna placed the fragment among those of uncertain placement of Book 2.

Decision concerning the identity of the person under attack has to be based on a convincing interpretation of the content of the fragment. O. Pecere (*RFIC* 104 (1976), 399–417) supported his selection of Sertorius with the assumption that mention of *secunda* ('successes') in addition to *adversa* ('reverses') fits in better with the military career of Sertorius; that the wording and arrangement of material of the fragment indicates a strong defence by Sallust against the criticism levelled at Sertorius. To strengthen his case he proposed to change *fortunam* (luck in warfare) of the third clause into *fortia* (brave deeds) to preserve concinnity with the neuter plural adjectives *adversa* and *secunda* of the preceding clauses. The consequent laudatory effect would support the correctness of the reference to Sertorius; it would also suggest but not confirm a context for the fragment—a denigratory campaign against Sertorius forming part of the propaganda fanfare which celebrated Pompeius' crossing of the Alps and his entry into Spain (Plut. *Pomp.* 18. 1; *Sert.* 18. 3–4). Pecere, however, followed La Penna in recommending placement of the fragment among those of uncertain placement of Book 2.

Pecere's argument for changing *fortunam* to *fortia* has been convincingly refuted by M. Scarsi, *Stud. Non.* 7 (1982), 239–45. In fact the substitution would entail a double paradox: inconcinnity is a prominent feature of Sallustian style, and *fortia facta* (deeds of bravery), an element of the *nobilis* tradition, would fit in better with Metellus than with Sertorius.

Scarsi, however, also favours a reference to Sertorius on the grounds that the military operations of Metellus deserved the label 'failures' and hence there was no need to resort to denigration. In her view the fragment forms part of a continuation of the Sallustian polemic against the *invidia scriptorum* who had denigrated Sertorius' exploits in the period preceding 80 BC by totally ignoring them. See notes on 1. 77.

The critics and in a sense Maurenbrecher himself have foundered on the assumption that the statement refers only to the years 79–78. My contention that the target was indeed Metellus Pius and that the fragment forms part of a report on the transfer of the Spanish command to Pompeius is based on the view that its wording covers the whole military career of the person under attack. Metellus, described as 'the greatest Roman of his time and held in highest repute' (Plut. *Sert.* 12. 5) had an extensive and variegated military career which involved victories in the Social War and a leading role in Sulla's victorious campaign in Italy in 83 and 82 (App. *BC* 1. 81, 84–8, 91–2; Dio, 30–5 fr. 106; Vell. Pat. 2. 28. 1; Plut. *Sull.* 28. 8; Oros. 5. 20. 5 and 7). See note on 1. 101, **Metellus.** The combination of the fear inspired by Sertorius' influence in Spain, the ambition of Pompeius, and the lack of Roman success in the first two years of the war provided strong material for the propaganda of Pompeius' supporters, and brought about the change in command.

**2. 17. noble of countenance, shameless in character.** The phrase *os probum*, derived from Varro (Syme, *Sallust*, 206 and n. 118) was used by Pliny, *NH* 7. 53, 37. 14 concerning the handsome looks of Pompeius, a feature remarked upon by several writers, notably Plutarch (*Pomp.* 2. 1). Seneca, *Ep.* 11. 4: 'Pompeius had the most sensitive cast of countenance; he always blushed in the presence of a gathering', adds a second aspect to the expression *os probum*—it places emphasis on the gentleness, dignity, modesty of the young man; the latter feature also figures in fr. 18 below (*modestus ad alia omnia*).

To this complimentary phrase Sallust added, in Syme's words, a damaging appendage—*animo inverecundo*—to produce a judgement which aroused savage indignation in Pompeius' freedman, Lenaeus, and which recalls the chiastic pungency of the historian's comment on Catiline: *satis eloquentiae, sapientiae parum* (*Cat.* 5. 3).

**2. 18. moderate . . . except in his thirst for power.** A careful wording: not an entirely negative picture, but this form of historical objectivity achieves Sallust's aim of stressing the factor he considered most dangerous to the state—the unscrupulous ambition of Pompeius. Caesar is more direct: 'urged on . . . by his desire that no one should be on the same level of authority with himself' (*BCiv.* 1. 4. 4). The statement of Velleius (2. 29. 3): 'in peace a citizen of temperate conduct except when he feared a rival' combines both elements of Pompeius' drive for power.

**2. 19.\* he had nevertheless . . . behaved insultingly.** A fragment cited also by Servius, *Aen.* 9. 631 and 10. 643. Editors have proposed a variety of candidates to which it could refer: Cethegus (de Brosses); Marcius Philippus (Gerlach); Licinius Macer (Dietsch); Pompeius (Kritz). Maurenbrecher placed it as 2. 23M in the section dealing with urban affairs in 76 and applied it to L. Sicinius, the turbulent tribune of that year. I follow Kritz in applying it to

Pompeius; see La Penna, *SIFC* 35 (1963), 33; Syme, 202 n.
97. Kritz put it in among Fragments of Uncertain Reference;
I believe this present context is appropriate.

   Valerius Maximus (6. 2. 8) tells the story of the aged
Helvius Mancia, a freedman's son who was prosecuting L.
Libo before the censors. In the course of the trial Pompeius
reproached Helvius with his humble birth and old age,
saying that he had been sent from the underworld to accuse
the defendant. The old man's spirited reply dwelt on
excesses of Pompeius' early career: 'I do indeed come from
the underworld . . . there I saw the bloody Gnaeus Domitius
Ahenobarbus . . . killed in the very prime of his youth on
your orders (see note on 1. 44–6). I saw Marcus Brutus . . .
complaining that his fate was first due to your treachery and
then to your cruelty (see notes on 1. 67. 7, 69 and 70). I saw
Gnaeus Carbo, the fiercest protector of your boyhood and
your father's property in his third consulship, bound in
chains . . . and protesting that contrary to all laws of right
and wrong, he had been slaughtered by you' (see note on
1. 44*).

   Appian's account indicates the deep feeling aroused in
Pompeius' contemporaries by the young general's cruelly
insulting treatment of Carbo: 'He ordered his officers to kill
all of the other [persons of distinction] without bringing
them into his presence; but Carbo, "the three times consul",
he ordered to be brought before his feet in chains, and after
making a public harangue at him, murdered him and sent his
head to Sulla' (*BC* 1. 96).

**2. 20.   He used to compete . . . .**   The combination of this
quite objective description of the dedication of a man who
wanted to emulate Alexander the Great (see note on 3. 86)
and the conduct described in the preceding fragment shows
again the way in which historiographical objectivity can be
used to emphasize less creditable aspects which are also
objectively presented, even if they are sometimes mis-
interpreted or dismissed.

**2. 21.   the tribune . . . by previous arrangment . . . vetoed a
law . . . concerning his return.**   Commonly interpreted as
referring to a law proposed by the consul Sulla concerning

Pompeius' return from Africa in 80 BC; thus, Maurenbrecher on 2. 21M; M. Gelzer, *Vom. röm. Staat* 2. 96 and n. 221; Broughton, *MRR* 2. 80; Smith, *Phoenix* 14 (1960), 1–13. Badian (*Hermes* 83 (1955), 107–18 argues that the fragment refers to the law by which Q. Pompeius Rufus superseded Cn. Pompeius Strabo in his command in 88 BC. He raises two constitutional points against the later date: (i) a *privilegium* was unnecessary to recall a commander; (ii) it is very doubtful if the Sullan legislation left tribunes the right to veto laws.

In *Hermes* 89 (1961), 254–6 Badian dealt with objections to his view. Broughton, *MRR* Suppl. 47, maintained that the phrase in Gellius 10. 20. 10: *de Cn. Pompei reditu* ('concerning the return of Cn. Pompeius') naturally refers to Pompeius Magnus. Badian's counter is not convincing: already in his earlier article (112 n. 6) he maintained that the *cognomen* Strabo rarely appears in the sources, and provided four examples: Liv. *Per.* 77; Val. Max 9. 7 ext. 2; App. *BC* 1. 63; Vell. Pat. 2. 20. 1. In all of these Cn. Pompeius, in two cases called proconsul, is mentioned in conjuction with Q. Pompeius, consular colleague of Sulla in 88; the identification is therefore certain even without the *cognomen*. In his reply to Broughton (254) Badian states that the nature of Gellius' lexical note made precise identification immaterial; he himself seems to have realized (255) that this reply was not sufficient to counter what he acknowledged was a telling objection. His cursory reply to points raised by Smith (*Phoenix* 14 (1960), 10–12) is also unsatisfactory, in particular his cavalier rejection of the view expressed by Adcock and Smith, with which I agree, that it is unlikely that in a portrait of Pompeius which belongs to Book 2, reference would be made to a detail in the career of Pompeius Strabo.

Badian, however, is correct in his view that whatever the reference of the fragment, both its content and Gellius' introduction are not sufficient to provide secure interpretation of an incident not recorded elsewhere.

Gellius calls Sulla's measure a *privilegium*, a legislative measure relating to a specific individual, which implies that here Sulla was proposing to exempt Pompeius to either his benefit or his detriment from an existing law, which was most likely the Cornelian law *de provinciis ordinandis* (Rotondi, *Leges Publicae*, 353). However, Gellius' criticism of Sallust for calling what was really a *privilegium* a *lex* is misconceived; he is using *privilegium* in the sense imperial jurists gave it (so J. Bleicken, *Lex publica* (Munich 1975), pp. 214 ff.). Acceptance of Gellius' view has given rise to some curious interpretations such as that of Maurenbrecher: Sulla, suspicious of Pompeius' intentions, concealed his doubts and proposed a law in favour of Pompeius' return with his army, forbidden by the Cornelian law, but arranged for Herennius to block its passge by *intercessio* (veto) or *obnuntiatio* (announcement of unfavourable omens).

The phrase *ex composito* ('by previous arrangement') does not make clear which were the parties involved. Given the probability (Badian, *Hermes* 83 (1955), 111 n. 4) that Herennius belonged to the *popularis* family from Picenum, the Pompeian stamping-ground, it seems to me more likely that Pompeius had arranged beforehand with the tribune to thwart, by whatever means, the passage of a law inimical to Pompeian interests.

**2. 22. at Narbonne . . . assembly of the Gauls.** This meeting at Narbonne, a city of Gallia Narbonenis, the southern province of Transalpine Gaul, took place in the course of Pompeius' journey to Spain to take up command against Sertorius. The date of his arrival in Spain is a matter of dispute (see notes on 2. 26–31). I accept the view that Pompeius spent the winter of 77 in Gaul and entered Spain early in 76. The object of the meeting referred to above was probably to devise a means of ensuring that the unrest in Gallia Narbonensis which Pompeius had quelled would not break out again. See note on 2. 82. 5, **I recovered Gaul.**

**2. 23–5.** Deal with urban political events in 76. The consuls for the year were Cn. Octavius and C. Scribonius Curio. The year was marked by the attempts of the tribune Cn. Sicinius to have the powers of the tribunate restored, a campaign opposed by the consul Curio (Cic. *Brut.* 216; Ps.-Asc. 189 St.).

**2. 23. He used to call him Burbuleius.** The consul Curio is certified as the butt of this joke by Val. Max. 9. 14. 5; cf.

Plin. *NH* 7. 55. The derider was probably the tribune Sicinius: Cicero, who describes him as a man 'of coarse but hilarious wit', gives an example of Sicinius' reaction to Curio's habit of reeling and swaying his whole body while making a speech (*Brut.* 217; cf. Quint. *Inst.* 11. 3. 129).

This fragment suggests that Sallust's treatment of Curio was a fairly detailed one. Curio had a variegated, even distinguished career. Tribune in 90, legate to Sulla in Greece in 86 (Plut. *Sull.* 14. 11; App. *Mith.* 39), in 85 he was given the task of restoring Nicomedes of Bithynia and Ariobarzanes of Cappadocia to their thrones (App. *Mith.* 60; cf. Gran. Lic. 35. 83C; Flor. 1. 40. 12). Praetor in 80, he proceeded towards the end of his consulship as proconsul to Macedonia where he served from 75 to 72. He may have been censor in 61 (*MRR* 2. 179) and was a member of the pontifical college from 60 to 53.

He receives mention in Sallust also at 1. 75, 2. 60, and in 3. 93–4. It is, however, not likely that Sallust had much personal praise for a man who had enriched himself during the Sullan proscriptions (Ps.-Asc. 89 St.).

**2. 24.   his colleague Octavius . . . suffering from gout.**   This fragment has been transmitted with book-number 3. Kritz consequently placed it among urban affairs of 73 (3. 83K); the possibility of a back reference to the urban affairs of 76 is a reasonable one, given Macer's outburst: 'Gaius Curio played the despot to the extent of ruining a guiltless tribune' (3. 36. 10). However, I follow Maurenbrecher, de Brosses, and Dietsch in assuming that III is an error for II, and assigning it directly to the urban affairs of 76.

**2. 25.   cease from pursuing that course of action.**   Both Kritz and Dietsch interpreted this as an attempt either to prevent a tribune from arousing the commons in assembly or to persuade an accuser not to proceed with a lawsuit. Maurenbrecher's application of it to the opposition of Curio to Sicinius' agitation concerning the tribunate seems a reasonable one.

**2. 26–34.**   Deal with events of the Sertorian War in 76. The order of events in this war from Pompeius' arrival in Spain to the death of Sertorius can be fairly reliably established on the evidence available. Lack of precise dating for specific events is, however, a serious problem. Only one event of this war can be dated with absolute certainty—Pompeius' letter written in late 75 and read in the senate in January 74 (2. 82 pt. D).

The traditional chronological framework—76–72 BC—for this five-year campaign period has been challenged over recent decades: R. Grispo (*Nov. Riv. Stor.* 36 (1952), 200–10) and Frassinetti (*Stud. Urb.* 49 (1975), 381–98) have argued for dating Pompeius' arrival in Spain and the battle of Lauro to 77, the battles of Valentia, the Sucro, and Segontia to 76, but have retained the traditional dates for the rest of the war. Bennett (*Historia*, 10 (1961), 459–72) and Spann, 116–18) have argued for 73 as the date of Sertorius' assassination, yet have retained the traditional chronology for the preceding years. Konrad, noting that the allocation of a different starting or ending point for the period must involve change in the traditional chronological framework, devoted a long appendix, 257–305) to supporting his contention that the period must be 77–73.

This is not the place to dilate on this topic; no unassailable case for change has been presented; see Scardigli, *Athenaeum*, 49 (1971), 259–70; G. Perl, 'Zur Chronologie der Königs-reiche Bythynia, Pontos und Bosporus', in *Studien zur Geschichte und Philosophie des Altertums* (Amsterdam 1968), 319. I have therefore followed Maurenbrecher's general order of the events and indicated where I have disagreed with him on details.

By the end of 77 Sertorius was master of Spain from the Sierra Morena to the Pyrenees. On the east coast between Nova Carthago (Cartagena) and the Ebro the only towns holding out against him were Lauro and Saguntum. Dianium was his naval stronghold and harboured his allies, the Cilician pirates. The second phase of the war opened with a struggle for the plain of Valentia. Pompeius' first moves in this contest were unsuccessful; he himself was to descend from the north; his quaestor C. Memmius was to land at Nova Carthago and march up from the south. Sertorius, anticipating that the east coast would be the decisive theatre, left Hirtuleius to watch Metellus in the southern province and posted Perperna, with Herennius in reserve, to prevent Pompeius from crossing the Ebro. He stationed himself in the upper Ebro valley where he could intervene either against Pompeius or Metellus. Pompeius forced a crossing of the Ebro and marched down to Saguntum. Perperna fell back on Valentia. Sertorius responded by laying siege to Lauro, the capture of which would secure Perperna and Herennius in Valentia.

Two engagements, the battles of Lauro and Italica, mark the progress of the Sertorian War for 76. The majority of the Sallustian fragments refer to an episode of the battle for Lauro, the sources of which are: Frontin. *Str.* 2. 5. 31; Plut. *Pomp.* 18. 4; *Sert.* 18. 5–11; App. *BC* 1. 109; Flor. 2. 10. 7; Obseq. 58; Oros. 5. 23. 6–9.

**2. 26.\* renowned among mankind.** A translation based on the reading *per mortales* (Codex Parisianus lat. 1836 reported in M. Adriaen's edition of the works of St Jerome—*Hieronymi presbyteri opera pars 1. 6*, (Turnhout 1970) instead of Maurenbrecher's *prae mortalibus* (2. 64M). The tone and content of this fragment celebrate the extraordinary loyalty to Rome of the Saguntines, who chose death rather than betrayal when overwhelmed by the Carthaginians under Hannibal in 219 BC. It was an example which was celebrated in succeeding literature (e.g. Liv. 21. 7. 3, 19. 10, 28. 39. 17; Plin. *NH* 3. 20; Pompon. 2. 92; Amm. Marc. 15. 10. 10. Silius Italicus' celebration of the Saguntines in *Pun.* 1. 329 ff., 634, 676; 2. 436, 660 ff.; 3. 15–16) contains traces of the Sallustian narrative. See D. Vessey, *CP* 69 (1974), 28–36.

**their devotion outstripping their resources.** Maurenbrecher thought in terms of Saguntine participation in support of Pompeius in the vicinity of Saguntum. He therefore places frr. 26 and 27 later in the narrative as 2. 64 and 65M. On the basis of references in App. *BC* 1. 110 and Plut. *Sert.* 19. 3 and 21. 1 some commentators have thought in terms of a battle of Saguntum. The Greek text of the passages mentioned has since been emended and the stronger probability is that they allude to the battle of Segontia which Gabba (*Comm. App.* 1 ad loc.) identified with Sigüenza on the upper Henares in the province of Guadalajara (*Itin. Anton.* 436. 5, 438. 12; see Spann, *Historia*, 33 (1984), 116–119; Konrad, 245 ff.).

Both Pecere (*SIFC* 50 (1978), 149–55) and La Penna (*SIFC* 35 (1963), 37) agree in connecting this fragment with the topic of local aid provided for the Roman armies operating in Spain. Pecere thinks in terms of the Saguntines' offer of help, psychological rather than physical, to a Roman army under difficulties in 76–75. I lean towards La Penna's alternative context: on his march south Pompeius headed for a town upon whose loyalty he could rely. I also assume that frr. 26 and 27 belong to the same context.

**2. 27.\*  of the Saguntines.** See note above.

**2. 28.\*  Sertorius had set up ... ambushes.** Servius, *G.* 2. 98 and *Aen.* 11. 896 cites part of this fragment. Transmitted without book-number, its placement as referring to the battle of Lauro is substantiated by Frontinus, *Str.* 2. 5. 31: 'After examining the ground they hid the above-mentioned forces by night in a neighbouring wood, posting the light-armed Spaniards in front as best suited to stealthy warfare, the shield-bearing soldiers a little further back, and the cavalry in the rear.'

Pompeius' efforts to raise the siege of Lauro were disastrous. Outwitted in a movement to seize a commanding height to the west of the city, he was severely defeated when attempting to crush Sertorius between his own army and the city (Plut. *Sert.* 18. 5–10). Later his foraging parties were enticed to their destruction, and a legion sent out to rescue them was annihilated (Frontin. loc. cit.; App. *BC* 1. 109).

**2. 29.\*  they rush ... from the rear.** The effectiveness of the ambush tactic was total. Frontinus provides a vivid picture: 'On learning [of the ambush] Pompeius sent out a legion under Decimus Laelius to reinforce his men, where-upon the cavalry of the enemy, withdrawing to the right flank, pretended to give way, and then, passing round the legion, assaulted it from the rear, while those who had followed up the foragers attacked it from the front also.'

**2. 30.\*  a great number ... the body of Laelius.** Emphasizes the complete success of Sertorius' tactics. The scholiast's mention of 'the soldiers of Hirtuleius' has given rise to an assumption that L. Hirtuleius, Sertorius' principal lieutenant, was present at Lauro. This officer, not a commanding officer in his own right, seems to have specialized in a type of roving commission. It may be, however, that the Hirtuleius mentioned was his brother Q. Hirtuleius. See *MRR* Suppl. 29.

**2. 31.\*  since Metellus . . . the hope . . . was a remote one.**  Dietsch convincingly refuted the opinion of earlier editors who, calling to mind material in App. *BC* 1. 68, believed this fragment referred to an incident in the civil war. Maurenbrecher's referral to the Sertorian and specifically to the context of the battle of Lauro is less open to objection. The débâcle at Lauro produced confusion in Pompeius, despair for the people of the town. Prospect of relief or rescue was remote, given Pompeius' disposition of the Roman forces.

**2. 32.\*  Ucurbis.**  Usually written as Ucubis, a town in farther Spain to the east of Italica. Maurenbrecher placed it as 1. 123M in a vague context of affairs relating to Metellus and Hirtuleius after the defeat of L. Manlius at Ilerda; see note on 1. 113.

Hirtuleius, even if he had been present at Lauro, returned once more to the south to prevent Metellus from joining Pompeius. At Italica he suffered defeat at the hands of Metellus. Reasons for this defeat are suggested in Frontin. *Str.* 2. 1. 2, 2. 3. 5; cf. Oros. 5. 23. 10.

**2. 33.  unimpaired, as far as supplies were concerned.**  Maurenbrecher's acceptance of Dietsch's interpretation of the Latin *copiis integra* as referring to a region whose resources had not yet been exhausted seems to be on the right track.

After his victory over Hirtuleius, Metellus, probably because of the lateness of the season, did not intervene on the east coast but marched to winter-quarters in Gallia Narbonensis which in the winter of 76 had not yet been reduced to penury (2. 82. 9).

**2. 34.\*  during the winter . . . augment his forces.**  We learn from Livy, 91 fr. 22W–M, that during the winter

break of 77/76 Sertorius had busied himself in preparing
weaponry, organizing supplies and reinforcements for the
next campaigning season. In the winter of 76/75 with
Pompeius spending 'the winter among the most savage of
foes' (2. 82. 5) and Metellus under more comfortable
conditions in Gaul, we can assume that Sertorius repeated
his practice of preparing for the next campaigning season.

   Maurenbrecher referred the Livy passage to the winter of
76/75. I follow Bieńkowski, *Chronologie*, 211; G. Stahl, *De
Bello Sertoriano* (Erlangen 1907), 65; Schulten, 78 ff.;
Frassinetti, *Stud. Urb.* 49 (1975), 382 n. 10 in rejecting the
statement in Maurenbrecher *Proleg.* 25 concerning the
Livian fragment.

**2. 35\*–6.**   Maurenbrecher allocated three fragments (his
2. 36\*, 37, 38M) to the Macedonian War in 76. His comment
on fr. 38 indicates that he placed Curio's Dardanian
campaign in 76. There are strong reasons for placing it in 75;
see note on 2. 60. Although certitude as to placement cannot
be guaranteed, I have placed two of Maurenbrecher's
fragments 36\* and 37M) in the Macedonian context and
shifted the third one (38M) to a different context as 2. 61.

**2. 35.\*   to Stobi.**   A town in Macedonia. It could have
figured in the operations conducted by the governor of
Macedonia, Appius Claudius Pulcher, in 77–76 against the
Thracians (see notes on 1. 115, **sick colleague**, and 1. 120–1)
or in the expedition of his successor C. Scribonius Curio
against the Dardani of Illyricum in 75. I have selected the
former.

**2. 36.\*   an impressive man.**   Kritz and Dietsch contented
themselves with rejecting de Brosses's view that Sertorius
was the man in question; they offered no alternative
candidate. Maurenbrecher's suggestion that the fragment is
part of an epitaph on the death of Appius is more
satisfactory. The fact that Appius was a noble would not
prevent Sallust from recognizing and appreciating service to
the Republic.

**2. 37.\*   a race fierce . . . subjection.**   That this refers to the
Dalmati, the people of Dalmatia, a country on the east coast

of the Adriatic, seems to be confirmed by Tertullian's statement: 'Sallust puts to flight the treacherous Mauri and the fierce Dalmati' (*De Anim.* 20).

**2. 38.\* Iapydia.** A region in the northern part of Illyria. The reference in this and the preceding fragment is to the Dalmatian expeditions carried out by C. Cosconius. Over about two years of campaigning Cosconius, as governor of Illyricum, occupied portions of the Dalmatian coast and captured Salonae (Cic. *Cluent.* 97; Eutrop. 6. 45; Oros. 5. 23. 23). See Introd. section 3.

**2. 39.\* informed through messengers of Orestes.** Cn. Aufidius Orestes, praetor in 77 (Val. Max. 7. 7. 7), consul in 71 (Eutrop. 6. 8. 15). In 76 as propraetor he governed the province of Asia (*CIG* 2349*b*); strong probability therefore attaches to Maurenbrecher's suggestion that Orestes conquered a tribe in his province—possibly Pamphylians or Pisidians with whom Servilius had fought in the recent past—and informed the senate of its surrender.

**2. 40–5.** Deal with urban affairs of the year 75.

**2. 40. who had commanded . . . reputation for wisdom.** For interpretation of Fleury MS col. 1 (AB) and the like see Introd. section 4 (*a*).

The first sentence of this fragment appears to be verbally clear but it does not provide satisfactory sense. Wölfflin thought in terms of a manoeuvre by Sertorius which cast scorn on Pompeius. Mommsen referred the words to the defeat of Pompeius at Lauro; Maurenbrecher left the matter open.

An attempt to provide a satisfactory context led G. Perl (*Eirene* 12 (1972) 324–9) to emend *idque illi in sapientiam cesserat* ('a gesture which had earned him a reputation for wisdom') to *idque illi in sapientia Ap. cesserat* ('and in this Appius had yielded to him in soundness of judgement'). With this emendation Perl suggests that the first sentence should now read: 'the commander of the Roman army in Macedonia [Scribonius Curio] dismissed one legion, despising its lack of loyalty, and in this case Appius had proved inferior to him in soundness of judgement.' The background he assumed for this incident is as follows: Appius Claudius (consul in 79) had waged war as governor of Macedonia against tribes threatening his borders. These battles had involved heavy losses which gave rise to mutiny in a Roman legion. Appius, who had long been in ill-health (see note on 1. 115, **sick colleague**) was not able to handle the situation and died shortly afterwards. His successor, Curio (consul in 76), took firm disciplinary action against the mutinous legion (Frontin. *Str.* 4. 1. 43). In this way he demonstrated the firm measures expected of a general in such crises.

Both the emendation and the background suggested to support it are based on assumptions which I find difficult to accept. Palaeographically, the emendation depends on Perl's contention that the Rustic Capital M at the end of SΛPIENTIΛM is really an Λ and P with abbreviation mark, producing ΛP., an abbreviation of Appius. The argumentation he uses to produce this result from a palimpsest which is practically illegible is not compelling. Perl notes that the *praenomen* Appius tends to be used on its own in references to the patrician branch of the *Gens Claudia* (e.g. 2. 60; 4. 54M) except in contexts of an official character or on the first introduction of the name (e.g. 1. 67. 22). He has to support his contention that AP (of which he can quote no other example) is an abbreviation of Appius by observing that the context which he has constructed removes any misunderstanding.

*idque illi in sapientiam cesserat*, which Hauler declared a certain reading is, as Perl points out with reference to Tac. *Germ.* 36. 1 and Curt. Ruf. 3. 6. 18, acceptable Latin. Perl's version involves acceptance of *id* as an adverbial accusative (a doubtful usage), while the use of *in* + ablative (*in sapientia*) instead of a plain ablative with an abstract quality like *sapientia* (as with *virtute, subtilitate, odio* in the examples he quotes on p. 327 n. 46) seems contrary to normal usage.

In his background reconstruction Perl's case depends heavily on his contention that Appius failed to deal firmly with a mutiny because he was seriously ill. The Frontinus passage on which the assumption is based makes no reference of any kind to Appius.

**L. Octavius.**   Sallust's judgement of this consul as apathetic and careless seems to be supported by the fact that he has

left little mark on history. Apart from notices concerning his
participation in minor contractual matters such as temple
maintenance (Cic. *2 Verr.* 1. 130), the sale in Rome of
the rights to collect tithes of corn, oil, and minor crops (ibid.
3. 18) and the formula *Octaviana* (ibid. 3. 152), a form of
legal action instituted by Octavius (a charge of 'Robbery
with Violence or Intimidation'), nothing else is known of his
consulship. Of his subsequent career we know only that he
was proconsul in Cilicia in 74 where he died early in his year
of office (Sall. *Hist.* 2. 82 pt. D; Plut. *Luc.* 6. 1).

**C. Cotta.**   Gaius Aurelius Cotta, born about 124 BC (Cic.
*Brut.* 301) into a distinguished plebeian *gens* (see Klebs,
*RE* 2. 229–30; Badian, *Historia,* 6 (1957) 321–2 = *Studies,*
63–4). A friend of the reforming tribune of 91, M. Livius
Drusus, Cotta stood for a tribuneship for 90 (Cic. *De Or.*
1. 25). Broughton (*MRR* 2. 26) does not name him among
the tribunes of 90, although Cicero (*De Or.* 3. 11) reports
that owing to personal animosity he was expelled from the
office of tribune. In the change of political climate after the
murder of Drusus, Cotta was charged before a *quaestio* (a
special commission) set up under the terms of the *Lex Varia,*
carried by Q. Varius Severus Hybrida, a tribune of 90. This
law provided for the setting up of an inquiry against those
who had encouraged the allies to revolt (Val. Max. 8. 6. 4).
Before the judgement was handed down, Cotta, along with
many 'of the most illustrious senators' who had been
charged under this law, went into exile (Cic. *De Or.* 3. 11;
*Brut.* 305; App. *BC* 1. 37).

After his return from exile in 82 (Cic. *Brut.* 311) Cotta
kept himself in the public gaze by participating in court cases
of political significance: in 79 he appeared against Cicero in
a case involving questions of liberty and citizenship (Cic.
*Caecin.* 97), and in 77 was chosen along with Q. Hortensius
to defend Cn. Cornelius Dolabella on a charge brought
against him by C. Julius Caesar (Cic. *Brut.* 317; Suet. *Iul.* 3).
His growing political influence would probably have been
augmented by his membership of the prestigious College of
Pontiffs (Cic. *Nat. D.* 2. 168; Vell. Pat. 2. 43. 1) and his
election to the praetorship of 78 (at the latest) would not
have caused surprise.

**but was through ambition . . . of individuals.** The Latin
version of this segment is quite corrupt and has given rise to
a host of conjectures, as Perl's *apparatus criticus* (*Eirene* 12
(1972), 325) clearly shows. Maurenbrecher's version: *sed
ambitione tum ingenita largitio⟨n⟩e cupiens gratiam
sing⟨ul⟩orum* . . . ('but because of his ingrained ambition
he was eager to curry the favour of individuals by bribery') is
not far removed from the more recent version of Perl
(*Eirene* 12 (1972), 329) based on a selection of alternative
conjectures: *sed ambiti⟨on⟩e tum ingenio largito⟨re⟩t
cupiens gratia singulorum* . . . ('but being through ambition
and by natural inclination a briber and desirous by the
goodwill of individuals . . .'). My translation is based on
Perl's version with the exception that I have substituted
*gratiae* for *gratia* on the model of *avidissimus gratiae* ('most
eager for private goodwill') 2. 43. 4 and *cupientissimus legis*
('most eager for the law') 5. 19M.

   This summary characterization of Cotta and the stress on
his ambition and the means by which he pursued his ends are
of crucial importance in interpreting Sallust's narrative of his
other activities and the speech of Cotta (2. 44).

**2. 41.   motion of the same speaker.**   Almost certainly the
consul Cotta: not many lines of text have been lost between
the fragments 39 and 40. It is likely that in the missing
passage Sallust spoke of measures which illustrated Cotta's
ambition.

**Publius Lentulus Marcellinus.**   Identification of this man as
P. Lentulus Spinther (consul in 57) is still a matter of
dispute: discussion and references in W. Jashemski, *The
Origins and History of the Proconsular and Propraetorian
Imperium* (Chicago 1950), 178–9; W. Drumann and P.
Groebe, *Geschichte Roms in seinem Übergang von der re-
publikanischen zur monarchischen Verfassung* (6 vols.;
Leipzig 1899–1929), 2. 340 (27); Münzer, *RE* 4. 20 and 238.

**quaestor.**   Jashemski's view that Lentulus was sent armed
with *imperium* as *quaestor pro praetore* is supported by
Badian (*JRS* 55 (1965), 119) who points out that the full
official status would be *pro quaestore pro praetore*; see

Balsdon, *JRS* 52 (1962), 134–5; McGushin, *Comm.* (1977) on 19. 1 comm.

**the new province of Cyrene.** Sallust's date of 75 for annexation was accepted by earlier scholars; more recent views favour 74, on the basis of Appian, *BC* 1. 111. Oost's suggestion (*CP* 58 (1963), 20, with nn. 51 and 52) that its formal organization into a province took place in 75, the arrival of the first governor in 74 seems a reasonable compromise.

**bequeathed to us by . . . Apion.** A bequest which took place in 96. The senate apparently accepted it in principle but made no move to take over direct control. It was decreed that the cities of the kingdom should be independent and left to themselves. It is not unlikely that some of the silphium (a plant which produced a gum-resin called *laser* much valued by the ancients as a condiment or medicine) which came to Rome in these years was from Cyrenaica. In time the supply dried up because the plants were destroyed when the *publicani* decided to turn the lands they rented over into grazing (Pliny, *NH* 19. 39, 22. 101).

**although that province . . . needed . . . less greedy manner.** My translation of this part of the fragment is based on the emended Latin version of Perl (*Klio* 52 (1970), 321 n. 3): C⟨um⟩ . . . *prudentiore quam* ⟨*adu*⟩*lescentis et minus q[uam] ille avide imperio co*⟨*nti*⟩*nenda fuit.* The version printed by Maurenbrecher: *q*⟨*uod*⟩ . . . *prudentiore quam* ⟨*illas*⟩ *per gentis et minus g*⟨*lo*⟩*riae avidi imperio co*⟨*nti*⟩*nenda fuit* ('required an administration more prudent than that practised among those people, exercised by someone less greedy for glory') endorses the appointment of Lentulus.

Sallust's criticism of the selection of the inexperienced and self-seeking Lentulus may reflect his suspicions about Cotta's motive for supporting the nomination. It is, however, undoubtedly based on the problems caused in Cyrene by the senate's long delay in organizing the king's dominion into a properly constituted province. The outcome of this neglect is illustrated by Plutarch's report on the visit of Lucullus to Cyrene in 86 (*Luc.* 2. 4). Lucullus found the people worn out by continual tyrannies and wars. The senate's attitude, based on its previous African experience with Jugurtha, and its reluctance, because of its rivalry with the equestrian order, to entrust the hereditary lands of Apion to the *publicani* was for Sallust an example of the unwillingness of the ruling oligarchy to face the responsibilities of imperial rule; it also underlined the decline of the senate as an effective organ of the Roman constitution.

On the state of Cyrene between 96 and 75 see Oost, *CP* 58 (1963), 13–16; on the tensions between factions in Rome, especially in the relations of the oligarchy and the *equites*, see Badian, *Historia*, 6 (1957), 318–46 = *Studies*, 34–70.

**Moreover . . . ⟨rivalries⟩ of the different orders.** Apparently in Sallust's view a determining factor in the senate's change of attitude towards Cyrene. It is likely that because of the continuous unrest in Cyrenaica the *publicani* were experiencing continuous difficulty. By 75 their demand for internal order in Cyrene was putting pressure on the home government.

Other reasons have been advanced: the annexation was part of the measures taken by M. Antonius to suppress piracy (e.g. Cary, *CAH* 9. 390); Lucullus (consul in 74) with his knowledge of the problems of Cyrene used his influence to secure the establishment of a regular Roman regime there (see e.g. Badian, *FC* 140 n. 1; *JRS* 55 (1965), 118). That these and other reasons could have played a part in the decision taken in 75 seems feasible. Sallust's narrative goes on to dwell on a motive which may well have been the decisive one: the factor of economic recession which dominates frr. 41–8 and fr. 82 makes for the probability that Cyrene was eventually constituted as a province in the hope of augmenting Roman revenues. With proper management a naturally fertile land (Strabo 17. 3. 21; cf. Caes. *BCiv.* 3. 5. 1) could, despite its economic distress, produce some improvement in Rome's revenues and grain supplies.

**2. 42.   an intolerable shortage [of corn].**   Such a crisis had been building up for some time. Distributions of subsidized corn had been abolished by Sulla in 81 (see note on 1. 48. 11, **the rations of slaves**); there is reason to believe that Lepidus' corn law of 78 (Gran. Lic. 36. 34–5C; see note on 1.54, **Octavius and Q. Caepio . . . requested to do so**) did not long survive its author; see note on 3. 36. 19, **that hastily enacted law . . . grain**. The situation was aggravated by the failure of the harvest in Gaul in 75 (2. 82. 9).

Underlying causes were pirate interference with transport, the probable neglect of the state corn-depots in Rome, and the failure of deliveries from Sicily to arrive safely and on time. Two years later the purchase of corn from Sicily was organized in every detail by decree on the initiative of the consuls (Cic. 2 *Verr.* 3. 163 and 173, 5. 52; Sall. *Hist.* 3. 36. 19).

**along the Sacred Way.** It appears that the consuls were acting as *deductores*, supporters who escorted a candidate from his house when he set out to canvass votes; cf. Q. Cic. *Com. Pet.* 34, 36. The route indicates that they were heading for the Forum and not the Campus Martius where elections for curule office were held. The attack on the consuls must have taken place early in the year.

The fact that both consuls were escorting Metellus may be significant: Cotta's presence could be explained by the close political relations between the Aurelii Cottae and the Caecilii Metelli (Badian, *Studies*, 36); that he persuaded his lethargic colleague to accompany them may be an example of his compulsive seeking after the favour of those capable of advancing his personal ambitions.

**Q. Metellus.** It is possible that Q. Caecilius Metellus Creticus failed in the election of 75. Broughton (*MRR* 2. 102 and 108 n. 3) has tentatively listed him among the praetors of 74 but Seager (*CR* 20 (1970), 11) has argued that the Q. Metellus referred to as urban praetor in Val. Max. 7. 7. 7 is Creticus and not Celer, as Broughton (*MRR* 2. 166) states, though he does not list him as *praetor urbanus*. In 74 the notorious Verres was the urban praetor. On this theory Creticus would have had to be praetor in 73 or 72, the latest possible year before his consulship of 69.

**the *cognomen* Creticus.** Metellus served with some distinction (*CIL*². 1. 595) as proconsul (68–65) in Greece and Crete, with command of the war against the pirates in Crete

(Cic. *Flac.* 30, 63, 100; Liv. *Per.* 98; Vell. Pat. 2. 34. 1). In the battle for Crete which is being referred to here he came into collision with Pompeius to whom many Cretans wished to surrender. Metellus refused to recognize Pompeius' right to receive their surrender and arrested L. Octavius, Pompeius' envoy in charge of the negotiations (Liv. *Per.* 99). Plutarch (*Pomp.* 29) gives a pro-Metellus account of this disagreement; Dio (36. 18. 1–19. 3) provides a negative characterization of Metellus and speaks disparagingly of his adoption of the *cognomen* Creticus.

**They then demolished the defensive wall.**   This last sentence of the fragment is grossly corrupt in the palimpsest. Maurenbrecher's printed version: *in⟨de⟩ . . . ⟨pu⟩gnaculum perve⟨nit?⟩* indicates his uncertainty. He reported the proposed emendations, including Pertz's *in propugnaculum* and even suggested one of his own, but would not commit himself to any of them. My translation is based on the solution proposed by Frassinetti (*Athenaeum*, 40 (1962), 97–8): *in⟨de⟩ propugnaculum perve ⟨rtit⟩*.

It may be that the mob used pieces of the rubble to attack the house. When Sallust was engaged in writing his historical works an incident very similar to this one took place at the end of 40 BC. The description by Appian (*BC* 5. 67–8) provides details which practically duplicate the incident of 75. In 40 the enraged mob blamed the triumvirs for a catastrophic shortage of food supplies. When Octavianus attempted to reason with them he was repeatedly stoned, as was M. Antonius who came to his rescue. They eventually took refuge in Antonius' house. (See Dio, 48. 31. 5–6; Perl, *Philologus*, 111 (1967), 138–40.)

**2. 43.  the senators acting promptly.**   We have no precise knowledge of the scale of the unrest indicated by the attack on the consuls, but it seems to have produced quick reaction from the government. Attempts to alleviate the shortage of corn included the quaestor Cicero's dispatch from Sicily of 'an enormous quantity of corn at a time of very high prices' (*Planc.* 64; Plut. *Cic.* 6. 1). Other extraordinary measures included the subsidizing of high corn prices out of individual purses as in the case of the aedile Q. Hortensius in this year

(Cic. *Brut.* 318; 2 *Verr.* 3. 215) and of the aedile M. Seius in 74 (Cic. *Off.* 2. 58; Plin. *NH* 15. 2, 18.16). It was also decided that the consul Cotta should attempt to pacify the people and recall them to a sense of duty.

**2. 44.** The speech that Sallust assigned to Cotta is very likely one that was actually delivered. However, Cicero's statement in the latter part of 46 BC that by that time no speech of Cotta was extant (*Orat.* 132) indicates that the speech as we have it was drafted by Sallust. Cotta was considered a leading orator of his time; he was deemed suitable enough to be a debating member in two of Cicero's works: *De Oratore* and *De Natura Deorum*; cf. Cic. *De Or.* I. 25; *Brut.* 183, 317. His style was described as acute and subtle, marked by accuracy, precision, and concentration on the main argument without the language of metaphor (Cic. *De Or.* 2. 29, 3. 31; *Brut.* 202, 317).

Sallust's version reflects these characteristics well enough to have caused some modern scholars to take it at face value as the attempt by a veteran politician, unjustly blamed for something for which he was not responsible, to exonerate himself and to recall a turbulent people to a sense of patriotism and trust in their government. In other words, that Sallust has here in an unbiased way perceived and given expression to the internal difficulties of the ruling oligarchy. Thus, Paladini, 109–10; Büchner, *Sallust*, 216–19; K. Büchner, *C&M* 9 (1973), 246–61; Malitz, *Hermes* 100 (1972), 359–86.

Other scholars are more sceptical. Sallust's first introduction of Cotta (see note on 2. 40, **but was through ambition . . . of individuals**) with its stress on the man's excessive ambition sounds a warning note; he had earlier (*Cat.* 38. 3) cautioned that each member of the ruling clique, under pretence of public welfare, was in reality working for his own advantage. See Earl, *Political Thought*, 108–9; Syme, *Sallust*, 200; Perl, *Philologus* 109 (1965), 75–82.

In the absence of narrative by which statements in the speech might be evaluated, careful analysis and interpretation of what Cotta says is imperative. The attitude of the speaker and the tenor of the speech demand close scrutiny.

**2. 44. [Introduction].** The Fleury MS col. 4 (BA) contains a corrupted version of the introduction to the speech and the beginning of the speech itself down to 'my own courage; in . . .'; the Codex Vaticanus Lat. 3864 contains all of the speech.

**in mourning garb.** The phrase *mutata veste* is a technical term indicating a change into a mourning garment (*toga pulla*) as a sign of some public or private grief (Cic. *Sest.* 26, 27; *Planc.* 29; Liv. 6. 20. 1–2). But since Cotta is very much distressed (*permaestus*) because of the unfriendly attitude of the people expressed in a number of accusations against him the toga in question is likely to have been a soiled one, *toga sordida*, worn by accused persons (Plut. *Cic.* 30; 31; Dio, 38. 16; Liv. 26. 29. 3, 45. 20. 10).

**instead of the goodwill he longed for.** The stress on *cupita voluntate* recalls *cupiens gratia singulorum* ('desirous of the favour of individuals') of 2. 40 which is the leading element of his attitude. It is a line of thought which indicates that Cotta is not prepared to accept personal responsibility for the unrest.

**2. 44. 1–5.** The tone and content of this section of the speech confirm the impression conveyed in Sallust's introductory remarks. Over half the speech is devoted to a plaintive outburst of disappointment at his failure to win the popularity he longed for, pained repudiation of the accusations levelled against him for lack of leadership in the crisis, a grovelling manipulation of the truth in order to elicit sympathy and support, and an offer of self-immolation which he knows will not come to anything. No word of reassurance or comfort to a suffering populace, no concrete proposal of any kind for the alleviation of their distress.

**2. 44. 1. encountered many dangers at home and abroad.** See note on 2. 40, **C. Cotta.**

**2. 44. 2. in these present troubles.** See notes on 2. 42 and §§ 6 and 7 below.

**taken everything else with it.** i.e. the courage, the endurance, and the energy which had enabled him to handle the problems of his earlier career.

**old age.** The Romans reckoned that old age, *senectus*, began after 60 years (Censorinus, DN 14. 2; Isid. *Etym.* 11. 2. 7). At this time Cotta was just approaching 50 years; the exaggeration, which he uses again in § 9, is one of the oratorical tricks to arouse the pity or the goodwill of the hearers—a *captatio benevolentiae*.

**2. 44. 3. a traitor to you.** Sallust uses the word *parricida* ('murderer of a near relation') which when used in connection with the *patria* can mean 'traitor'; see note on 1. 48. 24, **treason.** It is clear that the accusation *'parricida'* was hurled at Cotta during the period of unrest and could therefore carry both meanings. Cf. Sall. *Cat.* 51. 25; *nostri proditor*; note above on 1. 56, **'tyrant' and 'Cinna'.**

**twice born.** alludes to his return from exile, which was looked on as a second birth: thus Cicero, 'I am beginning a sort of second life' (*Att.* 4. 1. 8; cf. 6. 1. 4 and *Red. Sen.* 27).

**adequate punishment.** cf. Sall. *Cat.* 51. 15: 'I consider no torture sufficient for the crimes of these men.'

**well-known punishments of the damned.** cf. Sall. *Cat.* 52. 13; Virg., *Aen.* 6. 539–627.

**2. 44. 4. before your eyes.** See note on 2. 51.

**and as a magistrate.** According to Cicero (*Off.* 2. 59) Cotta, like L. Marcius Philippus, could boast that he had risen to all the highest magistracies without giving any entertainments as aedile. There is no record of what positions Cotta held prior to his attainment of the consulship.

**had need of my tongue . . . the use of them.** Sallust's use of *lingua* (tongue) which can be used in a bad sense may be significant. However Cotta's reputation as a defence counsel was well established. The validity of this assertion should be assessed in the light of Q. Cicero's statement: 'C. Cotta, a past master of electioneering, used to say that—he used to promise his help to all, but give it to those in whom he expected he was making the best investment' (*Comm. Pet.* 47).

**my gift of oratory.** My interpretation of Sallust's *callidam facundiam* ('my practised eloquence'); *callidam* has at times been interpreted as 'calculating', a meaning which the word can also bear.

**Most eager for private goodwill.**  With a touch of irony Sallust makes Cotta repeat the very trait which had been highlighted in 2. 40.

**When the state and I were overcome.**  Refers to his own exile and to the triumph of the anti-oligarchic factions in the political upheaval which followed the murder of the tribune. M. Livius Drusus. See note on 2. 40, **C. Cotta**.

**restored to me . . . and added . . . mark of distinction.** Inaccurate and another attempt at *captatio benevolentiae*: Cotta owed his return from exile to Sulla's victory in the civil war (Cic. *Brut.* 311).

**2. 44. 5.    even if I were to give up my life.**  cf. Cic. *Fam.* 1. 4. 3: 'If I were to sacrifice my life in defence of your honour, I should not appear to have balanced a fraction of what I owe you.'

**something that may be given and received as a gift.**  A literal translation of a compressed Latin sentence. One might paraphrase as follows: 'One cannot offer one's life to individuals, but an honourable life is a gift given to society in return for which one receives a good reputation and preservation of the goods fortune bestows.'

**2. 44. 6–8.**  Cotta now attempts self-exoneration. It is based on the self-evident truth that he and his colleague cannot be held responsible for a crisis which has been developing over several years. But the complaint of the people is not so much that a crisis has been allowed to develop as that the chief executive officers are taking no steps to deal with it. That Cotta was aware of his responsibility seems to be indicated by the fact that he does not seek to lay the blame on government officials in charge of the maintenance and distribution of the corn supply— aediles and the *quaestor Ostiensis*. He has no plan for alleviation; his first reaction is throw up his hands and rebuke the people for their violence in attacking their elected consuls.

**2. 44. 6.   Our commanders in Spain.**   Q. Caecilius Metellus Pius from 79 (see note on 1. 101, **Metellus**) and Cn. Pompeius from 77 (see note on 2. 26–32).

**are calling for pay . . .**   See note on the letter of Pompeius to the senate (2. 82).

**the defection of our allies.**   i.e. the Spanish peoples won over by the personality and attitude of Sertorius (Plut. *Sert.* 6. 4, 11. 1–3). This had an effect on the local provision of resources for war; cf. Sall. *Iug.* 84. 3, 86. 1.

**the flight of Sertorius through the mountains.**   Sertorius' tactic of avoiding pitched battles drove Metellus to distraction (Plut. *Sert.* 12. 6–7, 13. 2–4). Pompeius, too, took some time to counter Sertorius' guerrilla tactics.

**2. 44. 7.   Asia.**   A province which included the kingdom of Pergamum, Phrygia, Caria, Lydia, and the Ionian colonies of the coast and of the islands.

**Cilicia.**   On the south-east coast of Asia Minor between Pamphylia and Syria.

**Mithridates.**   See note on 1. 67. 8, **Mithridates . . . looking for an opportunity for war.** At about this time Mithridates was negotiating a treaty with Sertorius in Spain. (Cic. 2 *Verr.* 1. 87; Sall. *Hist.* 2. 91; Liv. *Per.* 93; Plut. *Sert.* 23–4; App. *Mith.* 68, 70, 112; Oros. 6. 2. 12; Ps.-Asc. 244 St.)

**Macedonia.**   Under the leadership of C. Scribonius Curio the border wars against the Thracian tribes had greatly expanded.

**the coastal regions of Italy and of the provinces.**   Infested by pirates whose HQ was on the south coast of Asia Minor; they had made vulnerable the seas between the Strait of Gibraltar and the Syrian waters. P. Servilius did succeed in destroying many of their strongholds between 78 and 76 but the vulnerability still remained. As a result trade was interrupted, revenues decreased, and prices rose. Cf. App. *Mith.* 92–3; Plut. *Pomp.* 24; Cassius Dio, 36. 20–3.

**the fleet . . . is much smaller.**   The fleet had had to be subdivided because of increased calls on its services: the transport of troops to distant theatres of war; defence of the coasts against pirates.

**2. 44. 8.   by treason or negligence on our part.**   Once again words which probably reflect reproaches or open accusations directed at the highest executive power.

**2. 44. 9–12.**   This second segment of Cotta's personal viewpoint repeats concepts already uttered. The solemn and anachronistic offer of self-immolation (§ 10) as a solution to the crisis is, as the warning which follows in §§ 11 and 12 indicates, an empty gesture; it is a device to deflect the need for real evidence of his personal blamelessness and to present himself as the victim of *fortuna* and the anger of the people.

**2. 44. 10.   what our ancestors . . . in hard-fought wars.**   Cicero (*Tusc.* 1. 89) lists a series of examples of self-immolation in Roman wars from 510 to 208 BC. The examples uppermost in Roman minds would probably have been those of the Decii: Decius Mus against the Latins in 340; his son against the Samnites in 295; his grandson against Pyrrhus in 279—this last being legendary rather than historical.

**2. 44. 12.   it was not for crime or avarice.**   Another probable echo of accusations made against him.

**2. 44. 13–14,**   The peroration of the speech sums up its duplicity and underlines the absence of a rallying call to joint efforts to remedy the situation. Cotta finishes as he began by reproaching the people for not doing what was expected of them. The tone and content of this final statement clearly convey Sallust's view that the problems of Republican governing will find no real solution from within the ruling oligarchy. The probable outcome of inability to cope receives vivid indication in the letter sent by Pompeius concerning government lack of action on this same crisis (2. 82).

**2. 44. 13.   in your own name . . . I beseech you.**   cf. Sall. *Iug.* 14. 25: 'Fathers of the Senate I beseech you in your own name . . .'.

**take thought for your country.**   A call to duty which should rather apply to the chief executive officers of the state. The appeal to 'the glory of your ancestors', a typical sentiment of the nobility, reflects the obtuseness of Cotta and of the oligarchy's view of the art of government.

**2. 44. 14. Imperial power.** *Summum imperium*, theoretically the rule of senate and people over the empire (cf. Tac. *Ann.* 1. 2). Cotta uses this constitutional feature, long ignored in practice, to accuse the people of being unwilling to risk their peace and prosperity when their imperial subjects are suffering war.

**2. 45.\*    any law . . . other than that which he carried in his consulship.** Available sources give no informtion of the effect, if any, of Cotta's speech. Nor do we have direct indication of the political programme of the consuls of 75. This fragment refers to the *Lex Aurelia de tribunicia potestate* and it suggests that much of the political discussion of this year was concerned with demands for the strengthening of tribunician power.

**against the wishes of the nobility.** Asconius, 78. 20–2, quotes Cicero's statement that the nobles were very hostile towards Cotta because he had added a small amount, not of power, but of status to the tribunate. Given Cotta's earlier career and his support of the tribune M. Livius Drusus (see note on 2. 40, **C. Cotta**), it is not absolutely clear whether Cotta belonged to the conservative nobility or did in fact share popular feeling on this question. Cicero's statement, part of his defence of the *popularis* tribune C. Cornelius, may have been designed to show that conservative nobles were opposed to moves, irrespective of their source, which impinged on their privileges. On the other hand Sallust makes the tribune Macer (3. 36. 8) describe Cotta as *ex factione media* ('from the inner circle of the nobility'); judgement as to the consul's political convictions will depend on the interpretation of that description which I discuss ad loc.

**that it should be permitted . . . other magistracies.** Restrictions placed by Sulla on the tribunate (see *MRR* 2. 75) included that which prevented holders of the tribunate from seeking further offices. The tribune Q. Opimius is said to have supported Cotta's law (Ps.-Asc. 255 St.) and that may have a bearing on his condemnation in the following year for using his veto contrary to the Cornelian law (Cic. *2 Verr.* 1. 155–6; Schol. Gronov. 341. 9; cf. H. W. Benario, *Historia* 22 (1973), 70.

On the expiry of his consulship Cotta governed Gallia Cisalpina as proconsul. Even though he had not waged what could truly be called a campaign—*nullo certo hoste* 'he met no regular foe', as Cicero says (*Pis.* 62)—he somehow won the bestowal of a triumph. However the *fortuna* which dogged his ambition and of which he complains in § 2 of his speech stayed with him, in that he died from the effects of an old wound on the day before he was due to celebrate his triumph at the end of 74 or early in 73 (Cic. *Pis.* 62; Asc. 14. 17–24).

**Note:** At the end of this section Maurenbrecher includes, as 2. 52M, an extremely corrupted fragment from cols. 5 and 6 (A) of the Fleury MS. Only a few letters have survived at the beginning of each line of col. 5 and at the end of each line in col. 6. Maurenbrecher guessed some connection with the material of the immediately pre-ceding columns of the manuscript but there is really no way of learning the subject-matter of the cols. 5 and 6. I have therefore decided to omit them from the text.

**2. 46–57.**   A segment which deals with the course of the Sertorian War in 75. The operations of this year formed a climax in the long-drawn-out conflict. Pompeius' main objective remained the domination of the east coast and the securing of the plain of Valentia, a target he had failed to achieve in the previous year. Metellus, who had wintered in Gaul, came into contact with Sertorius' lieutenant Hirtuleius at Segovia as he was on his way back to his province. The result of the battle of Segovia was to influence the course of the rest of the war. On the east coast two battles, those of Valentia and of the Sucro, illustrated on the one hand the gap in leadership quality between Sertorius and his remaining subordinate commanders, on the other the manner in which Pompeius' craving for personal glory affected his general-ship in a set battle. The final encounter of this campaigning year, that of Segontia amid the Celtiberian highlands, resulted in a defeat for Sertorius which turned out to have a crippling effect on his resources and strategy in subsequent years.

**2. 46. on the left the walls . . . on the right the River Turia.** We learn from 2. 82. 6 and Plut. *Pomp.* 18. 5 that Pompeius' victory at Valentia over the Sertorian generals Herennius and Perperna caused the death of 10,000 rebel troops including Herennius. Mention of Valentia and the River Turia make it certain that this fragment refers to this battle. It appears that the fighting took place outside the walls of the town after Pompeius had infiltrated from the coast along the narrow access way between the walls and the river on the north side of the town. See Schulten, *Sertorius*, 111 and n. 537.

**2. 47.*  the real ⟨blame⟩ must be attached to Perperna.** The crucial word to which the adjective *vera* ('true', 'real') refers has not been transmitted; the word *poena* ('offence', 'penalty') suggested by Mähly was rejected by Maurenbrecher who did not suggest an alternative. The lack of adequate preparation and tactics and, perhaps, reluctance to commit himself, which appear also to have marked Perperna's participation in subsequent battles, would justify the choice of some such word as Schulten's suggested *culpa* which I have included here.

**2. 48. It could be taken for an island.** Cicero (*Balb.* 5) states that his client, Balbus, served in Spain under Memmius, Pompeius' quaestor from the time of the latter's appointment, and that he was besieged in Carthago Nova. This fragment, part of a fairly detailed description of a place on the coast, could be part of Sallust's introduction to the narrative of this siege. Dietsch clinched his identification of this description with Carthago Nova by citing Livy, 26. 42 and Polybius, 10. 10.

Sertorius' absence from the battle of Valentia was most likely due to his presence at the siege of Carthago Nova. That the siege apparently lapsed in stalemate may have been occasioned by news of the battle of Segovia and its outcome. The battle of Valentia meant that Pompeius now had a firm base on the east coast; the defeat at Segovia meant that Metellus was free to combine with Pompeius.

**2. 49.\*   and on the flanks . . . men who were absolutely dependable.**   Sallust now turns his attention to the opening phase of Metellus' campaign of 75, the battle of Segovia in Celtiberia. To support his contention that Metellus wintered in 76/75 in Baetica, Spann (106 with nn.) takes up E. Cavaignac's suggestion (*REA* 30 (1928), 99) that the site of the battle was a Segovia in further Spain which is supposed to have been on the modern Rio Geril between Palma del Rio and Ecija. The outcome of the battle (Auct. *Vir. Ill.* 63. 2; Oros. 5. 23. 12; Florus, 2. 10. 7) was the fruit, as at Italica in 76, of superior tactics. Frontinus (*Str.* 2. 3. 5) provides the details: 'Metellus . . . had discovered that the battalions of Hirtuleius which were deemed strongest were posted in the centre. Accordingly he drew back the centre of his own troops to avoid encountering the enemy at that part of the line until by an enveloping movement of his wings he could surround their centre from all sides.'

**2. 50.   [soldiers on each side] . . . the enemy general.** Nonius transmitted *occurrere duci* where the dative *duci* is governed by the verb *occurrere* ('that rushed to confront the leader'). Assuming that both generals did the rushing Gerlach suggested *duces* for *duci* and Dietsch and Maurenbrecher printed *duces*. My translation retains *duci* as object of the verb and understands it as a collective for *ducibus*; in military language collective nouns such as *eques, pedes, miles* are commonplace. I also suggest the likely subject of the verb *occurrere*. See Garbugino, *Stud. Non.* 11 (1986), 33–4.

**missiles fell on Metellus' cloak and struck Hirtuleius on the arm.**   The above incident could have occurred in either of the two battles in which Metellus and Hirtuleius were opposed. Schulten (*Sertorius*, 104 n. 503) maintained that in the battle of Segovia Hirtuleius was killed, not wounded, and therefore referred the incident to the battle of Italica (see note on 2. 32, **Ucurbis**). Schulten's argument is not compelling in that it is possible to think in terms of a phase of the battle of Segovia preceding the death of Hirtuleius. Placement is by no means secure, but I have followed Maurenbrecher's viewpoint.

Metellus annihilated the encircled army, among them Hirtuleius the most able of Sertorius' lieutenants (Frontin. *Str.* 2. 7. 5). He was now free to combine with Pompeius and to participate in campaigns on the east coast and elsewhere. His presence was to have an important bearing on Sertorius' future plans of campaign.

**2. 51–4.** After the defeat at Valentia and the death of his fellow general, Perperna retreated south towards the Sucro. Sertorius, on receipt of news of the disaster at Segovia, presumably abandoned the siege of Carthago Nova and took up a position on the Sucro. Metellus was on his way to the coast with the intention of joining up with Pompeius who, elated with his achievement at Valentia, was hurrying to attack Sertorius before Metellus could share in the glory of expected victory. But the battle did not turn out as he anticipated.

**2. 51. in the evening.** Firm placement of just one word, (*vespera*) even with book-number supplied, is normally hazardous. I join Dietsch and Maurenbrecher in suggesting allocation to the battle of the Sucro because other sources stress that battle was joined late in the evening since both generals feared the arrival of Metellus: Pompeius wished to fight alone to avoid sharing his victory; Sertorius wanted to deal with only one antagonist at a time (Plut. *Sert.* 19. 3–4; *Pomp.* 19. 1–3).

**2. 52. acknowledge as men people who came away unarmed.** This fragment is transmitted also by Priscianus, 2. 511. The battle of the Sucro opened with Sertorius engaged against Pompeius' legate, Afranius, on his own right wing, while Pompeius was being victorious over the Sertorian left (Plut. *Sert.* 19. 5–6). To counter this, Sertorius put 'other generals' in charge of his right and took command on his left wing. He rallied the troops who were already in retreat with a mixture of encouragement and command, as this fragment suggests.

**2. 53.\* of above average height and build.** Sertorius rallied his left wing to such effect that he routed Pompeius' right. In the course of the fighting 'Pompeius, who was on horseback, was attacked by a tall man who fought on foot; when they came to close quarters and were at grips, the strokes of their swords fell upon each other's hands, but not with the same result, for Pompeius was merely wounded, whereas he lopped off the hand of his opponent' (Plut. *Pomp*. 19. 4). According to Appian (*BC* 1. 110), whose account of this battle is untrustworthy and contains the serious error of substituting Metellus for Afranius, 'Pompeius was wounded in the thigh with a spear.' Pompeius made good his escape by abandoning his horse, which had golden head-gear and ornamented trappings of great value (Plut. *Pomp*. 19. 5).

**2. 54.\*** **[they seized] his horse . . . trappings.** Plutarch (*Sert*. 19. 8) explains the circumstances of Pompeius' escape: the Libyans who had seized the horse were so busy distributing the booty and quarrelling with one another over it that they forgot about pursuing him.

Meanwhile the Sertorian right wing was routed and pursued into camp by Afranius, who was not able in the darkness to control his pillaging troops, who fell easy prey to Sertorius on his return from the other wing. In the morning Sertorius cancelled his plan to renew the battle when he heard that Metellus was approaching; he gave his army instructions to disperse and to assemble again at an appointed time and place (Plut. *Pomp*. 19. 6; *Sert*. 19. 11).

**2. 55–7.** After the battle of the Sucro Sertorius retreated from the coast to the Celtiberian highlands. The Romans followed but stretched their lines of communication and supply to an extent which made them vulnerable to guerrilla attacks. The decision was eventually reached that a pitched battle should take place. Plutarch (*Sert*. 21. 1) states that Sertorius was forced to give the Romans battle (ἠναγκάσθη), a statement which remains puzzling. But there is no doubt that a battle did take place—the battle of Segontia, the last pitched battle of the Sertorian War.

From sources other than Plutarch—Liv. *Per*. 92; App. *BC* 1. 110; Oros. 5. 23. 12—it appears that the battle consisted of three encounters: Metellus attacked and defeated Perperna while Sertorius and Pompeius fought in a different location, obviously not far distant, where Sertorius was victorious and Pompeius retreated; Metellus now clashed with Sertorius and eventually scored a decisive victory. This last encounter seems to be the only one dealt with in the surviving Sallustian fragments.

**2. 55. before Sertorius . . . draw up his troops for battle.** Maurenbrecher refers this to the preliminaries of the battle of Segontia. The wording of the fragment in my opinion points to the beginning of the final encounter: Sertorius, with some of his troops still involved in the pursuit of the retreating forces of Pompeius, now had to face Metellus with little time to make the necessary dispositions.

**2. 56. nor . . . support troops . . . organized assembled.** Placed, as 2. 102M, in fragments of uncertain placement by Maurenbrecher. I have risked placing it in the context of the last phase of the battle of Segontia on the assumption that it provides insight into the cause of Sertorius' difficulty. His problem of lack of adequate time properly to prepare for the final encounter with Metellus was compounded by the inefficiency of his subordinate officers.

**2. 57. Metellus was wounded by a blow from a javelin.** Plutarch's description of the consequences of this incident places it firmly within the context of Segontia and provides one reason for Roman victory: 'Then Metellus, who was holding his ground with a vigour that belied his years, and fighting gloriously, was struck by a spear. All the Romans who saw or heard of this were seized with shame at the thought of deserting their commander and at the same time were filled with rage against the enemy. So, after they had covered Metellus with their shields and carried him out of danger, they stoutly drove the Iberians back' (*Sert.* 21. 2–3).

Sertorius' defeat at Segontia was a turning-point in the war. His ability to fight pitched battles depended on sufficient numbers of heavy infantry and cavalry. Figures of Sertorian losses provided by the sources are as follows: at Italica, 20,000 (Oros. 5. 23. 10); at Valentia, 10,000 (Plut. *Pomp.* 18. 5); at the Sucro, 10,000 (Oros. 5. 23. 11); at Segontia Perperna lost 5,000 and Sertorius 3,000 (App. *BC*

1. 110). Sertorius' losses against Metellus at Segontia are not known, but were undoubtedly substantial.

It is granted that the least reliable numerical data transmitted by ancient writers are casualty figures (Brunt, *Manpower*, 694–7). Even if we admit as reasonable the 60,000 infantry and 8,000 cavalry estimated as Sertorius' total force at Lauro (Oros. 5. 23. 9), and if the reported casualty figures were halved, it would still mean that after Segontia Sertorius' resources were and would remain inadequate to face two Roman armies in a deciding encounter. Cf. Konrad, 145–6.

**2. 58.   after Varro heard these things, exaggerated in the manner of rumours.** Maurenbrecher assumed that *haec* ('these things') referred to an event in the war and used the fragment to provide a brief discussion of the part played by Varro in the Sertorian War. Varro did serve as a legate to Pompeius, and on the death of Pompeius' quaestor, Memmius, at Segontia (Plut. *Sert.* 21. 1), took over as proquaestor.

I find more attractive the idea that this fragment refers to the content of the fragment which follows; a decision as to what is the connection between them remains a problem. Spann, 211, suggests that it implies that Sallust had first-hand information about something Varro knew about only through rumours; he does not hazard an opinion as to what that 'something' might be. Garbugino (*Stud. Non.* 11 (1986), 36 n. 15) suggests a possible solution: Sallust's description of the triumphal celebration of Metellus presents a negative characterization of the man. There is the likelihood that rumours of Metellus' conduct were spread by members of Pompeius' staff, who had reasons for tarnishing the glory of Metellus. Varro, who in his *legationum libri* recalled the experiences of his first Spanish campaign and who as a member of Pompeius' staff shared his chief's feelings about Metellus may well have incorporated such rumours in his treatment of Metellus. The moral censure so evident in Sallust's version is also in keeping with Varro's well-known attitude to the simplicity and lack of pretension which marked the old-Roman way of life. In effect Sallust, who shared this outlook in his writing, may well have been commenting that the rumoured excesses known to Varro, whose works he would have read, were nothing unusual in the conduct of a member of the ruling nobility.

**2. 59.** My translation of this extensive fragment is based mainly on the version transmitted by Macrobius. There are three snippets from the fragment preserved in Nonius and one in Servius. Some of these offer a reading different from that of Macrobius and, where appropriate, I draw attention to them in the notes.

**2. 59. 1. But Metellus . . . farther Spain.** Maurenbrecher reports as fr. 2. 68*: *sed Metellus in volnere* ('but Metellus, wounded . . .') based on Donatus, Ter. *Andr.* 310. The word *volnere* is a correction for the meaningless *ulpie*. La Penna draws attention to Wessner's 1962 edition of Donatus where it is established that the correct reading is *sed Metellus in ulteriorem H* (= *Hispaniam*), thus making this snippet a citation of the beginning of this fragment. Maurenbrecher's 2. 68* should be eliminated, as he himself suggested in *Bursians Jahresbericht*, 113 (1902), 238.

**after a year.** Towards the end of the campaigning season of 75 (see notes on 2. 88 ff.) Metellus withdrew to winter-quarters in Gaul (Plut. *Sert.* 21. 8). The events described in this fragment took place after the 74 campaigning season when Metellus retired to winter-quarters in his province (Liv. *Per.* 93). Plutarch's briefer version provides better insight into the atmosphere behind the celebrations. Metellus, who placed an excessive reward on Sertorius' head and who disparaged him verbally, boasted beyond measure of a success 'which he once won over Sertorius'. No mention is made of the deeds of the campaigns of 75; his return to the safety of his province enabled him to indulge his personal extravagances in a celebration of his prowess.

**2. 59. 3. let down by a rope.** The Latin word *transenna* which I translate as 'rope' appears to have a primary meaning of 'snare', 'net', 'trap' judging from its use in Plaut. *Bacch.* 792; *Pers.* 480; *Rud.* 1236. Elsewhere it seems to have been given a meaning to suit the context in which it appears, Cic. *De Or.* 1. 162 'lattice'. In citing this passage Macrobius uses *in transenna* which indicates that he interpreted it as 'net' or 'sling' while Nonius, 180. 18, and

Servius. *Aen.* 5. 488, use the simple ablative of instrument *transenna*; Servius interprets the word as *funis extentus* ('stretched rope'), a meaning used by Amm. Marc. 20. 11. 22, 25. 6. 14 and incorporated as a definition in Isid. *Etym.* 19. 1; Nonius, interpreting on different lines, explains *transenna* as *fenestra* 'an opening'.

**crash of thunder.**    Nonius and Servius have just *machinato strepitu* ('artificially produced noise'); Macrobius' preservation of *tonitruum* provides the appropriate specification of the sound.

**2. 59. 4.    toga picta.**    A toga ornamented with Phrygian embroidery worn by generals in triumphs. Val. Max. 9. 1. 5, using these scenes as an example of luxury and pleasure-seeking, speaks of *palmata veste*, which probably refers to the *tunica palmata*, a flowered tunic worn under the toga by triumphing generals.

**2. 60–2.**    Deal with Macedonian affairs in 75. See commentary on 2. 35*–6. Problems concerned with the dating of these events, arising from apparent contradictions in the sources, are discussed in the notes to individual fragments.

**2. 60.    In the same year . . . at the beginning of spring.** According to Liv. *Per.* 92 and Eutropius, 6. 2. 2, Curio began a campaign in Macedonia as proconsul. Since he was consul in 76, this means that the three-year campaign allocated to him by Eutropius covered the years 75–73. I take 'the same year' to be 75. Pecere (*SIFC* 41 (1969), 71) feels that the time-frame is too restricted to allow a setting out from Italy at the beginning of the year, the suppression of unrest in Curio's army, and a campaign against the Dardani to be included in one year; he would therefore place the activities dealt with in this fragment in the year 74, thus compressing Eutropius' triennium into a two-year period.

The fragment has been transmitted with book-number, the validity of which is not in dispute. Curio's predecessor, Appius Claudius, died in 76 and it is entirely possible that Curio proceeded to Macedonia before the end of 76.

**with his whole army.** The point of this statement with the emphasis on *omni exercitu* will emerge after discussion of points raised by the following frr. 61 and 62.

**collected . . . payments agreed upon with Appius.** Clearly indicates that an agreement had been reached between the Romans and the Dardani in which it had been established that the latter would pay a tribute agreed upon with Appius. It is likely that the death of Appius encouraged the Dardani to ignore the pledged tribute and that the Romans realized that a quick and decisive show of authority was essential. Curio set out on the task of ensuring the honouring of the pledge; he did so only after enforcing on a rebellious legion compliance with Roman army discipline so that he could embark on the Dardanian enterprise with a full complement of troops—*omni exercitu.*

**by whatever means he could.** The expression *pecunias cogere* is generally used in connection with the normal collection of tribute; the addition here of *quibus modis* (Carrio) or *quibus rebus* (Pecere) 'by whatever means he could' implies that where necessary violent measures would be resorted to in the case of recalcitrant debtors. A report in Ammianus Marcellinus indicates the extent of coercion which Curio exercised; referring to methods used against the Moors by Theodosius, a general of the emperor Valentinian (second half of 4th cent. AD), Ammianus writes: 'But he had the hands of the leaders of the archers cut off and punished the rest with death, following the example of that strictest of leaders Curio, who put an end by a punishment of that kind to the ferocity of the Dardani' (29. 5. 22).

**2. 61.  that warfare in a restricted area would go on too long.** Maurenbrecher printed this as fragment 2. 38 and referred it to an incident described in Frontinus, *Str.* 4. 1. 43. I accept the reference to the Frontinus passage which reads: 'When the consul Gaius Curio was campaigning near Dyrrachium in the war against the Dardani and one of the five legions, having mutinied, had refused service and declared it would not follow his rash leadership on a difficult and dangerous enterprise . . .'. Maurenbrecher, on the basis of the phrase 'the consul Gaius Curio' placed the fragment in the section dealing with affairs of the year 76. He defended this placement in his vol. 1, p. 70, where he rejected the statements of Liv. *Per.* 92 and Eutropius, 6. 2. 2. As a consequence he had to interpret Eutropius' 'triennium' as coinciding with the years 76–74. In this he was followed by Münzer, *RE* 2. 864 6 ff. and Broughton, *MRR* 2.93. As Pecere (*SIFC* 41 (1969), 69) pointed out, Maurenbrecher rejected such evidence as the fact that M. Lucullus, who took up the Macedonian command at the expiry of Curio's triennium and 'as proconsul subdued the Thracians' (Liv. *Per.* 95; cf. Ruf. Festus, 7), could only have done so in 72 since he was consul in 73.

Regarding the Frontinus phrase 'the consul Gaius Curio', Gundermann, to whom Maurenbrecher devotes a highly misleading footnote, proposed in his Teubner edition of Frontinus (1888) in the apparatus to 4. 1. 43 to understand *consul* in the sense of *proconsul*; he referred in 4. 1. 45 to a similar substitution and in the *apparatus* of this latter passage referred to 4. 5. 16. In his preface, p. xv, he mentioned the usage as one of the 'peculiarities' or 'errors' in Frontinus relative to traditional historiography.

**2. 62. Their anger flared to a tremendous degree.** Maurenbrecher referred this (as fr. 2. 44M) to the period of unrest during the consulship of C. Aurelius Cotta in 75; see notes on 2. 42. I consider its application to the mutiny of one of Curio's legions more appropriate.

**2. 63–9.**   The sources for the campaigns conducted by the proconsular governor of Cilicia, P. Servilius Vatia (Isauricus), in the triennium 77–75 provide little factual detail. His first operations which occupied the years 77–76 were directed against eastern Lycia and Pamphylia—see 1. 115–19 with commentary. In 75, the last year of his command he appears to have moved inland from a base in Pamphylia along a route which took him over the mountain range against tribes living to the north of the Taurus. His main target was the region that took its name from the two towns of Old and New Isaura (Liv. *Per.* 93; Strab. 12. 6. 2, 14. 3. 3; Frontin. *Str.* 3. 7. 1; Flor. 1. 41. 5; Eutrop. 6. 3; Ruf. Fest. 12. 3; Amm. Marc. 14. 8. 4; Oros. 5. 23. 23).

**2. 63.   changed direction towards the city of Corycus.** On the basis of this fragment Maurenbrecher accepted the view that after Servilius' reduction of Lycia and Pamphylia he conducted a campaign against Cilicia Tracheia. This was a view held by other scholars also; it was based on source material which Magie (2. 1170 n. 23) regarded as misleading: he pointed out that in Liv. *Per.* 90 *Cilices* is apparently used as a synonym for pirates in conformity with the general tendency to designate them in general by this name; see App. *Mith.* 92. This tendency appears also in general references to Servilius' conquest of 'Cilicia' in Vell. Pat. 2. 39. 2; Eutrop. 6. 3. 5; Oros. 5. 23. 21; Ruf. Fest. 12. 3, where the word is used to denote his victories over the pirates. There is no firm evidence that Servilius succeeded even in entering Cilicia Tracheia, principal headquarters of the pirates.

I believe that here Sallust's source confused Lycian Corycus with Cilician Corycus which was famous for its saffron (Strab. 14. 5. 5; Servius, *G.* 4. 127). A similar mistake was made by Strabo's source at 14. 5. 5. The Lycian Corycus was on Servilius' route to the Taurus range, the mountains behind which lay his chief objective, the territory of the Isauri and adjacent peoples. From the extant material Servilius can be shown to have operated in two districts: a section of the Lycian and Pamphylian coast and the stretch of country extending from Lake Caralis to Isauria. There is no evidence concerning any other district. The Lycian–Pamphylian campaign was completed in 76 and Servilius was left with a base in Pamphylia for further operations. A march through the Taurus from Pamphylia would bring Servilius directly into the country of the Orondeis (see Cic. *Leg. Agr.* 2. 50) which forms the eastern boundary of Lake Caralis.

**2. 64.* Exhausted . . . to Pamphylia.** Maurenbrecher placed this as 1. 128M, assuming a reference to the land operations of the Lycian–Pamphylian campaign which he placed in 77. Kritz (2. 39K) assumed a reference to a pirate commander hard-pressed by Servilius in the same campaign. I find more appealing the probability that it refers to

Servilius' second campaign. There were two possible routes to the north from Lycian Corycus, both difficult and both necessitating hard fighting against the hillsmen en route. It may be that a first attempt to penetrate the Taurus proved unsuccessful, leading to a regrouping and fresh plans to solve the problem.

**2. 65.   they overtop . . . all the [mountains] around.**   Servilius did succeed in getting through the Taurus, a feat which would have been not only exhausting, but also would have evoked the awe aroused by stupendous mountain scenery. The reference is presumably to mountains or to peaks of a particular mountain which overtopped neighbouring features. This and the next three fragments seem to form part of an excursus on the region opened up to their view and on its inhabitants.

**2. 66.   except for areas watered by the Clurda.**   The name Clurda was used by Priscianus as an illustration of his point that some river names end in -*a*. The form of the name presented here is Hertz's correction of the corrupt forms present in the manuscripts; it was based on Plin. *NH* 5. 108 where two rivers are mentioned in connection with the city Eumeneia on the plain of the upper Maeander—*Cludro flumini adposita* ('close to the river Cludrus') and *Glaucus amnis* ('the River Glaucus'). Ramsay, *CB* 1. 354 and Ruge, *RE* 7. 1408, have concluded that the Cludrus was the channel which drained the waters from the springs at the foot of the mountains into the Maeander. See Magie, 2. 984 n. 21.

Dietsch suggested that this fragment is dealing with the nature of a region which, where the river flowed through it, became different from the surrounding plains region, in that swamps were formed. Attractive, but Dietsch himself would not vouch for its certitude.

**2. 67.   a race of nomads . . . pillaging . . . planting.**   I take this to refer to the Isauri, 'a people who lived in a wild, inaccessible region, broken by steep mountain ridges and deep ravines with occasional plains where grain could be grown' (Magie, 1. 289). Their settlements are called λῃστῶν κατοικίαι—'robbers' settlements'—by Strabo, 12. 6. 2.

**2. 68. They buy . . . chattels consecrated to the service of the gods.** I agree with Maurenbrecher's ascription of this to the Isauri, who bought the chattels from the pirates who had seized them as booty. Plutarch, *Pomp.* 24, gives a detailed description of pirate activity by land and sea, taking heavy toll of temples and sanctuaries hitherto inviolate. App. *Mith.* 92 details the pleasure pirates derived from their raiding activities on land and their habit of retreating from retaliation to mountain-fastnesses. Neither the pirates nor their Isaurian customers would have much reverence for the gods of Graeco-Roman religions. The pirates celebrated their own secret rites and apparently adopted the worship of the Persian god Mithras (Plut. *Pomp.* 24).

**2. 69.** This more extensive fragment provides considerable detail concerning the type of armed conflict in the Isaurian campaign of Servilius. It deals with the destruction of two cities, one of which is not named, the other being definitely called Isaura Nova. Despite the detail there are some matters which have given rise to scholarly debate, in particular the identity of the unnamed town and the manner of the defeat of Isaura Nova.

**2. 69. A. when the second watch was already well advanced.** For purposes of guard duty the Roman night was divided into four watches (*vigiliae*—a word also used to designate the individuals who performed the duty).

**they began fighting simultaneously from both sides.** It is clear that two enemy forces were engaging the Romans at the same time. The phrase *simul utrimque* used here was employed by Sallust in *Cat.* 45. 3 to describe an attack from both sides on the Allobroges on the Mulvian bridge—*simul utrimque clamor ortus est* ('a shout was raised from both sides at once'). Maurenbrecher surmised that one of the enemy armies was a relief force sent to raise the siege and was attacking the Romans from the rear while the townspeople who formed the other force attacked from the front. Hauler (*WS* 49 (1931), 139–40) suggested that the besieged townspeople formed two corps in order to attack the Roman simultaneously from opposite sides.

Either scenario is possible; the strategy demanded the

cover of darkness for the required troop movements and the surprise advantage of a simultaneous attack from both sides: Hauler (*WS* 16 (1894), 48–9 disagreed with Maurenbrecher's scenario on the ground that no sufficient detail was provided concerning the 'relief force'. Such detail could, however, have formed part of the preliminary narrative now lost.

**across the ditches . . . to surmount the rampart.** In the Republican period camp defence was a circuit of circum-vallation consisting of a trench (*fossa*), the earth of which was thrown inwards and formed, along with turf and stones, into a mound (*agger*) on the summit of which a strong palisade of wooden stakes (*sudes*; *valli*) was fixed, forming the rampart (*vallum*). There were four openings in the *vallum*, corresponding to the four gates of the camp. For the engagement depicted here cf. Caes. *BGall*. 3. 25. 1, 7. 72. 4.

**or with their shields.** Maurenbrecher (2. 87M) presented an earlier version *aut omni re* ('or by any other means'). With the help of more sophisticated deciphering devices Hauler changed this reading, which he had proposed in 1887 to *aut umbonibus* (literally, 'the bosses of their shields') (*WS* 49 (1931), 135–7. Cf. Val. Max. 3. 23: *modo umbonis impulsu, modo mucronis ictu depellens* ('casting [them] down, now by the impact of his shield, now by the thrust of his sword').

**2. 69. B.    shortage of water compelled them to surrender.** This statement of cause and the passage in Frontinus, *Str*. 3. 7. 1: 'Publius Servilius diverted the stream from which the inhabitants of Isaura drew their water, and thus forced them to surrender in consequence of thirst' have been referred to Isaura Vetus. Ormerod (*JRS* 12 (1922), 45–6) does so because of the probability that the detail *averso flumine* ('by diverting a river') was inserted by Frontinus, since this type of diversion was a well-known *strategema*; Frontinus has wrongly applied it in the case of an Isaurian town known to have surrendered because of the failure of its water supply. Ormerod interprets the sortie described in section A as a desperate attempt to regain possession of the town's water supply, which had been seized by the Romans. S. Sterrett

(*PAS* 3 (1888), 159) pointed out that the details given in no way correspond to the topographical details of Isaura Vetus (mod. Zengibar Kalesi) situated on the top of Assar Dagh. It was a town that did not depend on a river for its water supply, but partly on a cistern, largely on a spring outside the city walls (mod. Bel Bunar). He therefore refers the diversion of the river to Isaura Nova, a view which I discuss below.

Maurenbrecher believed that both Frontinus and Sallust nominated Isaura Vetus as the town which surrendered because of shortage of water. Since it was known on topographical grounds that this was inaccurate, he concluded that we have to concede that Sallust here, as often, has transmitted information which is false.

**the rural population sold into slavery.** A detail which, together with the unlikelihood that a Roman *vallum* would have been built on the steep mountainside above which the town stood or that the Romans would have been able to cut off the defenders from the spring just outside their walls, makes it most unlikely that Sallust's *oppidum* can be identified with Isaura Vetus. It also renders attractive Magie's suggestion that the target of attack was one of the many 'robbers' settlements' mentioned by Strabo 12. 6. 2. See Magie, 2. 1172 n. 24.

**Isaura Nova.** The site of this town has not been definitely determined. Sterrett (*PAS* 3 (1888), 149–50) placed it at Dinorna, about 32 kilometres north-east of Zengibar Kalesi. This identification was rejected by Jühtner and his associates (*Vorl. Bericht über eine Arch. Exped.* (Prague 1903), 51), who reported no trace of fortifications in the place nor indications that it was ever a town of any importance. Ramsay (*JHS* 25 (1905), 163–80) placed Isaura Nova on a hill near Durla, about 27 kilometres north-east from Zengibar Kalesi, a site accepted by Ruge, *RE* 9. 2055–6. This identification has, however, been complicated by Sterrett's application of Frontinus' *averso flumine* statement to Isaura Nova: W. M. Calder, *JHS* 48 (1928), 220 and *Klio* 23 (1930), 91), has shown that the stream on which Durla lies does not carry enough water to serve as a supply for the modern town, which derives its water from wells.

**for fear that by sending back their envoys.**   Maurenbrecher printed *ne de missione mutarent animos*—'lest they might change their minds about sending hostages'. DEMISSIONE had earlier been interpreted by Wölfflin as *ne dimissione* to produce: 'lest by dispatching envoys elsewhere the enemy might change their minds'. Hartel's version: *ne demissione mutarent animos* ('lest they might change from a mood of depression to one of over confidence') is attractive, but Hauler's fresh examination of the palimpsest convinced him that the genuine reading was *remissione* which I have translated above. See *WS* 49 (1931), 137. The implication is that if the envoys were returned, the Isaurians might well change their minds about honouring their promises to Servilius.

Livy wrote concerning a similar situation: *partim remissione obsidum captivorumque*—'partly, by restoring their hostages and captives'. The first sentence of section C also seems to confirm the acceptability of *remissione*.

**2. 69. C. refugees.**   Presumably Isaurians who had fled from other settlements after being attacked by the Romans. The defiant younger men of Isaura Nova referred to them as *socii* ('allies').

**all engines of war.**   The Latin word employed here, *tormenta*, is used to designate offensive engines of various kinds. Often, however, such artillery is specified separately as *ballistae* and *catapultae*. The *ballista* was used to project stones, the *catapulta* to shoot darts.

**2. 69. D. much experience of Roman strength.**   Refers most probably to the campaign of Marcus Antonius against the pirates of the eastern Mediterranean in 102 BC (Liv. *Per.* 68; cf. Cic. *De Or.* 1. 82; Plut. *Pomp.* 24. 10; Obsequens, 44). This offensive was supplemented by a law passed about 100 BC which excluded pirates from the ports of the Empire and of allied states (*SEG* 3. 378).

**the Great Mother.**   *Magna Mater*, one of several titles of Cybele, the great mother-goddess of Anatolia. Primarily a goddess of fertility and of the mountains, she was regarded

as the protectress of her people in war. Her worship was
brought to Rome about 205 BC.

**only a javelin's throw from the town's escape route.** The
MS reading is: *ex quo in fugam oppidi teli coniectus erat.* The
word *fugam* was rejected by scholars who attempted a
variety of conjectures. Maurenbrecher accepted Mommsen's
*iuga* to produce 'from the ridge of the town'. Frassinetti
(*Athenaeum* 40 (1962), 98–9) agreed with Hauler's point
that *fugam* should be retained if it makes sense; he
disagreed, however, with Hartel's interpretation 'if they
tried to escape' and suggested that *fugam* could mean 'to the
furthermost point of the town'. I have with Hauler kept to a
reasonably common meaning of *fuga* (way of escape, line of
flight)—e.g. Virg. *G.* 4. 443; *Aen.* 7. 24; Prop. 2. 30. 1; Liv.
8. 19. 7, 27. 18. 9. Moreover, metonymical usage occurs
elsewhere in Sallust—e.g. *Cat.* 8. 3 *scriptorum magna
ingenia*; 14. 1 *flagitiorum . . . catervas*; 24. 4 *servitia urbana
sollicitare.*

**2. 70–8.** This group of fragments deals with events of the
Sertorian war after Sertorius' defeat at Segontia down to the
withdrawal of the generals to winter-quarters late in 75.
Immediately after Segontia Sertorius ordered his Celtiberian
contingents to disperse, giving them instructions to collect
additional forces and to meet him in the vicinity of the town
to which he now retreated as if in flight, drawing Pompeius
and Metellus after him. He took refuge in this town which
Plutarch described as 'a strong town among the mountains',
and began to repair the walls and strengthen the gates. It
was not his intention to stand a siege but rather to distract
the Romans; the ruse succeeded because the Romans set
about investing the town while the Spanish contingents
escaped to safety and engaged in the collecting of reinforcements without interruption. Neither Plutarch (*Sert.* 21. 4)
nor Frontinus (*Str.* 2. 13. 3) name this town, but it was
almost certainly Clunia (Liv. *Per.* 92). When Sertorius
effected a junction with his new force after a spectacular
escape from Clunia he embarked on a guerrilla campaign
marked by some tactical success and causing serious disruption
of Roman logistics.

**2. 70–4.** The theatre of this autumn–winter campaign and indeed of the remainder of the Sertorian War was Celtiberia and neighbouring regions; the type of fighting involved the participation of Celtiberian contingents. I have interpreted this group of fragments as being elements of a general introduction to facets of Celtiberian character and training which underlay the devoted support given to Sertorius. Cf. E. Hauler 'Neue Bruchstüke zu Sallusts Historien', *Oesterreich Akad. d. Wissenschaften*, 113 (Vienna 1886), 649–50. The quality of service which involved unswerving loyalty (fr. 70) was expressed in the expertise in guerrilla tactics characteristic of these northern Spaniards (frr. 71, 72) whose fierceness and enthusiasm were matched by the attitude and expectations of their womenfolk (fr. 73). The Sertorian strategy of continuous harassment by land and the interception or destruction of Roman supply convoys was supplemented by similar tactics at sea where Roman seaborne supplies were cut off by ships available to the rebel forces (fr. 74).

**2. 70.\*  dedicate their lives . . . refuse to go on living.** Expressed by Valerius Maximus as follows: 'The Celtiberians even thought it a sacrilege to survive a battle if the one to whose safety they had devoted their lives had fallen' (2. 6. 11). Both Maurenbrecher (1. 125M) and Kritz (2. 20K) connected this fragment with Plutarch, *Sert.* 14. 5: 'It was the custom among the Iberians for those who were stationed about their leader to die with him if he fell.' Sallust applies this Spanish custom specifically to the Celtiberians.

**2. 71.  accustomed from boyhood to brigandage.** Maurenbrecher places this fragment as 2. 88 and Kritz as 2. 77; both refer it to Plutarch's general description of Spanish (Iberian) character in *Sert.* 14, although Kritz is dubious about the validity of the reference.

**2. 74.  in addition a few . . . craft.** A small naval force is implied; its origin is obscure. After his expulsion from Spain in 81 Sertorius had entered into alliance with Cilician pirates (Plut. *Sert.* 7.5; see notes on 1. 87–92) but this agreement was short-lived since they fought against each other in Mauretania (Plut. *Sert.* 9. 2–3). Sertorius' establishment of a naval base at Dianium (see note on 1. 114) indicates that he had some vessels in the seventies; whether these were supplied by Cilician pirates or were vessels lent by Mithridates in accordance with the treaty between him and Sertorius cannot be securely established—see note on 2. 91.

**2. 75–8.** To this group of Sallustian fragments we owe what little is known about details of Pompeius' operations after Sertorius' escape from Clunia. Plutarch simply reports that after this episode and Sertorius' subsequent harassment of the Roman armies Metellus retired to Gaul and Pompeius wintered among the Vaccaei (*Sert.* 21. 8; *Pomp.* 19. 11). But it appears that Pompeius and Sertorius continued to skirmish after Metellus departed for Gaul and before Pompeius retired to winter-quarters. Maurenbrecher's interpretation of these fragments, particularly concerning the theatre of operations, the chronology of events, the site of Pompeius' winter-quarters, is totally different from the implications of Plutarch's summary, and has affected the views of subsequent scholars.

**2. 75. the older men . . . to make peace and obey his orders.** The bulk of the Celtiberian cities allied with Sertorius were situated in the northern mountains; there still remained many cities in Celtiberia and the adjacent regions which had stayed neutral. Moreover, in a land in which warfare of some kind was practically a way of life, the older generations like those of Isauria (see 2. 69. D) were often prepared to accept some form of subjection as the price of peace. In addition even in the earlier wars the older generations of Celtiberia had urged peace with Rome (App. *Hisp.* 94, 100).

**they . . . separated . . . armed themselves.** Strabo, 3. 4. 17, speaks on similar lines of the independent spirit of Spanish women, particularly those of the Cantabri; Plutarch, *Mor.* 248 E, and Polyaenus, *Str.* 7. 48 deal with the warlike disposition of the Lusitanian women.

**Meo⟨riga?⟩.** Only the three first letters of a name, which may be that of the town under threat, have been preserved. Hauler pointed to Ptolemy's *Geography* 2. 6. 50 where a town in the region of the Vaccaei has been transmitted in the MSS sometimes as Lacobriga, sometimes as Meoriga. But our other tradition knows only the form Lacobriga (Plin. *NH* 3. 25; *Itin. Anton.* 395, 449, 454). Hauler is suitably cautious concerning his suggestion; the supplementation Meo⟨rigam⟩ and the setting of the events in the region of the Vaccaei remain quite insecure.

**2. 76. [The townspeople] . . . alliance in good faith.** Maurenbrecher (vol. 2. 100) states that the siege discussed in this fragment involved the town dealt with in the preceding fragment. He offers neither evidence nor argument and omits to mention that between 2. 75 and 2. 76 two columns of text, a narrative of about 150 words, has fallen out; in it the matter of the united efforts of the independent-minded women was probably examined in more detail. I consider Maurenbrecher's identification highly unlikely.

Maurenbrecher printed the beginning of this fragment as follows: '⟨*oppidani promiserunt . . . dierum*⟩ ⟨mora⟩ interposita si exempti forent, fide societatem acturos.' The words in italics were supplied by Maurenbrecher as a possible introduction, and the word ⟨mora⟩ ('delay') was conjectured by Wölfflin to agree with the transmitted *interposita*; the text thus constituted means: 'The inhabitants promised that, if the siege was raised, they would, after a delay of . . . days, enter into an alliance in good faith.'

Pecere (*SIFC* 50 (1978), 155–8) objects to Wölfflin's *mora* on two grounds: a request for delay could be justified on evidence of an objective impediment or internal difficulties; there is no hint of either in the received text. Secondly, a promise of loyal alliance would normally demand a satisfactory guarantee of adherence to the pact. Having noted a very similar situation in Dictys Cretensis 1. 12: 'Pelopidae in unum conveniunt *atque interposita iuris iurandi religione* ni Helena . . . redderetur bellum se Priamo inlaturos *confirmant*', Pecere suggested a reading which adopts the terminology italicized in the Dictys passage. He therefore presented: '*oppidani* ⟨confirmant religione iuris iurandi⟩ interposita si . . .' to produce the version I have presented in translation. His conjecture also suggests a solution to Perl's problem

concerning the word to which *interposita* should be connected
(*WZ Rostock* 12 (1963), 272–3).

**between him and Pompeius.**  The context clearly indicates
that *illum* ('him') is a reference to Sertorius. It has been
assumed because of the order of the words that *illum* is the
person addressed and that therefore it was Sertorius who
was besieging the town. This I do not believe can be
harmonized with Plutarch's description of the activity of the
two generals (*Sert.* 21) which Florus, 2. 10. 8, vividly
summarizes: 'then one army [Sertorius] devoting itself to
laying waste the countryside and the other [Pompeius] to the
destruction of the cities'.

**Then the Roman army was withdrawn.**  Maurenbrecher's
interpretation that Pompeius was forced to withdraw out of
fear of Sertorius, who had entered into an agreement with
the besieged townspeople, has been accepted by most
commentators after him. Perl, however, points out (loc. cit.)
that the reason for the Roman departure is given in the
fragment as *frumenti gratia* ('for the purpose of securing
supplies'). He assumes that Pompeius, who wanted to win
over more communities in northern Spain in order to
provide a base for a winter camp, began a siege against a
neutral town whose loyalty he won by a pact of friendship.
He raised the siege of the town and since he could not expect
maintenance from it to support a longer stay, he marched
away. It was for the protection of these and other allies that
he subsequently left Titurius with fifteen cohorts (one and a
half legions) in Celtiberia (2. 76).

   I find Perl's suggestions attractive, particularly the point
that the offer of alliance was made by Pompeius, not
Sertorius. The corrupt state of the transmission and the lack
of sufficient detail must, however, confine one to the realm
of conjecture.

**to the territory of the Vascones.**  Maurenbrecher accepted
this statement as confirmation that Pompeius set up his
winter-quarters among the Vascones and not the Vaccaei as
Plutarch (*Sert.* 21. 8) reports. He accused Plutarch of error
(see 2. 93M) occasioned by the fact that, after the separation
from Metellus, Pompeius went to the Vaccaei. Subsequent

scholarship: Stahl, *De Bello Sertoriano*, 76–7; Drumann–
Groebe, *Geschichte Roms* 4. 383 n. 3; T. Rice Holmes,
1. 149, 383; Schulten, 120; van Ooteghem *Pompée*, 119;
Gelzer, *Pompeius*, 49 has followed Maurenbrecher in
accepting Pompeius' first operations as being in the territory
of the Vaccaei, the winter-camp among the Vascones. The
fragility of this hypothesis is revealed in Schulten's (p. 120
n. 563) carefree remark that Plutarch's περὶ Βακκαίους is
naturally a confusion with *Vascones*.

This fragment makes quite clear that because of lack of
supplies and the continual threat from Sertorius a lengthy
winter-quartering among the Vascones was not possible.

**the hopes he had of Asia.**   Maurenbrecher's Latin version:
*ne ei perinde Asiae Galliaeque vaderent e facultate*, which
presumably means: 'lest accordingly the route to Asia and
Gaul be no longer available to him', implies that Sertorius
made the move to ensure that he was not cut off from the
east coast.

Like Hauler (*WS* 9 (1887), 31) I find more acceptable,
Hartel's conjecture *ne ei periret Asiae* ⟨*spes*⟩: 'that the
hope he had concerning Asia might not be lost to him', a
reference to the continuing negotiation with Mithridates
about a treaty which would bring Sertorius much-needed
reinforcement in money and ships.

After the word *Asiae* Hartel decided to start a new
sentence: *Atque vadi e facultate Pompeius* . . . ('because of
the convenience of the ford, Pompeius . . .'), which suggests
that because of a ford which was easy to cross Pompeius
interrupted his march for some days, not so much because
he was worrying about supplies of water in a parched region
(cf. Strabo, 3. 4. 12) as, being only a short distance away, he
might entice the elusive Sertorius to a pitched battle or be
able himself to mount a surprise attack on the rebel force.

**the Mutudurei and the [N]eores.**   Two communities obviously
adjacent to the Vascones who had retained their neutrality.
The exact location of the two peoples remains unknown.
Hauler's addition of [*N*] was based on Pliny's (*NH* 6. 29)
transmission of the name 'Neoris in Hiberia'. The fact that
these communities were not prepared to provide supplies

supports the point about the acute shortage which made a prolonged stay in the region by either army an impossibility.

**in battle-square formation.** The Latin phrase *agmine quadrato incedere* was applied to the line of march adopted when advancing through hostile country where surprise attacks were expected. Instead of advancing in extended, straggling columns the troops were kept in close, compact groups, flanking the baggage-trains on all four sides, ready to react immediately to danger from any quarter; cf. Sall. *Iug.* 105, 3–5.

**2. 77. He ordered . . . Titurius.** An order given by Pompeius as he was setting out with the bulk of his troops for winter-quarters among the Vaccaei. The provision of two winter-quarters served the purpose of conserving supplies in either region and of reassuring allies whose support was vital in the following year's campaign.

**2. 78. they invaded the fields of the Termestini.** A people of Termes (Ptol. *Geog.* 2. 6. 56) between Clunia and Numantia who were very friendly with Sertorius (Flor. 2. 10. 9). They are mentioned in Liv. *Per.* 54 and in Tac. *Ann.* 4. 45. 1.

This attack has been attributed to Pompeius' force on its way to winter-quarters. It seems more likely that Titurius' contingent, which faced a bleak winter in a region largely hostile or indifferent to their needs, made such raids when the necessity arose.

**2. 79–81.** I take these three fragments to be part of an introductory narrative to Pompeius' letter to the senate, the two major points of which are the crucial shortage of regular food supplies and money to procure such supplies and pay the troops.

**2. 79. many convoys had been destroyed.** Whatever arrangements were made for the provisioning of the Roman soldiers depended ultimately on the safe arrival of supplies. As Plutarch (*Sert.* 21) emphasized, Sertorius' tactic was to use the expertise of his Celtiberian guerrillas to cut off supply-trains; it was a tactic which in Plutarch's view brought about the decision of the Roman generals to separate into different winter-quarters. The threat remained operative even during the winter months; Pompeius' call for reinforcement was no doubt partially prompted by the necessity of finding some way to counter the cutting-off of his supply lines.

**2. 80\*–81.   money . . . provided to give Metellus the means.**   A serious problem facing any commander in the field was the regular availability of pay for his troops: non-payment over extended periods triggered unrest and even mutiny. Because Metellus' name is mentioned in fr. 80\* Maurenbrecher placed it as 2. 34\*M in 76. I prefer the present context: when Pompeius took over from Metellus it may be that he expected to inherit some of the funds allocated to Metellus to meet campaign expenses. It can be deduced from fr. 80\* that his expectations on this point were not met. His disappointment and disgust at the Roman treasury's failure to meet the shortfall are expressed in 2. 82. 2–3. His own efforts to remedy the situation included private borrowing (fr. 81) to an extent that exhausted both his means and his credit (2. 82. 9).

**2. 82.**   It is not unlikely that Sallust had seen the original letter sent by Pompeius to the senate. His version of it, however, is in keeping with his earlier portrait wherein he dealt with leading character-traits of that ambitious general (2. 17–20). The thrust of the letter is clear; the responsibility for the existing crisis is placed directly on the senate, which had sent a very young general into a very difficult war, a task undertaken by him more out of enthusiasm than discretion. Pompeius' version of his prowess and his service to the state is presented as an account to be settled by the governing body. The language in which the demands are couched, the barely concealed threats they contain are in keeping with the vanity and arrogance which were undoubtedly real traits of Pompeius' personality, even though Sallust, who detested the man, may have taken extra trouble to bring them into sharper focus in this context.

**2. 82. 1.   toils and dangers . . . since my early manhood.** In 83 BC Pompeius in his twenty-third year raised an army on his own responsibility in Picenum, where he checked Carbo the proconsul and marched to join Sulla, defeating the Marian officers C. Carrinas, T. Cluilius, and Iunius Brutus Damasippus on the way. He was saluted as Imperator by Sulla (Plut. *Pomp*. 6–8; Liv. *Per*. 85; Vell. Pat. 2. 29, 1–2). In 82 he drove the Marian general Carbo out of Etruria (see note on 1. 33*); sent by Sulla against Perperna in Sicily, he drove out Perperna and put the consul Carbo to death (see note on 1. 44*). In 81 he vanquished the Marians in Africa under Domitius Ahenobarbus whom he put to death, and was saluted in the field as Imperator (see note on 1. 45).

**in my absence.** In a period of acute shortages and unrest in Rome (see note on 2. 44. 6–8) the senate, which from the outset had been reluctant to support Pompeius' appointment to Spain, had not been willing to allocate a disproportionate share of meagre resources to any one theatre of war. Pompeius' mode of expression contains an arrogant implication that if he had been nearer at hand the senate would not have had the courage to refuse his requests.

**in spite of my youth, having exposed me.** An attack on the inconsiderate nature of the senate in appointing him to such a difficult task. The word *proiectum* is used here precisely to designate an action ill-considered and ill-advised; cf. Sall. *Iug*. 14. 21. The words 'in spite of my youth' emphasize that since the senate alone was responsible for his nomination no blame could be attached to him since he was too young to foresee and to evaluate the risks. Hence the responsibility of aiding him lay entirely with the senate.

**to a most cruel war.** Sallust's *saevissimum bellum* is described by Cicero as *durissimum*, 'most difficult' (*Balb*. 5) and 'a very extensive and most dangerous war' (*Leg. Man.* 62).

**the most wretched of all deaths.** A common theme; cf. Homer, *Od*. 12. 341–2; Thuc. 3. 59. 3; Dion. Hal. Ant. *Rom*. 6. 86; Liv. 27. 44. 8, 21. 41. 11.

**an army which deserves your highest gratitude.** Reference to the army's service to its country, a factor which receives no mention in Pompeius' list of successes (§ 6) is here used to strengthen his accusations against the senate: the more meritorious the loyalty of the troops, the more odious the attitude of the government.

**2. 82. 2. the Roman people.** The senate's negligence concerning affairs in Spain is presented as a danger to the state.

**the means of meeting even one year's expenses.** Cotta's speech (2. 44. 6–8) gives a reasonably accurate account of the scale of the difficulties facing the government at this time; Pompeius, however, is naturally concentrating on his particular problems.

**2. 82. 4.  I admit . . . with more eagerness than discretion.** The only personal blame that Pompeius will accept; even that is excusable because of his age (§ 1).

**only a titular command.**  A title without an army, which he provided out of his own resources. A mixture of exaggeration and downright lies. Plutarch sets the picture straight: 'Pompeius, therefore, who kept his army (the one allocated to him by the senate for the war against Lepidus, see note on 1. 68) under his command, tried to get himself sent out to reinforce Metellus, and although Catulus ordered him to disband his soldiers, he would not do so, but remained under arms near the city, ever making some excuse or other, until the senate gave him the command on the motion of Lucius Philippus' (*Pomp.* 17. 3).

**within forty days.**  The speed (*celeritas*) with which Pompius conducted his campaigns was especially remarked on. Thus of his African campaign in 81 Plutarch remarks: 'It took him only forty days all told, they say, to bring his enemies to naught' (*Pomp.* 12. 8); much the same sort of time is allotted by Cicero to the pirate war conducted by Pompeius in 67 (*Leg. Man.* 34–5).

**drove an enemy . . . at the very throat of Italy from the Alps into Spain.**  Gross exaggeration, if not outright distortion of the facts. Sertorius is presented as having removed himself from Spain with the intention of attacking Italy—something which never happened even if it were ever part of Sertorius' intention. The cliché 'at the very throat' or its equivalent *supra caput* occurs in Cic. *Mur.* 79; Sall. *Cat.* 52. 24; Liv. 3. 17. 2, 4. 22. 6.

**a route different from that which Hannibal had taken.** App. *BC* I. 109 reports: 'Pompeius courageously crossed the Alps, not with the expenditure of labour of Hannibal, but by opening another passage around the sources of the Rhône and the Eridanus (Po). These issue from the Alpine mountains not far from each other.' Determination of Pompeius' route depends on agreement concerning Hannibal's route. If Hannibal, as many assume, crossed the Alps by the Little St Bernard Pass then the route chosen by Pompeius is to be sought in the Cottian Alps (Mont Genèvre) a shorter line of communication between the valley of the Po and Gaul. If the pass over the Cottian Alps (Mont Genèvre) is assumed for Hannibal then for Pompeius the available route was through the Col d'Argentière which according to Jacobs–Wirz–Kurfess would fulfil all the stipulations implied in the Sallust–Appian reports.

**2. 82. 5. I recovered Gaul.** A gross exaggeration. No general revolt broke out in Transalpine Gaul. Disturbances of the peace did occur at several places; the cantons of the Volcae-Arecomici and the Helvii in Gallia Narbonensis were deprived of their independence by Pompeius and placed under Massilia. See note on 2. 22, **at Narbonne . . .**

**Lacetania.** The country of the Lacetani, 'a remote people living in woodlands' (Liv. 34. 20. 2) in the extreme north-east of Spain. The name is also presented as Laeetania (Plin. *NH* 25. 17) and Laletania (Mart. 1. 49. 22). See G. Barbieri, *Athenaeum* 31 (1943), 113–21.

**the Indicetes.** Another Spanish people of the north-east, bordering on the Lacetani (Plin. *NH* 3. 21).

**the first onslaught of the victorious Sertorius.** The battle of Lauro which is discussed in the notes on 2. 28–31. Pompeius did survive that encounter but suffered enormous losses.

**in spite of the rawness of my troops.** A mendacious protection of his reputation: his troops were experienced campaigners. See note on § 4, **only a titular command.**

**not in the towns nor in boosting my own popularity.** That is, by indulging his troops with more comfortable quarters. It has been suggested that Pompeius, with malice aforethought, contrasted himself with the other Roman general Metellus (mentioned only once, § 9), who was justifiably exposed to criticism for his foolish ostentation and self-indulgence. See notes on 2. 59.

**2. 82. 6. Why I need enumerate battles . . . ?** A careful avoidance of detail because of his own remarkably poor performance. The examples he can quote with safety are few and have to be carefully worded.

**the taking of the enemy's camp at the Sucro.** Pompeius' implication that this was a significant feat is an impudent fabrication. Details of the battle of the Sucro are dealt with in the notes on 2. 51–54. Pompeius himself suffered an ignominious defeat; the so-called occupation of the enemy's camp was due to his lieutenant, L. Afranius, and was a very brief affair which Pompeius was forced to abandon.

**the battle at the River Turia . . . and the city of Valentia.** The separate elements of this, the only totally successful engagement conducted by Pompeius, are presented as if each were a great feat in itself. Details are touched on in the notes on 2. 46 and 47.

**2. 82. 7. either, if victorious, can march into Italy.** A hypothetical situation conveying a threat more explicitly formulated later (§ 10). If Sertorius were to emerge victorious in Spain, he could well transfer the war to Italy; more seriously, if Pompeius conquered Sertorius he would be free to repay the injustices received from the senate and the privations they had thereby suffered.

**2. 82. 8. by abandoning the interests of the state for my own.** Makes more explicit the vague threat of § 7. Pompeius is, as it were, subject to surges of anger as he dwells on the effects of the senate's negligence. His final contemplation of the situation (§ 9), which involves not only the spectre of continuing famine but also personal ruin for himself, results in a threat which is unmistakable in its intent and its inevitability (§ 10). In this final sentence of the letter

Pompeius covers the full range of emotional stress—from a cry for help to a threat which is precise in its articulation and deadly serious.

**2. 82. 9.   Last year Gaul provided Metellus' army.**   The fact that Metellus also was forced to rely on local supplies to maintain his army indicates that reasons other than political were responsible for the lack of support about which Pompeius is complaining. He implies that the government's failure to supply him was due to political bias. It appears, however, that logistic problems in the field (fr. 79) and economic problems at home were the main reasons for lack of supplies.

**2. 82. D.   at the beginning of the following year.**   i.e. 74, the year of the consulship of L. Licinius Lucullus and M. Aurelius Cotta, the brother of Gaius (consul in 75).

**the consuls agreed.**   Namely the consuls of the preceding year, Gaius Aurelius Cotta and L. Octavius.

**because of the interests of the state.**   That the decision to provide money and reinforcements for Spain was motivated and expressed as being for the supreme good of the state is probably true to some extent. However, the way in which the sentence has been formulated clearly conveys the thinking of Sallust. The consuls are affected by Pompeius' threat to return to Italy because of its probable effect on their status and opportunity for glory; Lucullus in particular, who had ambitions concerning the command against Mithridates, feared lest he be ousted by Pompeius (Plut. *Luc.* 5. 2–3).

**and were backing their words with deeds.**   A statement illustrated by the activity of Antonius against the pirates in the second half of 74 (note on 3. 6). The view that this should be changed to a negative statement—'but did not match their words with deeds'—(D. R. Shackleton Bailey, *Mnem.* 34 (1982), 356; Diggle, *PACA* 17 (1983), 59–60) is therefore untenable.

**2. 83–91.***   The placement and interpretation of this group of fragments depend wholly on a decision concerning the dating of events connected with the content of 2. 83, which refers to the dispute over the succession to the Bithynian throne after the death of Nicomedes Philopator. The king had bequeathed his kingdom to Rome (Liv. *Per.* 93; App. *Mith.* 71; Eutrop. 6. 6. 1). The Roman senate's acceptance of the legacy and its decision to turn Bithynia into a Roman province so alarmed Mithridates of Pontus that he took up arms, advanced into Bithynia with his major force and sent smaller armies against Asia, Cappadocia, and Phrygia.

For many decades the date of the death of the last Bithynian king and of the outbreak of the so-called third Mithridatic War, which was a consequence of events connected with the death, has been a matter of serious dispute. Two dates have been put forward for the beginning of the Mithridatic War—74 BC, which has remained the majority view, and 73 BC which was first mentioned as a possibility by W. Ihne, *Römische Geschichte* 6 (Leipzig 1886), 70 n. 2, who did not pursue the matter further. It was Th. Reinach who drew attention to evidence provided by the royal Bithynian coinage, a tetradrachm bearing the name Nicomedes and dated 224 in the Bithynian Era which began, as he believed then (*Trois royaumes de l'Asie Mineure* (1888), 132) in October 297, which would make 224 equivalent to the Roman twelve-month period 1 October 74–1 October 73. The consequence, namely that the Roman campaign in Bithynia could not have begun earlier than 73, was accepted by E. Meyer, *RE* 3. 516; C. Brandis, *RE* 3. 524; W. Kubitchek, *RE* 1. 635. In 1908, however, Reinach changed his mind and dated the beginning of the era to October 298, with the consequence that the coinage evidence pointed to a date earlier than 73 for the outbreak of the war (Waddington–Babelon–Reinach, *Recueil général des monnaies* etc. (Paris 1904–8), 217–18).

A revival of support for Reinach's first position is indicated in more recent research—e.g. W. H. Bennett, *Historia*, 10 (1961), 469 ff.; B. McGing, *Phoenix* 38 (1984), 12–18. The most persistent advocate for a return to 73 BC for the outbreak of the Mithridatic War is G. Perl, *Philologus* 111 (1967), 383–8; *BIRT* 15 (1967–8), 29–38; *Studien zur Geschichte und Philosophie des Altertums* (Amsterdam 1968), 229–330; *VDI* 109 (1969), 39–69. Perl's basic argument is that if Sallust's statement on 2. 83 can be reconciled with the evidence of Eutropius 6. 6. 1 ('in the consulship of L. Licinius Lucullus and M. Aurelius Cotta [i.e. 74 BC] Nicomedes king of Bithynia died and in his will made the Roman people his heir') and of the coinage, then the date 73 BC can be firmly established for the outbreak of the war. This view is based on a series of assumptions which in my opinion have not been established as fact. His main point, that the retention of the ostensible dating by Sallust in 2. 83 of the year 75 (based on book-number and Maurenbrecher's placement of this material before the Spanish campaign of autumn/winter 75) involves rejection of the clear and unequivocal dating provided by Eutropius and the coins, is quite misleading. We have noted that the evidence of the coinage is by no means unequivocal; Perl's presentation of the evidence, impressive in its detail, does not provide compelling reasons for accepting the contention that Reinach's first position was the correct one. Secondly, Perl's approbation of the singular accuracy of Eutropius' practice of dating by consular-years (*Studien zur Gesch.* 308) in no way provides grounds for assuming that Eutropius is referring to the last quarter of 74.

Fragment 2. 83 has been transmitted by Priscianus as belonging to Book 2. The fragility of Perl's argumentation concerning Eutropius and the Bithynian coinage would be considerably discounted if he could show that the content of 2. 83 belongs to the end of 74 and hence to Book 3 of the *Histories*. This he attempts to do. From a detailed examination of the reliability of Priscianus' transmission of book-numbers in his citations from the *Histories* (*Philologus* 111 (1967), 285–8) he recommends that the transmitted book-number 2 in this case should be changed to 3. Once again his argument is plausible but not compelling. He begins by admitting that the book-number of only one of the 57 citations from Sallust's *Histories* has been unanimously questioned by editors (see note on 4. 8M). He therefore conducts a statistical survey of Priscianus citations from fifteen works of eleven other Latin authors ranging from Cicero to Juvenal.

He worked on the categories 'correct', 'uncertain', 'false'.

Numbers cited are 'uncertain' where more than half the manuscripts are in agreement; where all or the majority of manuscripts disagree the cited number is false. On such statistical criteria he estimated that an average error percentage by Priscianus was just under 10 per cent; hence one should reckon on five or six errors among the 57 Sallustian citations, or in exceptionally favourable circumstances on two or three errors.

Further comment on this procedure as a sure basis for change is unnecessary. I simply refer to the criteria for critical analysis discussed in the note on 2. 16, **in their gossip . . . they were destroying**, and add that Perl failed to point out that of Priscianus' nine manuscripts eight show support for the transmitted number, 2; the remaining MS (*G*) failed to mention any number. Given these circumstances, I readily share the view expressed by Broughton in *MRR* 2. 106: 'I see no certain solution, but believe that the weight of evidence on the whole supports the earlier date.' Accordingly I follow his chronology of the activities of Lucullus' command between the years 74 and 69 (ibid. 108).

Maurenbrecher (vol. 2. 89 and 228–9) ignored the evidence of Eutropius and reported the group 2. 83–91 (= 2. 71–9M) under the rubric *res Asiae* ('Asian affairs'), placing it before the narrative of Curio's Macedonian campaign and the expedition of Servilius against the Isauri. This was an allocation presumably approved by Rice Holmes, 1. 400–1, and Bloch, *Didascaliae*, 73. I agree with Perl's view that the material should rather form part of *res urbanae* (city affairs) in a continuing context with the affairs of 74 discussed in note on 2. 82. D. This would fit in with the date indicated by Eutropius; moreover, the loss of a bifolium (Maurenbrecher; Bloch, *Didasaliae*, 66) or possibly two bifolia (Perl, *BIRT* 15 (1967–8), 32 ff.) of the Fleury MS between the end of the report of 2. 92. D. and the narrative of M. Antonius' campaign against the pirates in 3. 6 makes possible a reasonably detailed treatment at the end of Book 2 of the preliminary material relating to the Mithridatic War.

**2. 83. Opposing them . . . many who wished . . . to prove.** The Roman senate justified its acceptance of Nicomedes' bequest on the grounds that there was no

legitimate heir to the kingdom. Many in Bithynia protested
that there was an heir-apparent, a son of Nicomedes and
Nysa (cf. 4. 69. 9M) whose cause Mithridates espoused to
justify his invasion of Bithynia. The fragment deals with the
willingness of many Bithynians to come to Rome and argue
against those, probably including the envoys sent to Rome,
who maintained the legitimacy of the son of Nysa.

**2. 84–91.** Since the outcome of the senate's decision to
accept Nicomedes' legacy and to establish Bithynia as a
province was the third Mithridatic War, which plays a
prominent part in the narrative of Books 3–5, Sallust took
the opportunity to provide a characterization of Mithridates
Eupator which apparently dealt with his physical and
psychological make-up and his activity in the period preceding the outbreak of a war which had been threatening for
a long time. In this Sallust followed a method he had
practised in his monographs: he did not interrupt the
narrative of crucial events with digressions on personal and
political detail concerning the protagonists or with incidental
factors such as topography; these he dealt with in a
preliminary treatment as in *Cat.* 5; *Iug.* 5 ff., 17 ff., 63, 95.
Cf. the portrait of Pompeius in *Hist.* 2. 17–20.

**2. 84.*** **one cannot speak except with concern.** The
sentence in Seneca *Ben.* 4. 1. 1 which connects Sallust with
the phrase *cum cura dicendus* reads as follows: *potest videri
nihil tam necessarium aut magis, ut ait Sallustius, cum cura
dicendum* ('no [point] can seem so essential or to need, as
Sallust puts it, such careful treatment'). de Brosses and
Gerlach assumed that the Sallustian fragment was *magis
cum cura dicendum* ('should rather be expressed with care')
and placed it in the preface at the beginning of Book 1. Kritz
and Dietsch expunged it from the *Histories* on the ground
that Seneca had in mind Sallust's passage in *Iug.* 5. 4. 1.
Wölfflin (*Hermes* 9 (1875), 23–4) showed from a series of
examples, including Seneca, *Prov.* 5. 9 and *Tranq.* 14. 10,
that the Sallustian phrase was *vir cum cura dicendus*; in this
phrase the word *cura* which has several shades of meaning is
to be interpreted in line with the context. Wölfflin went on
to pinpoint the probable reference to Mithridates by quoting

a statement concerning the king in Vell. Pat. 2. 18. 1: *Vir neque silendus neque dicendus sine cura* ('a man about whom one cannot speak except with concern nor yet pass over in silence'). My translation of the fragment is based on this parallel.

**2. 85.\*   Artabazes . . . the founder of the kingdom of Mithridates.**   Florus (1. 40. 1) states that Artabazes succeeded Aeetas the first king of Pontus and that he was sprung from one of the seven Persians who had destroyed the pseudo-Smerdis. The history of the Mithridatidae is beset with difficulties; the sources have preserved material which is fictitious in its details. The family was indeed of Persian origin but Ed. Meyer, *Gesch. d. Königr. Pontos*, 31–2, has shown that the claim that the Pontic monarchs had ruled over the kingdom in the Persian period and that they were descended from one of the conspirators who murdered the Magian Smerdis (Polybius, 5. 43. 2; Diodorus, 19. 40. 2; Florus, 1. 40. 1: Auct. *Vir. Ill.* 76) is a fiction. Likewise the statement that the Mithridatic line was descended from Darius (Sallust 2. 85; Justin 38. 7. 1; Tacitus *Ann.* 12. 18. 3) is without foundation. Cf. Magie, 2. 10.

**2. 86–8\*.**   Fragments which illustrate the thinking behind Sallust's introductory phrase, *vir cum cura dicendus.* When Mithridates V Euergetes was assassinated in Sinope (120/1 BC) a last will and testament, probably forged, appointed his wife—who may have played a part in the assassination—to rule in the name of their two sons, Eupator and Mithridates Chrestos. At that time Mithridates Eupator was 11 years old. How much truth there is in the stories of plots against him as a boy, his escape from the court and subsequent wanderings cannot be determined. In physique, in physical prowess, in temperament he in fact conveyed a larger than life image and this provided the writers of his court with the opportunity, after the manner of late Hellenistic historiography, to enhance with romantic and thrilling detail the story of their patron.

  One fact can be fixed: sometime before 115 BC (*OGIS* 139) a *coup d'état* ended the rule of his mother, who spent the rest of her life in prison; the two boys were left to rule the kingdom until Chrestos was removed by his older brother.

**2. 86. of a cruel disposition.** '[Mithridates] was blood-thirsty and cruel to all' (App. *Mith.* 112).

**2. 87.\* after removing his mother by poison.** The tradition has it that by Mithridates' orders there died or lingered in perpetual captivity for real or alleged treason his mother, his brother, the sister he had married, three of his sons, and three of his daughters. Variations in detail of the reporting of these acts should cause no surprise. Appian (*Mith.* 112) agrees with Sallust in stating that Mithridates was 'the slayer of his mother' but he does not specify the method used.

**2. 88.\* killed both a brother and a sister.** The scholiast's comparison of Mithridates with Medea who murdered her two sons to punish Jason for deserting her is kept in balance with his selection of Sallust's reporting of Mithridates' murder of his brother and sister. Having removed his mother, the young king married his sister and at first shared the rule with his brother. Both were removed when Mithridates could brook neither rival nor equal. Plutarch (*Luc.* 18) lists 'out of many women' sisters and wives whose death was caused by Mithridates.

**2. 89.\* huge stature . . . weapons of a comparable size.** Appian (*Mith.* 112) provides detail, some probably apocryphal: 'He had a large frame, as his armour which he himself sent to Nemea and to Delphi shows, and was so strong that he rode on horseback and hurled his javelin to the last, and could ride a thousand stades (120 miles) in one day, changing horses at intervals. He used to drive a chariot with sixteen horses at once.' On 'weapons of comparable size' see Florus 1. 7. 4.

**2. 90. As a result of the Fimbrian revolt.** When Marius died in 86 L. Valerius Flaccus was appointed to the vacant consulship and also took over the command against Mithridates (first Mithridatic War). On his journey to the East Flaccus lost some of his men and some deserted to Sulla (see note on 1. 27–9). He also so alienated his army that the soldiers mutinied, killed Flaccus, and illegally appointed his legate C. Flavius Fimbria as their commander. The most detailed account of the mutiny is in App. *Mith.* 52–3; cf. Liv. *Per.* 82; Plut. Luc. 7. 2; Oros. 6. 2. 9.

Fimbria had success against Mithridates' son at Miletopolis, pinned down Mithridates himself at Petane, and sacked Cyzicus and Ilium (85 BC). When his army was taken over by Sulla Fimbria committed suicide at Pergamum (Diod. 38. 8; Liv. *Per.* 83; Strab. 13. 1. 27; App. *Mith.* 59–60).

**there were present at the court.** Orosius, 6. 2. 12, reports that Fannius and Magius fled as deserters from Fimbria's army to Mithridates; that it was at their urging that Mithridates arranged through envoys a treaty with Sertorius; that, to cement the treaty, Sertorius sent M. Marius to Mithridates and that the king appointed Marius to replace the commander Archelaus who had gone over to Sulla. Appian (*Mith.* 68) gives a different, and doubtful, version in which, both here and in ch. 70, he wrongly names Marcus Marius as Marcus Varius: 'Lucius Magius and Lucius Fannius were members of Sertorius' faction and when Sertorius concluded a treaty with Mithridates he sent Marcus Varius to him as general and the two Lucii, Magius and Fannius, as counsellors.'

**compliance in discussions.** The kind of deference which Mithridates expected and which influenced his decision-making is stressed by Plutarch: 'Mithridates, eager to send envoys to him, was incited to do so most of all by the foolish exaggeration of his flatterers. These likened Sertorius to Hannibal and Mithridates to Pyrrhus, and declared that the Romans, attacked on both sides, could not hold out against two such natures and forces combined, when the ablest of generals was in alliance with the greatest of kings' (*Sert.* 23. 3).

**respected and favoured by the king.** Illustrated by the closing sentence of Mithridates' address to his troops before setting out for the invasion of Bithynia in 74: 'Do you not see', he added, 'some of their noblest citizens (pointing to Varius [Marius] and the two Lucii) at war with their own country and allied with us?' (App. *Mith.* 70).

**2. 91.\*   They arrived . . . more quickly than Mithridates expected.**   A reference to the return of the envoys whom Mithridates had sent to Sertorius (Plut. *Sert.* 23. 4). The envoys were accompanied by Sertorius' quaestor Marcus Marius at the head of a contingent of troops (Plut. Sert. 24. 3; Oros. 6. 2. 12). On the discussions between Mithridates and Sertorius see Gabba, *Comm. App. Lib.* 1. 518. The terms of the treaty and the date of its ratification are matters of dispute. Plutarch's report on Sertorius' comment on the difference between Bithynia and Cappadocia and the province of Asia (*Sert.* 23. 6) would indicate that the treaty deliberations took place before the death of Nicomedes Philopator of Bithynia.

**2. 92–112.**   These are fragments of uncertain placement in Book 2. I begin with fragments placed by Maurenbrecher in the text of Book 2 (frr. 92–6); these I have relegated to this section because I feel that Maurenbrecher's placements cannot be satisfactorily justified. Thereafter I more or less follow Maurenbrecher's order, but try as far as possible to deal in a connected context with what I consider to be related fragments.

**2. 92.   truly expert in the art of war.**   The first two words of this three-word fragment *belli sane sciens* are uncertain. Maurenbrecher (2. 18M) accepted Lindemann's conjecture *belli sane* and I have translated it as above. His referral of it to Pompeius is, however, too daring: it could equally apply to Sertorius or to Metellus.

**2. 93.   whom King Leptasta . . . charge of treachery.**   Dietsch hypothesized that since Sertorius supported the king of Mauretania against Ascalis, pretender to the throne, the king sent to Sertorius a legate whom he accused of treachery. Maurenbrecher (2. 20M), objecting that such an incident properly belongs to Book 1, substituted a conjecture that the fragment referred to an incident in Pompeius' campaign in Africa. No evidence concerning an incident involving Leptasta is extant.

**2. 94.   addressing many meetings . . . in the Circus Maximus.**   The *Ludi Apollinares*, games instituted in honour of Apollo four years after the battle of Cannae (212

BC) were held annually on 6–13 July (Liv. 25. 12; Macrob. *Sat.* 1. 17. 25–30). It was a period in which public meetings were not normally held; the fact that meetings were held on this occasion indicates a period of political unrest. Maurenbrecher (2. 48M) ascribes it to the unrest occasioned by Cotta's law concerning the tribunate in 75 and the activity of the tribune Q. Opimius—see note on 2. 45, **that it should be permitted . . .** The period dealt with in Book 2 was beset with a variety of political problems; it is not possible to fix precisely on the year and on the personage involved in this case.

**2. 95. and the serious [situation] . . . under control.** There is not enough information provided here to justify Maurenbrecher's (2. 51M) referral to the popular unrest which occurred during Cotta's consulship (see note on 2. 42).

**2. 96. with too much confidence in himself.** Another statement far too vague to pinpoint precisely. Maurenbrecher (2. 53M) referred it to some legate of Sertorius who had ignored his instruction not to meet the Romans in pitched battle; he suggested Herennius or, better, Perperna. Reasonable, but the number of possible references in Book 2—e.g. Hirtuleius at Italica; Pompeius at Lauro; Pompeius at the Sucro—inhibits positive selection.

**2. 97–102.** Indicate operations on or near a river. Two such battles figure in Book 2—Valentia (River Turia) and Sucro (River Sucro). The meagre content of the fragments, the paucity of detail concerning the battles, the lack of proper names of place and protagonists make firm allocation of any one of these fragments hazardous. One must confine oneself to speculation.

Maurenbrecher speculated that 2. 97–9 (= 2. 99–100M) might form part of the narrative of the battle of Valentia. I believe that 2. 99 and 2. 100 (= 2. 100 and 4. 67M) are parts of the description of a single incident.

Fragment 2. 100 has been transmitted with book-number (2). Kritz, who places it in his Book 2 follows de Brosses in attributing it to the sudden rout of Cotta beneath the walls of Chalcedon. He did so on the basis of App. *Mith.* 71.

Maurenbrecher, on the basis of an analogy with the Plutarchan description of the battle of Tigranocerta, put the fragment into Book 4. He does not specify a Plutarchan passage, but as Garbugino (*Stud. Non.* 11 (1986), 55 n. 79) suggests, it was very likely *Luc.* 28. 6.

La Penna (*SIFC* 35 (1963), 40) considered Kritz's analogy with the Appian passage as reasonably close, but doubted that the operations around Chalcedon which took place at the end of summer 74 would have been narrated in Book 2. He also rightly rejects Maurenbrecher's vague identification with the Plutarchan treatment of Tigranocerta as compelling enough to justify correction of the transmitted book number.

My belief that 2. 99 and 100 deal with the same incident is strengthened by the probability that Sallust's description depended heavily on Thucydides' treatment of the slaughter of the Athenian force at the River Assinarus in Sicily: 'Once there they rushed in, and all order was at an end, each man wanting to cross first, and the attacks of the enemy making it difficult to cross at all; forced to huddle together, they fell against and trod down one another, some dying immediately upon the javelins, others getting entangled together and stumbling over the articles of baggage, without being able to rise again. Meanwhile the opposite bank, which was steep, was lined by the Syracusans who showered missiles down upon the Athenians' (Thuc. 7. 84. 3).

The possibility that 2. 97–100 formed part of the narrative on Valentia is most attractive: in the absence of Sertorius, the ineptitude of his lieutenants Perperna and Herennius caused panic and defeat and great loss of life. See note on 2. 46–57; cf. Pecere, *SIFC* 50 (1978), 158–60.

**2. 101. He extended the wall . . . to a swamp.** Maurenbrecher does not comment on this fragment—2. 107M. La Penna's suggestion of a possible reference to Sucro (*SIFC* 35 (1963), 36) is acute. He suggests that the swamp mentioned could have been that of Albufera close to which Schulten (113 and n. 537) persuasively places the battle. The wall could have been erected to defend Sertorius' camp, but in the absence of precise indication of camp-site La Penna counselled caution.

**2. 102.    all the wounded bodies on rafts.**    The codices of
Arusianus Messius read: *omnia sacrata corpora in rates
imposuisse*, where the word *sacrata* ('consecrated') caused
Wölfflin to suggest *sacrata pecora* ('sheep'); Kritz understood *sacrata corpora* to be priests ('bodies consecrated to
the gods'). Maurenbrecher (2. 110M) retained *sacrata*; his
explanation that it referred either to people emigrating from
their native land or inhabitants fleeing from an enemy is
unsatisfactory. Dietsch, more perceptively, suggested that
*sacrata* be changed to *sauciata* ('wounded'), a conjecture
which has received recent affirmation by Mazzarino's (*Maia*,
33 (1981), 64–7) discovery that a version of the fragment in
the miscellaneous Codex Vat. Lat. 7179 has preserved
*s . . ciata*, with two letters missing because of a tear in the
manuscript. This version I have translated, but I cannot
hazard a guess as to what is being referred to.

**2. 103–105.**    I believe these fragments refer to a pitched
battle on land. The content, which indicates tactical manoeuv-
ring and desperate and confused fighting, could refer to the
battle of Segovia between Metellus and Hirtuleius, on which
see the notes on 2. 49 and 50, or to the battle of Segontia on
which see the note on 2. 55–7. The meagre narrative details
which have survived do not permit a more definite reference.

**2. 106–7.**    Refer to siege operations and hence could be
applicable either to Lauro (see notes on 2. 28–9) or Clunia
(see general comment on 2. 70–8).

**2. 106.    They were letting bread . . . in baskets.**    The
codices present: *E muris canes sportis dimittebant*. The word
*canes* ('dogs') caused problems: Mähly corrected it to *panes*
('bread'), Lipsius to *cives* ('citizens'). Kritz kept *canes* on the
assumption that the word did not refer to the animals but
was an animal-name used for military machines or instru-
ments on the pattern of *aries* ('ram') for battering-ram;
*corvus* ('raven') for a grapnel; *grus* ('crane') for a siege-
engine; *scorpio* ('scorpion') for a quick-firing piece of
artillery. In order to accommodate the use of *canes* as
equivalent to *harpagones* (poles fitted with hooks), suggested
to him by Isidorus' use of *canicula* as equivalent to *ferreus*

---

*harpago*, an iron hook used to extract articles from deep mud (*Etym* 15. 4), Kritz had to change *sportis* ('baskets') to *spartis* (ropes made from fibres); unfortunately the fragment was cited by Nonius precisely to illustrate his lemma SPORTAS. Dietsch suggested *arenas* ('sand') recalling Sertorius' use of a contrived dust-storm to out-manoeuvre the Characitani (Plut. *Sert.* 17) or *caena* ('mud') recalling the effect on besiegers of hot mud thrown down from the walls (*Curtius* 4. 3. 25).

I have translated Maurenbrecher's version but I am by no means convinced that it is what Sallust wrote.

**2. 108. comparable to a bull.** Gerlach and Kritz joined this fragment with 2. 13 apparently for no other reason than that both fragments deal with a bull. Dietsch, followed by Maurenbrecher (2. 109M) rejected Kritz's placement and suggested reference to animals much smaller than a bull. But where in Book 2 this would have arisen I cannot imagine.

**2. 109. so they are dismissed . . . evidence produced.** A fragment which occurs also in Donatus, Ter. *Hecyr.* 528; *Phorm.* 205; Servius Dan., *Aen.* 2. 61. *Fiducia*, which I have translated as 'brazen self-assurance', is assumed to have been used in a derogatory sense. There is no clue as to the nature of the accusation or the identity of the persons involved.

**2. 112. and the Carthaginians bring . . .** Neither the content nor the location of this fragment is recoverable. Two places in the narrative of Book 2 may be relevant: the excursus on Sardinia—see note on 2. 9, **The Balari . . . the Corsicans**; or the introductory material on Carthago Nova— see note on 2. 48.

# BIBLIOGRAPHY

(a)   *Editions of the Sources of Indirect Transmission*
*Adnotationes super Lucanum*, ed. I. Endt (Stuttgart 1969).
AMPELIUS, *Liber memorialis*, ed. E. Assman (Stuttgart 1976).
ARUSIANUS MESSIUS, *Exempla locutionum*, ed. H. Keil (in *Grammatici Latini* 7; Leipzig 1880), 439–514.
AUDAX, *Excerpta*, ed. H. Keil (in *Grammatici Latini* 7; Leipzig 1880), 320–62.
AUGUSTINUS, *De civitate Dei*, ed. B. Dombart and A. Kalb (Turnhout 1955).
CAPER, *De dubiis nominibus*, ed. H. Keil (in *Grammatici Latini* 5; Leipzig 1868), 571–94.
CHARISIUS, *Artis grammaticae libri*, ed. C. Barwick (Leipzig 1964).
CLEDONIUS, *Ars grammatica*, ed. H. Keil (in *Grammatici Latini* 5; Leipzig 1868), 10–79.
*Commenta Bernensia*, ed. K. Usener (Leipzig 1967).
DIOMEDES, *Artis grammaticae libri III*, ed. H. Keil (in *Grammatici Latini* 1; Leipzig 1857), 300–529.
DONATUS, *Commentum Terenti*, ed. P. Wessner, 3 vols. (Stuttgart 1962–3).
EUTYCHES, *Ars de verbo*, ed. H. Keil (in *Grammatici Latini* 5; Leipzig 1868), 447–89.
FESTUS, *De verborum significatu*, ed. A. Thewrewk de Ponor and W. M. Lindsay (Leipzig 1913).
GELLIUS, *Noctes Atticae*, ed. M. Hertz and C. Hosius (Leipzig 1903).
ISIDORUS, *Isidori Hispalensis Episcopi Etymologiarum sive Originum XX* (OCT; Oxford 1911).
JEROME [Eusebius Hieronymus], *Commentariorum in Abacus prophetam*, ed. M. Adriaen (Turnhout 1970).
——*Epistulae*, ed. I. Hilberg (in Corpus Scriptorum Ecclesiasticorum Latinorum, 54; Vienna 1910).
——*Onomastica Sacra* ed. F. Wutz 1914 (in Texte und Untersuchungen zur Geschichte der altchristlichen Literatur 3: 11).
LACTANTIUS, *Divinae Institutiones*, ed. S. Brandt (in Corpus Scriptorum Ecclesiasticorum Latinorum 19; Vienna 1890).
LYDUS [John the Lydian], *De Magistratibus*, ed. R. Wünsch (Stuttgart 1967).
MACROBIUS, *Saturnalia*, ed. J. Willis (Leipzig 1970).

MACROBIUS, 'Excerpta Bobiensa de Macrobii Theodosii' ed. H. Keil (in *Grammatici Latini* 5; Leipzig 1868), 631–55.

MARTIANUS CAPELLA, *De nuptiis Philologiae et Mercurii*, ed. J. Willis (Leipzig 1983).

NONIUS, *De compendiosa doctrina libri*, ed. J. H. Onions and W. M. Lindsay (Leipzig 1903). I quote according to Mercier's pagination.

PHILARGYRIUS, IUNIUS, 'Explanatio in Bucolica', ed. H. Hagen (in *Appendix Serviana*; Leipzig 1902), 323–87.

PLACIDUS, in *Glossaria Latina* ed. W. M. Lindsay and others (in Nouvelle Collection de Textes et Documents; Paris 1926).

POMPEIUS, *Commentum artis Donati*, ed. H. Keil (in *Grammatici Latini* 5; Leipzig 1868), 95–312.

PORPHYRION, *Commentum in Horatium Flaccum*, ed. A. Holder (Innsbruck 1894).

PRISCIANUS, *Institutionum grammaticarum libri*, ed. M. Hertz (in *Grammatici Latini* 2–3; Leipzig 1855–9).

PROBUS, *Catholica*, ed. H. Keil (in *Grammatici Latini* 4; Leipzig 1862), 3–43.

——*Instituta artium*, ed. H. Keil (in *Grammatici Latini* 4; Leipzig 1862, 47–192.

PS.-ACRON, *In carmina Horatii commentarius*, ed. O. Keller (Leipzig 1902).

QUINTILIANUS, *Institutionis oratoriae libri*, ed. L. Radermacher (Leipzig 1907–35).

RUFINIANUS, 'De figuris sententiarum et elocutionis', ed. C. Halm (in *Rhetores Latini minores*; Leipzig 1863), 3–21.

RUFINUS, *De numeris oratorum*, ed. H. Keil (in *Grammatici Latini* 6; Leipzig 1874), 565–78.

*Scholia Bembina*: 'Die Scholien des Codex Bembinus zum Terentius', ed. F. Umpfenbach, in *Hermes* 2 (1867), 337 ff.

*Scholia Bernensia ad Vergili Bucolica atque Georgica*, ed. H. Hagen (Leipzig 1867).

*Scholia Bobiensia*, ed. T. Stangl (in *Ciceronis orationum Scholiastae*; Vienna 1912), 73–179.

*Scholia Gronoviana*, ed. T. Stangl (in *Ciceronis orationum Scholiastae*; Vienna 1912), 277–351.

*Scholia in Iuvenalem vetustiora*, ed. P. Wessner (Leipzig 1931).

*Scholia in Statii Thebaidem*: 'Die Statiusscholien', ed. A. Klotz, in *ALL* 15 (1908), 485–525.

*Scholiorum Veronensium in Vergilii Bucolica, Georgica Aeneidem fragmenta*, in Thilo–Hagen, 3.

SENECA *De beneficiis*[2] ed. C. Hosius (Leipzig 1914).

—— *Epistulae*[2] ed. O. Hense (Leipzig 1914).
SERVIUS, *Servii grammatici in Vergili carmina commentarii* (*et scholia quibus commentarius auctus est*), ed. G. Thilo (Leipzig 1884–1887; repr. Hildesheim 1961).
SOLINUS, *Collectanea rerum memorabilium*[2] ed. T. H. Mommsen (Berlin 1895).
SUETONIUS, *De grammaticis et rhetoribus*, ed. E. Brugnoli (Leipzig 1966).
VEGETIUS, *Epitoma rei militaris*, ed. C. Lang (Stuttgart 1967).
VICTORINUS, *Explanationes in rhetoricam M. Tulli Ciceronis*, ed. C. Halm (*in Rhetores Latini minores*; Leipzig 1863), 155–304.

(*b*)  *Modern Works*
(See also the Abbreviations list)
ALHEID, F., 'Oratorical Strategy in Sallust's Letter of Mithridates Reconsidered', *Mnem.* 41 (1988), 67 ff.
BADIAN, E., 'The Date of Pompey's First Triumph', *Hermes* 83 (1955), 107 ff.
—— 'Caepio and Norbanus: Notes on the Decade 100–90 BC', *Historia* 6 (1957), 318 ff.
—— 'Waiting for Sulla', *JRS* 52 (1962), 47 ff.
—— 'Roman Politics and the Italians', *Dialoghi di archeologia* (1972), 373 ff.
BENNETT, H., *Cinna and his Times* (Menasha, Wis. 1923).
BIEŃKOWSKI, P. R. v., 'Kritische Studien über Chronologie und Geschichte des sertorianischen Krieges', *WS* 13 (1891), 129 ff. and 210 ff.
BLOCH, H., 'The Structure of Sallust's *Historiae*: The Evidence of the Fleury Manuscript', in S. Prete (ed.), *Didascaliae: Studies in Honor of A. M. Albareda* (New York 1961), 59 ff.
BRUNT, P. A., 'Italian Aims at the Time of the Social War', *JRS* 55 (1965), 90 ff.
—— *Italian Manpower 225 BC–AD 14* (Oxford 1971).
—— *The Fall of the Roman Republic and Related Essays* (Oxford 1988).
BÜCHNER, K., *Sallust*[2] (Heidelberg 1982).
CARNEY, T. F. *A Biography of C. Marius*, *PACA* Suppl. 1 (1961), 98 ff.
CICHORIUS, C., *Römische Studien* (Leipzig 1922).
CLAUSEN, W., 'Notes on Sallust's "Historiae"' *AJP* 68 (1947), 293 ff.
CRINITI, N., *M. Aimilius Q. f. M. Lepidus: 'ut ignis in stipula'* (Milan 1969).

DRUMANN, W., and GROEBE, P., *Geschichte Roms in seinem Übergange von der republikanischen zur monarchischen Verfassung*, 6 vols. (Leipzig 1899–1929).

EARL, D. C., *The Political Thought of Sallust* (Cambridge 1961).

FLACH, D., 'The Structure of Sallust's *Historiae*', *Philologus* 117 (1973), 76 ff.

FRASSINETTI, P., 'Su alcuni frammenti delle *Historiae* di Sallustio', *Athenaeum* 40 (1962), 93 ff.

—— 'I fatti di Spagna nel libro II delle *Historiae di Sallustio*', *Stud. Urb.* 49 (1975), 381 ff.

GABBA, E., *Appiani Bellorum civilium liber primus* (Florence 1958).

—— 'Spartaco', *Athenaeum* 58 (1969), 379 ff.

GARBUGINO, G., 'Il I libro delle "Historiae" di Sallustio', *Stud. Non.* 5 (1978), 39 ff.

—— 'Note al II libro delle "Historiae" di Sallustio', *Stud. Non.* 11 (1986), 31 ff.

GASPAROTTO, G., 'Sull'ordine di frammenti delle "Historiae sallustianae"', *Atti e Mem. dell'Accad. Patavina 83* (1970–1), 67 ff.

GUARINO, A., *Spartaco*: analisi di un mito (Milan 1979).

HOLMES, T. R., *The Roman Republic I.* (New York 1923).

KATZ, B. R., 'Two Fragments of Sallust', *RhM* 124 (1981), 332 ff.

—— 'Notes on Sertorius', *RhM* 126 (1983), 44 ff.

—— 'Sertorius' Overlooked Correspondent?', *RhM* 126 (1983), 359 ff.

KEAVENEY, A., *Sulla: The Last Republican* (London 1983).

KLINGNER, F., 'Über die Einleitung der Historien Sallusts', *Hermes* 63 (1928), 165 ff.

KONRAD, C. F., 'Why not Sallust on the Eighties?', *AHB*2 (1988), 12–15.

LABRUNA, L., *Il console 'sovversivo': Società e diritto di Roma*, 2 (Naples 1975).

LA PENNA, A., 'Il significato dei proemi Sallustiani', *Maia* II (1959), 23 ff.; 89 ff.

—— 'Le "Historiae" di Sallustio e l'interpretazione della crisi repubblicana', *Athenaeum* 41 (1963), 201 ff.

—— 'Per la ricostruzione delle "Historiae" di Sallustio', *SIFC* 35 (1963), 5 ff.

LEPORE, E., 'I due frammenti Rylands delle Storie di Sallustio', *Athenaeum* 28 (1950), 280 ff.

LINTOTT, A. W., *Violence in Republican Rome* (Oxford 1968).

McGING, B. C., *The Foreign Policy of Mithridates Eupator King of Pontus* (Leiden 1986).

McGUSHIN, P., C. *Sallustius Crispus: Bellum Catilinae. A Commentary* (Leiden 1977).

MEISTER, K., 'Der Sklavenaufstand des Spartakus: Kritische Anmerkungen zu einer neuen Deutung', in H. Halcyk (ed.), *Studien zur alten Geschichte* (Rome 1986), 633 ff.

MOMMSEN, T. H., *History of Rome*, 4, transl. W. P. Dickson (London 1868).

OGILVIE, R. M., *A Commentary on Livy 1-5* (Oxford 1965).

OOST, S. I., 'Cyrene, 96-74 BC', *CP* 58 (1963), 11 ff.

OOTEGHEM, J. VAN, *Pompée le Grand: Bâtisseur d'empire* (Brussels 1954).

ORMEROD, H. A., 'The Campaigns of Servilius Isauricus against the Pirates', *JRS* 12 (1922), 35 ff.

—— *Piracy in the Ancient World* (Liverpool 1969).

PARONNI, P., *Pomponii Melae De chorographia* (Rome 1984).

PARTHEY, G., AND PINDER, M. (eds.), *The Antonine Itinerary (Itinerarium Antoninianum)* (Berlin 1848).

PASSERINI, A., *Studi su Caio Mario* (Milan 1971).

PECERE, O., 'Su alcuni frammenti delle "Historiae" di Sallustio', *SIFC* 35 (1963), 5 ff.

—— 'Su alcuni frammenti delle "Historiae" di Sallustio', *SIFC* 41 (1969), 61 ff. = *Omaggio a E. Fraenkel* (1968).

—— 'Note sui frammenti di Sallustio', *SIFC* 50 (1978), 131 ff.

PERL, G., 'Die Zuverlässigkeit der Buchangaben in den Zitaten Priscians', *Philologus* 111 (1967), 283 ff.

—— 'Zur Chronologie der Königsreiche Bithynia, Pontos und Bosporus', in *Studien zur Geschichte und Philosophie des Altertums* (Amsterdam 1968).

—— 'Sallusts politische Stellung', *WZ Rostock* 18 (1969), 379 ff.

—— 'Sallust und die Krise der römischen Republik', *Philologus* 113 (1969), 201 ff.

RADITSA, L. F., 'Historical Commentary on the Letter of Mithridates', Diss. Columbia (1969).

RAWSON, E., 'Sallust on the Eighties?', *CQ* 37 (1987), 163 ff.

ROTONDI, G., *Leges publicae populi Romani* (Milan 1912).

SCARDIGLI, B., 'A proposito di due passi su Sertorio', *A&R* 15 (1970), 174 ff.

—— 'Sertorio: problemi cronologici', *Athenaeum* 49 (1971), 229 ff.

—— 'Considerazioni sulle fonti della biografia plutarcea di Sertorio', *SIFC* 43 (1971), 33 ff.

—— 'Note sui frammenti di Sallustio', *SIFC* 50 (1978), 131 ff.

SMITH, R. E., 'Pompey's Conduct in 80 and 77 BC', *Phoenix* 14 (1960), 1 ff.

STAHL, G., *De Bello Sertoriano*. Diss. Inaug. (Erlangen 1907).

STAMPACCHIA, G., *La tradizione della guerra di Spartaco da Sallustio a Orosio* (Pisa 1976).

——'La rivolta di Spartaco come rivolta contadina', *Index* 9 (1980), 99 ff.

STIER, H. E., 'Der Mithridatesbrief aus Sallusts Historien als Geschichtsquelle' in *Festschrift F. Altheim* (Berlin 1969).

TAYLOR, L. R., *The Voting Districts of the Roman Republic* (Rome 1960).

WISEMAN, T. P., *New Men in the Roman Senate* (Oxford 1971).

VAN DEN HOUT, M. P. J., *Frontonis Epistulae* (Leiden 1954).

# INDEX

Actaeon 187
Aemilii 29, 115
Aemilius Lepidus Porcina, M. 134
Aemilius Lepidus M. (cos. 78) 23, 136,
    149
  activity in Etruria (78 BC) 33–4,
    128–32
  canvass for popular support 33,
    127–8
  corn law of 127, 208
  failure of attack on Rome and escape
    to Etruria 148–51
  flight to Sardinia 151–2
  last stand against Triarius 190
  speech to the Roman people 28–32
Aemilius Lepidus Livianus, Mam. (cos.
    77) 39, 147, 149, 153
Aemilius Lepidus, M. (cos. 46) 136
Aesernia 89, 111
Afranius, L. 221–2, 246
Africa 94, 96, 102, 108–10, 173, 243
African Sea 45, 185
Albufera 257
Alexander (the Great) 194
allies 26, 30, 85–8
Allobroges 231
Alps 59, 87, 244–5
ambition 24, 36, 75, 78, 81
Amisus 14
Anas (River) 170, 173
Ancona 87, 98, 116
Annius Luscus, M. 164–5, 168
Antiochus III (the Great) 29, 115
Antistius, P. 139
Antonius, C. (cos. 63) 144
Antonius, M. (cos. 99) 144, 234
Antonius Creticus, M. (praet. 74) 208,
    247, 250
Antonius, M. (cos. 44) 137, 144, 146,
    166, 210
Apion, see Ptolemy
Apollo 46, 61, 187, 255
Appuleius Saturninus, L. 35, 127, 138
Apulia/Apulians 89, 99
Aquillius, M'. (cos. 101) 54
Aquinus 176
Arausio 154

Archelaus 254
Arecomici 245
Ariobarzanes 197
Aristaeus 187–8
Arretium 119
Artabazes 60
Ascalis 167, 255
Asculum 149
Asia/Asia Minor 27, 57, 98, 215, 240
Asia (Roman province) 51, 92, 215,
    248, 255
Assinarus (River) 257
Athens/Athenians 97, 257
Atlanteos 188
Atlas (Mts.) 188
Attaleia 182
Aufidius Orestes, Cn.203
Aurelii Cottae 209
Aurelius Cotta, C. (cos. 75) 15, 49
  arouses hostility of nobles 52, 217
  career outline 205–6
  speech to the Roman people 50–2,
    211, 244
Aurelius Cotta, M. (cos. 74) 60, 247,
    256
Aurelius Cotta, C(?) or (M?). 168–9
Augustus (Octavianus) 20, 146–7, 210
Aventine 24, 81
Averro 177

Baelo 169
Baetica 220
Baetis (River) 165, 172
Balari 46, 187
Basilica Aemilia 135
Belleia 168–9
Bithynia/Bithynians 60, 254–5
  kingdom bequeathed to Rome 248
Bocchus of Mauretania 110
Bogud of Mauretania 110
Brundisium 99, 161
Bulla Regia 110
Burbuleius 48, 196

Cabeira 14
Cadiz 40, 165
Caeciliana 176

Caecilii Metelli 209
Caecilius Metellus Pius, Q. (cos. 80)
    42–3, 184–5, 215, 217, 244
  commander in Social War and
    senatorial envoy for peace 94–6
  excesses of private conduct criticized
    53–4, 224–5
  ineffectual leadership against
    Sertorius (79–77 BC) 175–80, 198
  loses Spanish command to Pompeius
    190–3
  military career summarized 173–7
  success against Hirtuleius at Italica
    201
  total victory at Segovia 220
  valiant part in battle of Segontia
    222–3
Caecilius Metellus Creticus, Q. (cos.
    69) 50, 209
  military career summarized 209–10
Caecilius Metellus Celer, Q. 134, 178
Caecilius Metellus Nepos, Q. 134
Caecilius Vicus 176
Caepio, see Servilius
Caesar, see Iulius
Calagurris 174
Cales 161
Calidius, Q. 180
Callaecia 177
Calpurnius Lanarius 40, 164
Calpurnius Piso, Q. (cos. 67) 115
Campania 100, 119
Campus Martius 209
Canary Islands 166
Cannae (battle of) 255
Cantabri 237
Cappadocia/Cappadocians 97, 245, 255
Capua 98, 150, 161
Carbo, see Papirius
Caria 215
Carrinas, C. 102–3, 184, 243
Carthage/Carthaginians 24–5, 46, 63,
    75, 187, 199, 259
Carthago Nova 164, 219, 221
Castra Caeciliana 176
Castulo 155, 183
Catiline, see Sergius
Cato, see Porcius
Catulus, see Lutatius
Celtiberia/Celtiberians 46, 56, 58, 174,
    180, 188, 222, 235–7, 241
Ceos 187
Cethegus, see Cornelius

Chaeronea 97
Chalcedon 256–7
Chelidonian Islands 182
Cicero, see Tullius
Cilicia 51, 152, 181, 205
Cilicia Tracheia 229
Cilician Corycus 229–30
Cilician pirates 181, 198, 215, 229, 231,
    236–7
Cimbri 31, 120, 154
Cinna, see Cornelius
Circeii 93
Circus Flaminius 108
Circus Maximus 61, 255
citizenship 30, 86–90, 107, 118–19
civil war(s) 23, 25, 36, 39, 81, 129, 135,
    159, 173
Claudius, Appius (mil. trib. 87) 94
Claudius Marcellus, C. (praet. 80) 134
Claudius Marcellus, M. (cos. 51) 24, 77
Claudius Pulcher, Appius (cos. 79) 38,
    54, 202–3
Clodius Pulcher, P. (trib. 58) 23, 72
Cluilius, T. 243
Clunia 235, 237, 241
Clurda (River) 55, 230
Clusium 102
Col d' Argentière 245
Colline Gate (battle of) 102–6, 163,
    184
Conisturgis 43, 177
constitution/constitutional 26, 28, 108,
    114, 135, 147, 153, 195, 208, 217
Contrebia 181
Coralis 187
Cornelii (slaves manumitted by Sulla)
    107, 123
Cornelius (clerk) 31, 217
Cornelius, C. (trib. 67) 217
Cornelius Cethegus, P. 38, 145, 193
Cornelius Cinna, L. (cos. 87) 33, 37,
    116, 128
  association with Papirius Carbo
    159–60
  reign of terror under Cinna and
    Marius 94–7, 105–6, 131, 144, 146
Cornelius Cinna, L. (son of above) 138
Cornelius Dolabella, Cn. 126
Cornelius Lentulus Marcellinus, P. 49
Cornelius Merula, L. 107, 144
Cornelius Scipio Asiaticus, L. (cos.
    190) 115, 161
Cornelius Scipio (Africanus)

Aemilianus, P. (cos. 147) 84
Cornelius Scipio Asiaticus (Asiagenus),
  L. (cos. 83) 98–9
Cornelius Sisenna, L. 66–7, 70–1, 91,
  102
Cornelius Sulla L. (cos. 88)
  abdication of dictatorship 112
  abolition of corn doles 118, 208
  first march on Rome 92–3
  in first Mithridatic war 27, 97–8
  portrait of 32–3, 126
  reign of terror 103–7
  second march on Rome 40, 99–102,
  161
Corsa 47, 189
Corsica/Corsicans 46, 185–7, 189
Corycus 43–4, 54, 182, 229
Cosa 38, 148, 150–1, 184, 190
Cosconius, C. 13, 203
Cossura 109
Cotta, see Aurelius
Cottian Alps 245
Crassus, see Licinius
Crete 185, 188, 210
Cunei 177
Curia Hostilia 139
Curio, see Scribonius
Cybele 234
Cyprus 23
Cyrene (goddess) 46
Cyrene/Cyrenaica (Roman province)
  49, 187
Cyrnian 187
Cyrnos 187
Cyzicus 14, 254

Daedalus 46, 187–8
Damasippus, see Iunius
Dalmatia/Dalmati 13, 49, 202–3
Dardania/Dardani 202, 207
Dardanus (Peace of) 54, 95, 98–9
Darius 60
debt 24, 80
Decii 216
Decius Mus 216
Dianium 181, 198, 237
Didius, T. (cos. 98) 39, 154–7
Dipo 42, 177
discord 24, 35, 76, 78, 84, 142
Domitius Ahenobarbus, Cn. 109–10,
  194, 243
Domitius Ahenobarbus, L. (cos. 94)
  138

Domitius Calvinus, M. 41–2, 170–4,
  180
Drusus, see Livius
Durla 233
Duris (River) 177
Dyrrhachium 26, 99, 227

Ebesus 164–5
Ebro (River) 198–9
Elysian fields 166
Elysium 40
Emerita 177
Epirus 98, 115
Eporedia 155
Etruria:
  dominated Rome under the Tarquins
  24, 80
  in civil war of the eighties an area of
  recruitment and fierce fighting
  100–2
  loyal to Lepidus in peasants' revolt
  128–9
  recruiting ground for Sertorius 161
  savagely treated in Sulla's reign of
  terror and later 103, 119
  scene of Lepidus' last stand in Italy
  149–51
Eumeneia 230
Eurytheia 187
extraordinary commands 152–3

Faesulae 128, 131, 143
Fannia 94
Fannius, C. 23, 69–70, 90
Fannius, L. 254
Flaccus, see Fulvius; Valerius
Flavius Fimbria, C. 95, 253–4
Florence 87
freedom 26, 28, 30, 32, 107, 114, 117,
  133, 136, 140
Fregellae 88–9
Fufidius, L. 31, 41, 123, 169–71, 173–4
Fulvius Flaccus, M. (cos. 125) 88–9

Gaddir 46
Gallia/Gaul 24, 59, 77, 131, 139
  Gallia Cisalpina 100, 102, 131, 148–
  9, 154, 156–7, 180, 195, 218
  Gallia Transalpina 131, 156–7, 180,
  195, 245
  Gallia Narbonensis 195, 201, 245
Geminius 93
Geryon 46, 186–7

Gibraltar 165
glory 24, 60, 78, 114
Gracchi, *see* Sempronius
Greece 97–8, 197
Guadaljara 200
guerrilla tactics 215, 241
Gulf of Valencia 165
Gutta 101

Hannibal 20, 59, 115, 199, 245, 254
Helvii 245
Helvius Mancia 194
Henares (River) 200
Hercules 186–7
Hermes 187
Herodotus 68, 71
Herennius, C. (trib. 80) 47, 59, 196,
    199, 219, 256–7
Hiempsal 89
Hirpini 89
Hirtuleius, L. 48, 53, 157, 198
    defeated at Italica 201
    defeated and killed at Segovia 200–1
    excellent military record in years 80–
    78 BC 170, 173, 180
Hispania Tarraconnensis 187
Homer 40, 66
Hortensius, Q. 205, 210

Iapydia 49, 203
Iarbas 110
Iberians 188
Icarus 188
Ichnusa 45, 186
Ilerda 43, 180
Ilians 187
Ilienses 187
Ilium 187, 254
Illyria, Illyricum 13, 202–3
*imperium* 37, 114, 130, 145, 147, 153,
    155–6, 217
Indicetes 59, 245
Insteius, L. 157
*interrex* 37, 147
Ioläes 187
Iolaus 46, 187
Isaura Nova (New) 55, 228, 231, 233–4
Isaura Vetus (Old) 228, 232–3
Isauria 229
Isauri 228, 230–1, 234
Isles of the Blest 165–6
Italica (battle of) 199, 201, 220, 256
Italy 26–7, 51, 59–60, 86–7, 92, 98–9,
    103, 109, 150, 152, 157, 173, 244,
    246–7
Iulius Caesar, C. (cos. 59) 115–16, 126,
    205
Iulius Caesar Strabo, C. 144
Iulius Caesar, L. (cos. 90) 144
Iunius Brutus D. (cos. 77) 114, 147,
    153
Iunius Brutus Damasippus, L. 101–2,
    139, 184, 243
Iunius Brutus, M. 131, 138, 148, 150,
    153, 194

Lacobriga 177, 184, 238
Lacetania 59, 245
Laelius, D. 48, 200
Lamponius, M. 101
Langobriga 177
Latins 26, 85–6, 88–90
Latium 30, 89, 100, 119
Lauro (battle of) 198–201, 245, 256
Lenaeus 47, 193
Lentulus, *see* Cornelius
Lepidus, *see* Aemilius
Lepini (Mts.) 101
Leptasta 61, 255
Lex:
    Aurelia de tribunicia potestate 217,
        256
    Cornelia de provinciis
        ordinandis 196
    Gabinia de bello piratico 115
    Iulia de civitate latinis (et sociis)
        danda 90, 118
    Plautia de reditu Lepidanorum 138
    Varia de maiestate 205, 214
liberty 26, 29, 34, 36, 38, 78
Libo, L. 194
Libya 186–7
Licinius Crassus L. (cos. 95) 87
Licinius Lucullus, L. (cos. 74) 60, 166,
    207–8, 247
Licinius Macer, C. 193, 197, 217
Liguria 47, 189
Lilybaeum 109
Livius Drusus, M. 88, 92, 119, 127, 132
Livius Salinator 40, 164
Lucania/Lucanians 89, 94, 100–1
Lucretus Ofella, Q. 101–3, 110–11
Lucullus, *see* Licinius
Ludi Apollinares 254
Lusitania/Lusitanians 42, 151, 167,
    169, 173–6, 178, 180, 237

Luscius, L. 119
Lutatii 29
Lutatius Catulus, Q. (cos. 102) 106,
145
Lutatius Catulus, Q. (cos. 78) 23, 66,
105–6, 115
led government forces against Lepidus
at Rome and at Cosa 38, 136, 148,
150–1
sent with Lepidus to deal with unrest
in Etruria 33, 128–9, 143
Lycia 43, 182, 228–9
Lycian Corycus 229
Lydia 182, 215

Macedonia/Macedonian 13–14, 23, 51,
54, 99, 115, 126, 147, 152, 154–5,
181–3, 202, 215, 226
Macer, see Licinius
Madeira 16
Maeander (River) 230
Magius, L. 254
Magna Mater 234
Magnesia 115
Mallius Maximus, Cn. (cos. 105) 154
Manlius, C. 120, 143
Manlius, L. 180, 201
Marcellinus, see Claudius
Marcius Censorinus, C. 101–2, 184
Marcius Philippus, L. (cos. 91) 34, 213
career sketch of 132
formulates SCU against Lepidus 38,
145–8
speech to the senate 34–8, 112–14,
132–3
Marcius Rex, Q. 120
Marius, C. (cos. 107, 104–100, 86) 139,
142, 154
flees Italy during Sulla's march on
Rome 26, 93–4
reign of terror after counter-coup of
Cinna and Marius 94–7, 131, 173
Marius, C. (cos. 82) 27, 35, 103, 108,
116, 139, 159, 162
Marius Gratidianus, M. 27, 105–6,
110, 254–5
Marrucini 89
Marsi 89
Massilia 189, 245
Mauretania 41, 54, 61, 110, 164, 167–9
Mellaria 168–9
Memmius, C. 198, 219, 224
Mercury 186

Meoriga 57, 237–8
Metellinum 176
Metellus, see Caecilius
metus hostilis 74, 77–8, 81–2
metus Punicus 77–8, 81
Miletopolis 254
Milyas 182
Minos 46, 188
Minturnae 93–4
Mithras 231
Mithridates VI Eupator 26, 36, 51, 60–
1, 92, 95, 97–9, 139, 237, 240, 247–
55
Mons Sacer 24, 81
Moors 164, 167, 171–2
Mucia 134
Mucius Scaevola, Q. (cos. 95) 87, 139
Mulvian bridge 231
Musa Dagh 182
Mutina 38, 148, 150
Mutudurei 57, 240

Narbonne 47, 196
Neores 57, 240
Nicomedes III Philopator 197, 248,
250, 255
Nola 109, 111
nomenclator 28, 107
Nora 186
Norax 186–7
Norba 115, 149–50
Norbanus, C. (cos. 83) 161
Numantia 241
Numidia/Numidian 46, 109–10, 189

Octavius, C. (later, C. Julius Caesar
Octavianus) 210
see also Augustus
Octavius, Cn. (cos. 87) 94, 107, 144
Octavius, Cn. (cos. 76) 196–7
Octavius, L. (cos. 75) 48–9, 60, 204,
247
Octavius, L. (officer of Pompeius) 210
Octavius, M. 33, 127
Olbia 187
Olisipo 177
Olympus 43, 182
Opimius, Q. (trib. 75) 217, 256
Orestes, see Aufidius
Orchomenos 97
Orondeis 229

Pacciaecus 167–8
Pallantia/Pallantians 46, 187–8
Pamphylia/Pamphylians 52, 182, 203
Paphlagonians 97
Papirius Carbo, Cn. (cos. 85, 84, 82) 27, 116
  against Sulla's rise to power 98, 100–2
  flight to Africa 102
  put to death at Lilybaeum 109, 194, 243
Papirius Carbo Arvina, C (?) (praet. 83) 139
Papirius Carbo, C (?) (praet. 81) 111
Peligni 89
Pergamum 254
Perperna Veiento, M. 109, 138, 181
  fled Sicily in 82 BC 109, 243
  failure at battle of Valentia 52, 199, 218–19
  involved in defeat at Segontia 222–4
Perseus, king of Macedon 29, 115
Petane 254
Phaselis 43, 182
Philip V of Macedon 29, 115
Philippus, see Marcius
Phocaeans 189
Picentines 89
Picenum 99, 102, 120, 150, 195, 242
Piraeus 97
Pisidia/Pisidians 43, 182, 203
Piso, see Calpurnius
Pityussian Islands 164, 168
Po (River) 25, 87
Pompeiians 89
Pompeius Magnus, Cn. (cos. 70) 100, 138, 180, 185, 210, 215
  characterization of 47, 193–4
  command against Lepidus 148–50
  command in Spain 190
  expelled Marians from Sicily 109
  exploits in Africa 109–10
  letter to the senate 58–60, 242
  part in battles of Lauro 192–201, 245, 256; of Valentia 218–19; of the Sucro 221–2; of Segontia 222–4
  Sallust's attitude to 17–18
  winter campaign in Celtiberia 57–8, 236, 238–41
Pompeius Strabo, Cn. (cos. 89) 142, 149, 157, 195
Pompeius Rufus, Q. (cos. 88) 142, 195

Pompaedius Silo, Q. 89, 94, 149, 173
Pontius Telesinus 101, 103
Pontus 60–1
Porcius Cato, M. (cos. 195) 23, 67–70
Porcius Cato, M. (praet. 54) 23, 72, 116, 137
Porcius Cato, L. (cos. 89) 157
Porto Santo 166
Portus Cale 177
Portus Cosanus 151
Portus Herculis 151
Praeneste 67, 100–3, 110–11, 139
proscribed 28, 31, 35, 107, 116, 141, 190
proscription 31, 106, 116, 118, 120, 197
Ptolemy Apion 49, 207–8
publicani 207–8
Pyrrhus 29, 115, 216, 254

quaestio 87, 205

Rhône (River) 245
Rome 24, 51, 86, 96, 98–9, 108, 130–1, 136, 143, 147–8, 155, 160–1, 183–4, 199, 235, 248
Romulus 29, 115

Sacred Way 209
Sacriportus 27, 100–1, 108
Saguntum/Saguntines 48, 198–200
Salinator, see Livius
Salonae 203
Sandaliotis 45, 186
Samnium/Samnites 89, 94–5, 100–3, 184
Sardinia 45–6, 113, 138, 151–2, 185–9
Sardus 186
Saturninus, see Appuleius
Scipio, see Cornelius
Scirtus 31, 123
Scribonius Curio, C. (cos. 76) 13, 153, 196–7, 202–4, 215, 226–8, 250
Scordisci 155
secession of plebs 24, 79–80
Segontia (battle of) 173, 198–9, 218, 222–4, 235, 258
Segovia (battle of) 218–21, 259
Seius, M. 211
Sempronia 114
Sempronii 25, 84, 88, 92
Sempronius Gracchus, C. 86, 119, 127
Sempronius Gracchus, Ti. 87–8, 108
senatus auctoritas 146

*senatus consultum ultimum* 132, 135–6, 143, 148
Septimius 42, 172–3
Sergius Catilina, L. 28, 105–6, 110–11, 114, 120, 136–7, 141, 143, 193
Sertorian War 48, 152, 167, 199, 218, 222, 224
  chronology of 197–8
  factors governing strategy and tactics for 79–77 BC 174–6
Sertorius 97, 138–9, 152, 184, 196, 202, 215, 240
  absence from Valentia battle 219
  campaigns against Metellus (80–77 BC) 167–81, 198
  character and early exploits 153–6
  in civil war against Sulla 159–62
  in Maurentania and elsewhere 164–7
  in Social War 156–9
  mixed fortunes at Segontia 222–4
  treaty with Mithridates 215, 240, 254–5
  victory at the Sucro 221–2
Servilius Vatia, P. (Isauricus) (cos. 79) 13, 43, 55–6, 99, 126, 175, 181–2, 188, 203, 215, 228–32, 250
Servilius Caepio, Q. 33, 127
Servilius Caepio, Q. (cos. 106) 154
Setia 100–1
Sicily 46, 108–9, 154, 186, 209–10, 243, 257
Sicinius, Cn. (trib. 76) 193, 196–7
Sierra Morena 198
Signia 101
Sisenna, *see* Cornelius
slaves 24, 30–2, 97, 107, 117–18, 160
slogans 113–15, 124, 133
Social War 16, 85, 87, 89, 92, 95, 118, 153, 163, 192
Spain 39–41, 51, 53, 58–9, 138–9, 147, 152, 154–5, 157, 162–3, 165, 167, 170–1, 173–4, 180–1, 190, 192, 195, 198, 200, 243–4, 246–7
Spartacus 96
Spoletum 102
Stobi 49, 202
Sucro (River) 59, 198, 218, 221–2, 246, 256–7
Suessa 161
Sulla, *see* Cornelius
Sullani 27, 125, 130
Sulpicius Rufus, P. (trib. 88) 35, 91, 139

Sulpicius Rufus, Ser. (cos. 51) 24, 77
Syracusans 257
Syria/Syrian 115, 125

Tachtali Dag 182
Tagus (River) 176
Tarentum 43, 115, 147
Tarquinius 24, 80
Tarquitius, C. 157
Tarraconnensis 169
Tarrhi 47, 189–90
Tarrula 31, 123
Tartessus 46, 186
Taurus (Mount) 55, 188, 228–30
Teanum 98–9, 161
Terentius Varro, M. 224
Terentius Varro Lucullus, M. 228
Termestini 58, 241
Terracina 93
Teutones 120
Thespians 187
Thessaly 99
Thorius Balbus, L. 174
Thracian 147, 171, 181, 183
Thucydides 13–14, 68, 71, 84, 132, 257
Tifata (Mount) 98
Tigranocerta 257
Tingis 167, 169
Titurius Sabinus, L. 58, 239, 241
treason 32, 125, 213
Trerus (River) 100
tribune of the plebs 24, 31, 81, 118
tribunician power 34, 124, 130, 142, 217
Troy 46
Tullius Cicero, M. (cos. 63) 120, 134, 141, 143, 146, 149, 166, 205, 210
Tullius Cicero, Q. 213
Turia (River) 52, 59, 219, 246, 256

Ucurbis 48, 201
Umbria 100–2
Urbinus, C. 53

Valentia 52, 59, 198–9, 218–21, 246, 256
Valerius Flaccus, L. (cos. suff. 86) 96, 116, 253–4
Valerius Triarius, C. 190
Valerius Serverus Hybrida, Q. (trib. 90) 205
Varro, *see* Terentius
Vascones, 57, 239–40

Veii 86
Venusini 89
Vercellae 106
Verres, C. (praet. 74) 209
Vestini 89
Vesuvius 96
Vettius 30, 120

Via Appia 100–1, 161
Via Latina 100
Volcae 245
Volaterrae 109, 111, 119

Zenicetes 182